1994

Evening Standard

LONDON RESTAURANT GUIDE

Dad,

We had difficulty in getting you a Retirement Present, after all what can you give the man who has everything? (1 thought a Cessna 178 but Alex didn't think an aircraft was such a good idea). We know that you + Gill will be going to Shows / Concerts / Opera's / Plays etc. etc. + thought that a meal out would compliment each performance. Why not try somewhere new each time.

Much love David + Alex.

1994

Evening Standard

LONDON RESTAURANT GUIDE

Fay Maschler

To Reg Gadney

First published in Great Britain in 1993 by
PAVILION BOOKS LIMITED
26 Upper Ground, London SE1 9PD
Text copyright © Evening Standard 1993
Maps and design copyright © Pavilion Books 1993

The moral right of the author has been asserted.

Designed by Alyson Kyles

Additional testing and reporting: Dee McQuillan
Wine Reviews: Andrew Jefford
Commissioning Editor for the Evening Standard: Joanne Bowlby

A CIP catalogue record for this book
is available from the British Library.

ISBN 1 85793 0142

Printed and bound in Great Britain by
Butler & Tanner Ltd, Frome and London

2 4 6 8 10 9 7 5 3

This book may be ordered by post
direct from the publisher. Please contact
the Marketing Department.
But try your bookshop first.

Maps designed by Lovell Johns Limited
10 Hanborough Business Park, Long Hanborough
Witney OX8 8LH

CONTENTS

INTRODUCTION

L ONDON HAS BECOME an exuberant city for eating out. Defying a recession that has floored other businesses, restaurants are booming. Of course, there have been casualties – some to be lamented, some that just make you think 'and high time too' – but as one door closes, another opens. Reasons for this welcome state of affairs include more realistic rents being wrested from landlords, a more creative approach on the part of prospective restaurateurs towards what constitutes premises, for example, seeing the potential in pubs and greasy spoons, a greater awareness and acceptance by the public of eating out as a pleasurable pastime and, most importantly, the flourishing of a generation of intelligent, inquisitive, peripatetic and, in some instances, glamorous British chefs who possess a mapgie mentality where ingredients and methods are concerned. Their approach to cooking is untrammelled by tradition or rigid customs and these men and (increasingly) women, some self-taught, seize the opportunities presented by the availability of global produce to create singular, appetizing and occasionally original recipes. Their endeavours, overlaying a restaurant culture which still owes a great deal to immigrant and imported talent, has put London at the centre of the gastronomic map.

This bold claim is not to suggest that you sacrifice yourself and your wallet on the altars of haute cuisine: eating out should be affordable and it should be fun. There *are* grand restaurants in London well worth saving for but the interesting developments have been in the mid-price, often spacious, easygoing places that formerly were talked about wistfully as the privilege of those countries where eating out is seen as a natural part of the way of life. This guide identifies and celebrates such establishments. It also evaluates classic and long-standing restaurants and clears a path through the thicket of ethnic offerings. Although the guide contains completely original reviews and appraisals, it is, to some extent, the distillation of what must be more than 3,000 meals eaten over a period of twenty-one years. It is written not by a team of inspectors nor as a result of a consumer survey but by an experienced, dedicated and enthusiastic eater-out keen to pass on the news.

As Beatrix Potter said of Pigling Bland, restaurants are 'hopelessly volatile'; since the date of going to press there will inevitably be a few changes in the close on 300 places reported on here. If there seems to you a place omitted that should be included, please write to the publisher and say why (but not if you are the restaurant owner or his or her mother).

Prices: The price given for each restaurant is a guide as to the cost of a three course meal for one person with half a bottle of wine (or appropriate drink), tax and service. Frugal diners may well find it possible to eat for less. Lovers of fine wine and those who consider a meal incomplete without aperitifs and digestifs will doubtless pay more.

Newcomers: This is a list of restaurants that opened after 1st January 1992.

Eros: I am frequently asked which are my favourite restaurants. The Eros award given to twenty London restaurants answers the question. The list, which will be compiled annually, reflects not just the best cooking in London – although in many cases it coincides – but something more; a recognition of the restaurants that joyfully succeed in what they set out to do, be that classic French food served with grace and style, a neighbourhood place all neighbourhoods would like to have, consistent high standards in a notoriously fluctuating area such as Chinatown, positive enlightenment concerning authenticity or regionality of a cuisine or an awareness that eating out appeals to the peacock in ourselves and others – but that peacocks also want to eat well.

Fay Maschler

FAY MASCHLER

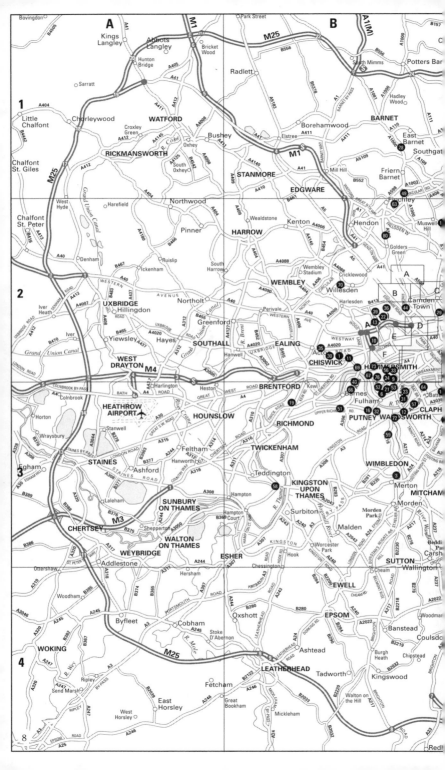

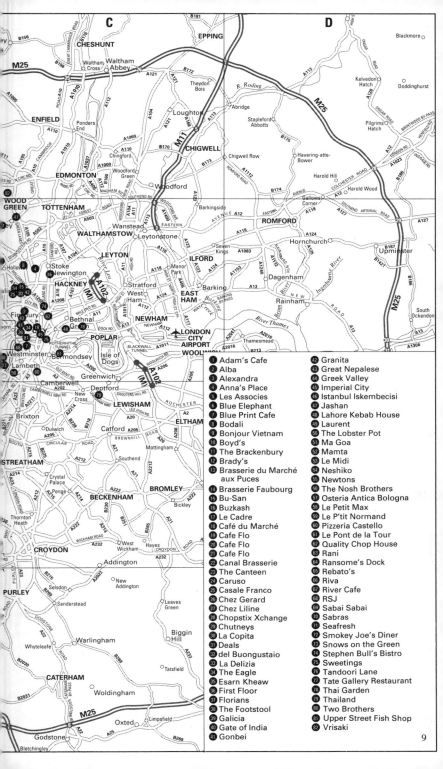

C   **D**

1 Adam's Cafe
2 Alba
3 Alexandra
4 Anna's Place
5 Les Associes
6 Blue Elephant
7 Blue Print Cafe
8 Bodali
9 Bonjour Vietnam
10 Boyd's
11 The Brackenbury
12 Brady's
13 Brasserie du Marché aux Puces
14 Brasserie Faubourg
15 Bu-San
16 Buzkash
17 Le Cadre
18 Café du Marché
19 Cafe Flo
20 Cafe Flo
21 Cafe Flo
22 Canal Brasserie
23 The Canteen
24 Caruso
25 Casale Franco
26 Chez Gerard
27 Chez Liline
28 Chopstix Xchange
29 Chutneys
30 La Copita
31 Deals
32 del Buongustaio
33 La Delizia
34 The Eagle
35 Esarn Kheaw
36 First Floor
37 Florians
38 The Footstool
39 Galicia
40 Gate of India
41 Gonbei

42 Granita
43 Great Nepalese
44 Greek Valley
45 Imperial City
46 Istanbul Iskembecisi
47 Jashan
48 Lahore Kebab House
49 Laurent
50 The Lobster Pot
51 Ma Goa
52 Mamta
53 Le Midi
54 Neshiko
55 Newtons
56 The Nosh Brothers
57 Osteria Antica Bologna
58 Le Petit Max
59 Le P'tit Normand
60 Pizzeria Castello
61 Le Pont de la Tour
62 Quality Chop House
63 Rani
64 Ransome's Dock
65 Rebato's
66 Riva
67 River Cafe
68 RSJ
69 Sabai Sabai
70 Sabras
71 Seafresh
72 Smokey Joe's Diner
73 Snows on the Green
74 Stephen Bull's Bistro
75 Sweetings
76 Tandoori Lane
77 Tate Gallery Restaurant
78 Thai Garden
79 Thailand
80 Two Brothers
81 Upper Street Fish Shop
82 Vrisaki

9

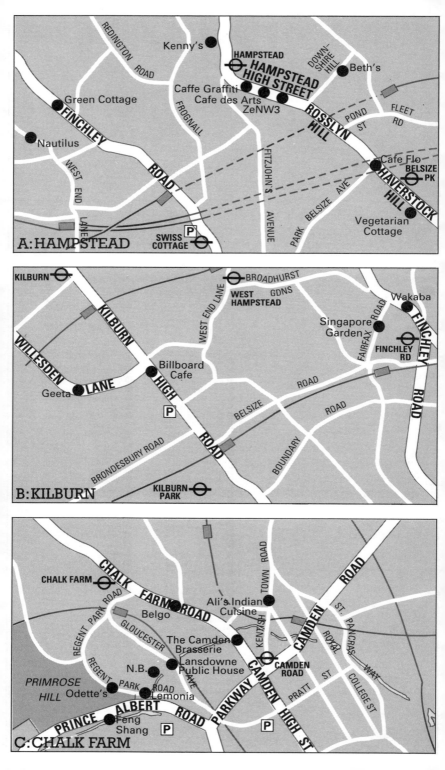

A: HAMPSTEAD

REDINGTON ROAD
Kenny's
HAMPSTEAD
HAMPSTEAD HIGH STREET
DOWN-SHIRE HILL
Beth's
Green Cottage
FINCHLEY ROAD
Nautilus
WEST END LANE
Caffe Graffiti
Cafe des Arts
ZeNW3
FROGNALL
FITZJOHN'S AVENUE
ROSSLYN HILL
POND ST
FLEET RD
Cafe Flo
BELSIZE PK
HAVERSTOCK HILL
PARK
BELSIZE AVE
Vegetarian Cottage
SWISS COTTAGE

B: KILBURN

KILBURN
BROADHURST
WEST HAMPSTEAD
GDNS
Wakaba
WILLESDEN LANE
KILBURN
WEST END LANE
Singapore Garden
FAIRFAX ROAD
FINCHLEY RD
FINCHLEY ROAD
Geeta
Billboard Cafe
HIGH ROAD
BELSIZE ROAD
ROAD
BRONDESBURY ROAD
BOUNDARY
KILBURN PARK

C: CHALK FARM

CHALK FARM
CHALK FARM ROAD
TOWN ROAD
CAMDEN ROAD
Ali's Indian Cuisine
REGENT PARK ROAD
Belgo
GLOUCESTER
KENTISH
ST. PANCRAS
The Camden Brasserie
CAMDEN
ROYAL
PRIMROSE HILL
REGENT PARK ROAD
N.B.
Lansdowne Public House
CAMDEN ROAD
CAMDEN HIGH ST
Odette's
AVE
Lemonia
CAMDEN
COLLEGE ST
PRINCE ALBERT ROAD
Feng Shang
PARKWAY
PRATT ST
ROYAL WAY

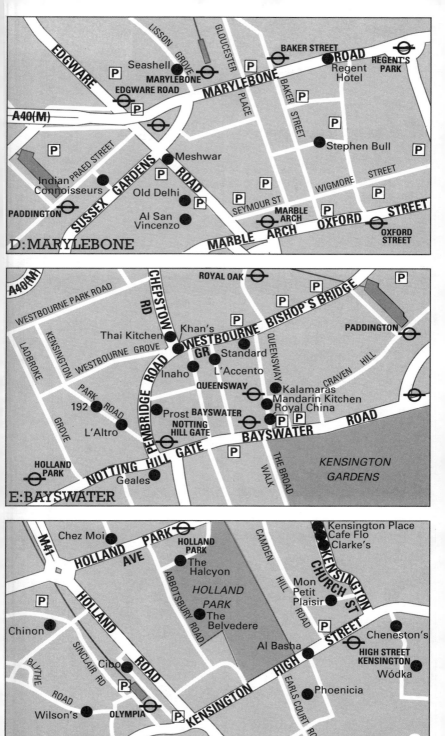

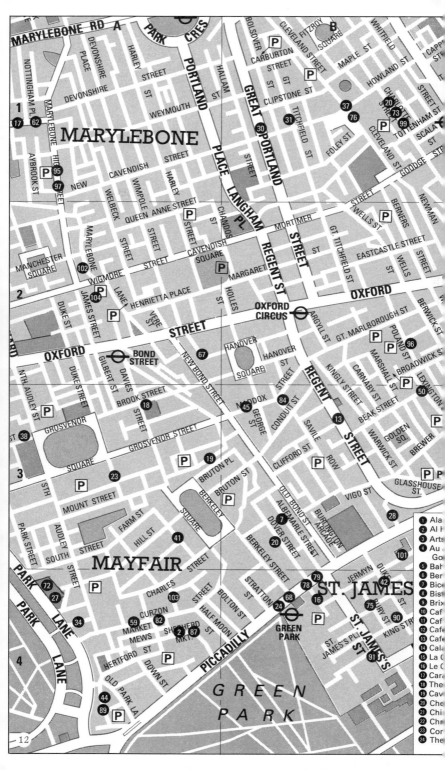

A map page showing the MARYLEBONE, MAYFAIR, and ST. JAMES'S areas of London.

Partial legend (right side):

1 Ala
2 Al H
3 Arts
4 Au
  Go
5 Bak
6 Ber
7 Bice
8 Bist
9 Brix
10 Caf
11 Caf
12 Cafe
13 Cafe
14 Cala
15 La C
16 Le C
17 Cara
18 The
19 Cav
20 Che
21 Chi
22 Chr
23 Cor
24 The

12

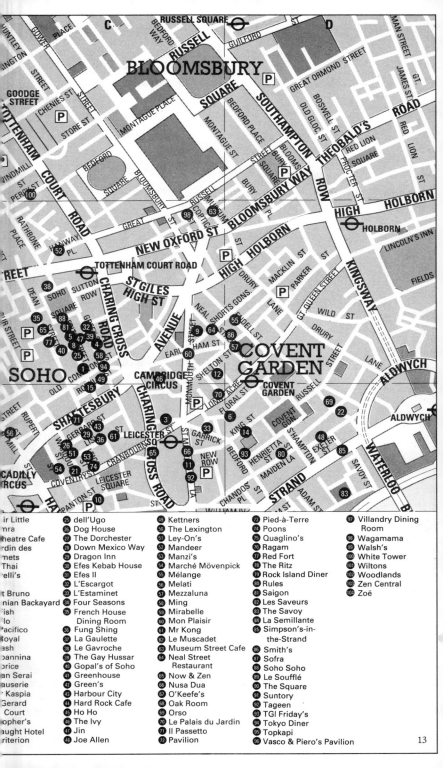

13

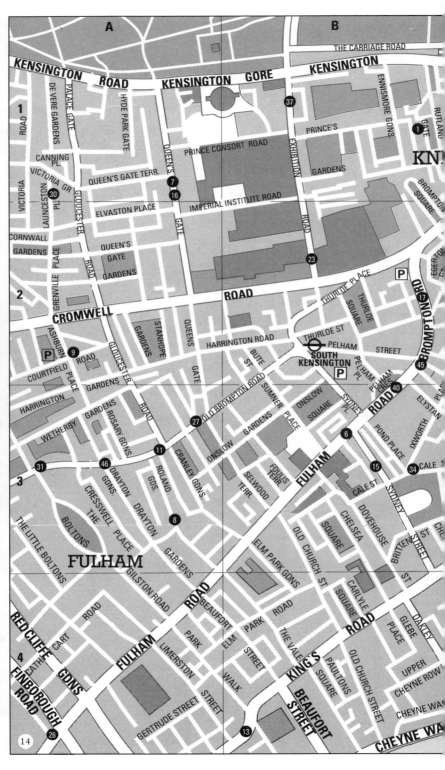

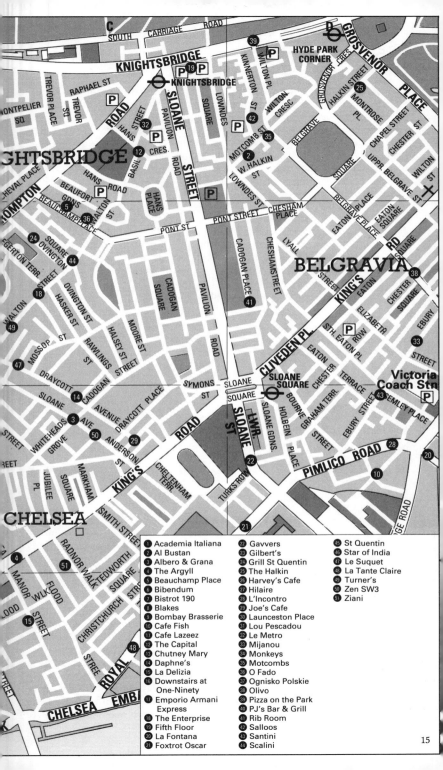

1. Academia Italiana
2. Al Bustan
3. Albero & Grana
4. The Argyll
5. Beauchamp Place
6. Bibendum
7. Bistrot 190
8. Blakes
9. Bombay Brasserie
10. Cafe Fish
11. Cafe Lazeez
12. The Capital
13. Chutney Mary
14. Daphne's
15. La Delizia
16. Downstairs at One-Ninety
17. Emporio Armani Express
18. The Enterprise
19. Fifth Floor
20. La Fontana
21. Foxtrot Oscar
22. Gavvers
23. Gilbert's
24. Grill St Quentin
25. The Halkin
26. Harvey's Cafe
27. Hilaire
28. L'Incontro
29. Joe's Cafe
30. Launceston Place
31. Lou Pescadou
32. Le Metro
33. Mijanou
34. Monkeys
35. Motcombs
36. O Fado
37. Ognisko Polskie
38. Olivo
39. Pizza on the Park
40. PJ's Bar & Grill
41. Rib Room
42. Salloos
43. Santini
44. Scalini
45. St Quentin
46. Star of India
47. Le Suquet
48. La Tante Claire
49. Turner's
50. Zen SW3
51. Ziani

15

Academia Italiana

24 Rutland Gate, SW7

071-225 3474 **£10 (Bring your own wine)**

'Of more than academic interest'

This is one of London's great quirky lunch palaces, an airy bow-windowed room, very plainly furnished, above the exhibition space of Italy's recently acquired cultural showcase in Rutland Gate. No licence nor any corkage exists so regulars bring their own wine (water or soft drinks are available). Menus are simple, rarely more than ten choices from salads and pasta and farinaceous dishes which, in Italy certainly, would only constitute half of a lunch even during the summer months. In winter there are stews and roasts. The cooking is simple and well-flavoured: seasonal vegetables with olive oil; quail and mushrooms with an inspired amount of pepper on salad leaves; a torta of leek rather like a quiche, and tiramisu made quite perfectly with proper mascarpone cheese. Service is pleasant and the atmosphere is agreeable, but perhaps the Academia is not the right place for power lunchers – no credit cards are accepted.

OPEN: Tues-Sat. **HOURS:** 12.30-2.30pm. **CLOSED:** Christmas Day and Bank Holidays. **CREDIT CARDS ACCEPTED:** None. **NUMBER OF SEATS:** 30. **SERVICE:** Optional. No smoking until after 2.00pm. Wheelchair access (assistance available). Galleries can be hired. **NEAREST TUBE STATION:** Knightsbridge. MAP REF: 14/B1

L'Accento

16 Garway Road,
Notting Hill Gate, W2

071-243 2201 **£20**

'A good value set price menu – on which you tend to build up your bill'

Restaurant success in the Notting Hill Gate/Westbourne Grove area must be looked at in context: there seems to be a greater than average willingness on the part of residents to disport themselves in bars, cafes and restaurants. Quite run-of-the-mill places can be swamped by custom. The reception for L'Accento was rapturous among other restaurant critics, qualified from me, but subsequent visits and reports from friends have proved that there is substance to the huge popularity of L'Accento. Value, as evidenced by the set price menu of £10.50 for two courses, is one attraction but a more important one is the robust quality of the cooking led by Andrea Beltrami. Osso bucco and bollito misto figured on one standard menu (subject to regular change). Dishes of the day will often include an item such as rich tangy stewed rabbit served with fresh polenta and buttered cabbage. Roast skate with brown butter exemplifies their spirited way with fish. Seasonality seems to be paid little heed with a pumpkin-stuffed pasta offered in May. Risottos and pastas are well-handled and, to my mind, make the best first courses, particularly black cuttlefish risotto if it is on offer. Should you encounter a rather lackadaisical attitude concerning the dessert menu with some of what is promised being unavailable, settle for vin santo with cantucci biscuits. The wine list is interesting and notably reasonable. An almost spiteful lack of softness in the spare, bare decor means that noise is a problem or a blessing, depending on how you view noise.

OPEN: Mon-Sun. **HOURS:** 12.30-2.30pm and 6.30-11.30pm (6.30-10.30pm Sun). **CLOSED:** Bank Holidays. **CREDIT CARDS ACCEPTED:** Visa, Access, Mastercard. **NUMBER OF SEATS:** 70. **SERVICE:** 10%. **SET PRICE LUNCH AND DINNER:** £10.50. Wheelchair access (but not lavatory). 12 tables outside. Private room seats 30. **NEAREST TUBE STATION:** Queensway/Bayswater.   MAP REF: 11/E

Adam's Cafe

77 Askew Road, W12

081-743 0572   **£22**

'Another greasy spoon transformation scene; this time into Tunisian'

Sausage, egg, bacon, beans and a slice by day, Thai by night is now quite commonplace. At Adam's Cafe artfully draped cloths and candles and mounds of couscous make the caff conversion into sunny Tunisia. Various couscous are the mainstay of a short menu which also offers grilled fish and lamb stews. Choose a Tunisian salad, a brik a l'oeuf or the same filo pastry wrapped round minced beef to start, sticky pastries to finish. The cheapness constitutes quite a lot of the charm of this husband and wife enterprise but there is a nice sincerity to it. Having opened unlicensed, the owners remain amenable to the idea of BYO, but there are now Moroccan, Tunisian and French wines available.

OPEN: Mon-Sat. **HOURS:** 7.30pm-12.00am. **CLOSED:** Bank Holidays and 2 weeks in August. **CREDIT CARDS ACCEPTED:** None. **NUMBER OF SEATS:** 60. **SERVICE:** Optional. Wheelchair access (but not lavatory). Private room seats 24. **NEAREST TUBE STATION:** Ravenscourt Park.   MAP REF: 8/B2

Alastair Little

49 Frith Street, W1

071-734 5183   **BAR £25; RESTAURANT £35**

'Where eclecticism took root'

I do believe that Alastair Little would like to change the look and feel of his sparse Soho restaurant. But I also suspect that part of him just cannot understand why people should want protection from draughts, and to have softer surfaces and sleeker service. At heart he is the eternal student and while his peers – and those who can afford to eat at his gaff – might appreciate some of the appurtenances of the good life he is still focused completely on the food and the excitement of new dishes, new discoveries. The scholarly approach informs his menus. A book he has read, or a dish he has eaten in another restaurant, often an ethnic one, will be transmuted into an offering on the list which is changed in part for every meal and tends to be stronger on first courses. Where once he seemed daringly to go where no white chef had been before, the eclectic approach has now become commonplace in restaurants, but Little still often has the edge. The way the Japanese do things influences his cooking of fish as in the thoroughly salted line-caught bass served with parsley salad. Increasingly there are Italian dishes on the menu often mutating through various manifestations e.g. a dish of chickpeas and pasta served first as a garnish, on another menu as a gratin, on the downstairs bar menu with a change of pasta. Little teaches some courses in Italy and typically returns having learned a good deal himself. Sometimes there is a straining for effect or an ingenuous amount of simplicity for the price charged. I have had some great meals at Alastair Little and some decidedly unremarkable ones. In that way he is more like a home cook than a chef. However, as a chef who has worked with him said, 'He's one of the few who have been cooking for a long time and are still interested in food.' The wine list is as changeable and adventurous as the menu. Service can have Marxist tendencies.

OPEN: LUNCH: Mon-Fri. DINNER: Mon-Sat. **HOURS:** 12.00-3.00pm and 6.00-11.30pm. **CLOSED:** Bank Holidays. **CREDIT CARDS ACCEPTED:** Visa, Access, AmEx. **NUMBER OF SEATS:** 35 in Restaurant, 20 in Bar. **SERVICE:** Optional. **SET PRICE LUNCH:** £10 in Bar, £20 in Restaurant. Bar can be booked privately and seats 16. **NEAREST TUBE STATION:** Tottenham Court Road/Piccadilly Circus/Leicester Square.

MAP REF: 12/C2

Alba

107 Whitecross Street, EC1

071-588 1798   **£27-£30**

*'A good deed (Piedmontese food) twinkling
in a barren area'*

Handy for the Barbican it may be, but Alba merits more leisurely appraisal than that allowed by pre- and post-performance eating. This particularly holds true in late autumn, the porcini and truffle season. (The Piedmont town of Alba is in the heart of truffle country.) Headily-scented white truffle grated onto something non-combative such as risotto, tagliatelle or scrambled eggs is one of life's purest pleasures. On a more prosaic note, there are dishes that are not run-of-the-Italian-restaurant-mill such as tongue with salsa verde, pepperoni in bagna caôda, pasta filled with ricotta and spinach dressed with a walnut sauce, risotto with radicchio, pot roast stuffed veal, and hard Italian cheeses served with pears. The grilling of fish is well-handled. Espresso and/or vin santo served with cantuccini (hard nut biscuits) may be the best mode of completing a meal. The wine list is strong on Piedmont and Tuscany. The look is pink and plain but this sits happily with an establishment that is sympathetically serious about food, not trying to make any statement of intent beyond that.

OPEN: Mon-Fri. **HOURS:** 12.00-3.00pm and 6.00-11.00pm. **CLOSED:** Bank Holidays. **CREDIT CARDS ACCEPTED:** All major cards. **NUMBER OF SEATS:** 45-50. **SERVICE:** 12.5%. Wheelchair access (but not lavatory). **NEAREST TUBE STATION:** Barbican/Moorgate. MAP REF: 8/C2

Al Basha Restaurant

222 High Street Kensington, W8

071-938 1794 £25

'Lebanese food with a sort of a view of Holland Park'

In the good old days before the Department of Trade ordered every estate agent's thesaurus to be put on a bonfire, these particularly creative writers would have described the Al Basha restaurant as 'affording fine views across Holland Park' at the very least. Few would have been able to resist exaggerating a strip of paved ground outside the restaurant into 'the perfect location for al fresco dining'.

In reality you would have to be a first cousin of the giraffe to see much of the park, and the pleasures of eating lunch outside may be diminished by the heavy traffic that rumbles along High Street Kensington. The real attractions of Al Basha are its long list of meze and the good manners of the staff, rather than its similarity to Xanadu. It is a large place that, come nightfall, can seem gloomy until halfway through a bottle of the remarkable Lebanese wine Chateau Musar.

Although the selection of meze found in Lebanese restaurants across London is similar, Al Basha's chefs produce brighter flavours and better portions than many. Potatoes fried with spices, coriander and garlic, lamb's tongue with a lemon sauce and purée of grilled aubergine (moutabal) are full of character and the more familiar items are not humdrum. As the meal begins with freshly baked bread and a basket of raw vegetables the appetite may not hold out for one of the plainer main courses of lamb or chicken cooked on a charcoal grill.

OPEN: Mon-Sun. **HOURS:** 12.00pm-12.00am (12.00pm-1.00am Sat-Sun). **CREDIT CARDS ACCEPTED:** Access, AmEx, Diner's Club, Mastercard, Visa. **NUMBER OF SEATS:** 180. **SERVICE:** 15%. **SET PRICE LUNCH:** £12.50. Wheelchair access (but not lavatory). 15 tables outside. Private room seats 60. **NEAREST TUBE STATION:** High Street Kensington. MAP REF: 11/F

Albero & Grana

Chelsea Cloisters,
89 Sloane Avenue, SW3

071-225 1048/9 £28

'The most evolved Spanish food in London'

Chef Angel Garcia came to London having secured a Michelin star in Madrid at the restaurant Luculo. In order to impose on London restaurants some imaginative and authentic Spanish cooking this achievement seems almost an exaggerated prop, so hokey and pathetic is most of what is offered in that name. The food at Albero & Grana – the name signifies the ochre and red colours associated with the sand and matador's cape of the bull-ring – is quite unlike the *Eldorado* offerings of most of London's Iberian restaurants. Some of the dishes even turn out not much like their menu titles but although Garcia has studied in France his cooking has not taken on the gelded, attenuated style associated with much modern cooking in Spain. It is original, in so far as one can use that description for any flourish of dishes.

Lasagne of black pudding (morcilla) is a sandwich of rectangles of grassy green pasta enclosing meat, the whole pinned together with a rosemary twig and served with a froth of green pepper sauce. The process of escabeche – marinating sauteed ingredients in an acidic medium – is applied to items as varied as duck liver and oysters. The technique implicit in a soufflé is brought to bear on unlikely ingredients such as wing of skate. Meat main courses are sensibly more straightforward – particularly to be appreciated in Segovian lamb – but nevertheless thought through; almonds as well as apples with duck breast, endives gracing a dish of veal kidneys. Caramelized rice pudding and apple and cinnamon millefeuille show how highly developed is Spanish patisserie. Such food deserves a more comprehensive, better list of Spanish wines and also more committed service.

The front part of Albera & Grana, vividly decorated in the namesake colours, is a better than usual tapas bar that also serves fish and shellfish grilled a la plancha.

OPEN: LUNCH: Mon-Sun. DINNER: Mon-Sat. **HOURS:** 12.30-3.30pm (1.00-5.00pm Sun) and 6.00pm-12.00am. **CLOSED:** Bank Holidays. **CREDIT CARDS ACCEPTED:** All major cards. **NUMBER OF SEATS:** 130. **SERVICE:** Optional. Lounge separated by cast iron screen seats 25. **NEAREST TUBE STATION:** South Kensington/Sloane Square.

MAP REF: 14/C3

Al Bustan

27 Motcomb Street, SW1

071-235 8277 £22

'Fastidious Lebanese food in splendid surroundings'

My theory about the high standards of cooking in Lebanese restaurants in London concerns its 'purity'. No zealous Western entrepreneur has decided to popularize, sanitize, burlesque or streamline Lebanese food in the way that happens with most other cuisines. In a world of food opportunism Lebanese cuisine remains fairly uncorrupted. The luxurious Al Bustan in Belgravia is as good a place as any to prove my point. It has the additional bonus of the owner's wife being the chef. A show of interest in the menu may produce the offer to prepare some specials such as vine leaves stuffed with cooked, spiced lamb served with roasted lamb on the bone or slices of highly spiced grilled lamb wrapped in warm unleavened bread. From the printed menu include fried chicken livers with pomegranate molasses in your spread culled from the long list of cold and hot first courses. As is commonplace in this tradition the meal begins with a bowl of salad vegetables – justifying the cover charge – and, here, notably light, hot sesame bread. Finish with equally light pastries. Wines, including the Lebanese wines, are uniformly expensive. An aperitif of arak followed by freshly squeezed juice might be the answer. Service is formal and proficient.

OPEN: Mon-Sun. **HOURS:** 12.00pm-12.00am. **CLOSED:** Christmas Day and Boxing Day. **CREDIT CARDS ACCEPTED:** All major cards. **NUMBER OF SEATS:** 65. **SERVICE:** Optional, £2 cover charge. **SET PRICE LUNCH:** £15. **SET PRICE DINNER:** £20. 4 tables outside. **NEAREST TUBE STATION:** Knightsbridge.   MAP REF: 14/D1

Alexandra
(previously Café Normand)
507 Kingston Road, SW20

081-542 4838   **£25-£28**

'A family run corner of Normandy in Raynes Park'

Chef/proprietor and proud father of Alexandra, Eric Lecras previously worked at Le P'tit Normand in Southfields. His own venture is small, personal and faithful to the butter, cream and Calvados school of cooking. Dishes which change daily are listed on a blackboard and frequently include, as you might expect, moules Normandes, crêpes Dieppoise, canard Vallée d'Auge and their version of tarte Tatin named after the restaurant (and the little girl). The dishes are competently cooked, if sometimes constructed rather too economically. It is a sweet place decorated almost as hopelessly as you would find in France. In that country there would be an even greater number of disparate items made of beaten copper tacked onto the wall.

OPEN: LUNCH: Tues-Fri, Sun. DINNER: Tues-Sat. **HOURS:** 12.00-2.00pm and 7.00-10.00pm. **CREDIT CARDS ACCEPTED:** Visa, Access, Mastercard. **NUMBER OF SEATS:** 50. **SERVICE:** 12.5%. **SET PRICE LUNCH:** £10.55 or £12.75. 5 tables outside. Private room seats 32. **NEAREST TUBE STATION:** South Wimbledon.   MAP REF: 8/B3

Al Hamra Restaurant

31-33 Shepherd Market, W1

071-493 1954/6934   **£25**

'Meze on the pavement in Shepherd Market;
it could almost be Beirut'

The mix of twee and sleaze that characterizes Shepherd Market can be forgotten at Al Hamra, one of the better Lebanese restaurants in London. The best use you can make of it is securing a table outside on a fine day. However, a corner site and liberal use of plants makes the interior also attractive. Any indignation over the hefty cover charge (£2.50 per person) tends to die down with the arrival of the array of raw vegetables and warm Lebanese bread. It is a healthy D.I.Y. start to a meal which should concentrate on a choice from the forty or so small dishes such as moutabal (aubergine purée), fattoush (bread salad), batrakh (smoked cod's roe), bastorma (thick bresaola), sojuk sadah (lamb sausages), firri (grilled quails), and pay less attention to the main courses of charcoal-grilled meat and poultry. The unabashed carnivore will add to the first list the various hors d'oeuvres based on raw lamb and its liver. Lebanese wine – when available – is the best value as French wines tend to be over-priced and not well chosen. Arak is an alternative but not to be recommended if you are lunching and have plans for the afternoon – apart from the obvious one that might, if not staring you in the face, at least be cruising past.

OPEN: Mon-Sun. **HOURS:** 11.00am-12.00am. **CLOSED:** Christmas Day and New Year's Day. **CREDIT CARDS ACCEPTED:** All major cards. **NUMBER OF SEATS:** 75. **SERVICE:** Optional, £2.50 cover charge. **SET PRICE LUNCH AND DINNER:** £20 plus drink. Wheelchair access (but not lavatory). 4 tables outside. **NEAREST TUBE STATION:** Green Park.   MAP REF: 12/A4

Ali's Indian Cuisine

81 Kentish Town Road, NW1

071-284 2061/2   **£10-£15**

'A better and more winsome than usual local Indian'

Ali's, a small restaurant with vaguely colonial decor and notably agreeable staff, stands quite high in the league table of local Indians. 'Ali's Specialities', for example murgh makani and gosht kata massalla, are carefully prepared. The chicken dish is tender and creamy, the flavourings in the lamb identifiable. Crisply fried onions used as a garnish is symptomatic of the lengths gone to that most comparable restaurants do not. Piped music is intrusive and relentless.

OPEN: Mon-Sun. **HOURS:** 12.00-3.00pm and 6.00pm-12.00am (12.00pm-12.00am Sun). **CLOSED:** Christmas Day. **CREDIT CARDS ACCEPTED:** Visa, Access, AmEx. **NUMBER OF SEATS:** 35. **SERVICE:** Optional. **SET PRICE LUNCH:** £5.50. Wheelchair access (but not lavatory). Private room seats 16. **NEAREST TUBE STATION:** Camden Town/Kentish Town.   MAP REF: 10/C

Al San Vincenzo

30 Connaught Street, W2

071-262 9623 £30

*'A singular Italian restaurant; neither
trattoria nor trendy'*

In many ways Vincenzo Borgonzolo is an Italian restaurateur marching to
the sound of a different drum. The relatively complex food owes nothing to
fashion which in these days of crostini with everything comes as a relief.
Renouncing a set price menu in favour of an à la carte has somehow loosened
up the atmosphere in the small, warmly decorated dining room managed by
Vincenzo's wife, and contributed new fluidity and grace to the cooking.
Why this should be so I can't imagine but the latest meal at Al San Vincenzo
conveyed that Cheam – where the Borgonzolos previously ran a restaurant –
has been forgotten. They are now at ease in their location up West. The
menu changes regularly. Should you be offered oricchiette freschi al
putanesca, the firm traditional pasta of Apulia dressed with black olive
pesto, capers, chilli and Parmesan, take it. Pasta in general is interestingly
sauced. Seize also the two types of Italian sausage served with sprouting
broccoli. Game in season is well-handled and the kitchen shows
commendable brio when it comes to dealing with offal including hot salted
tongue served with Italian pickles. A quintessentially casalinga dish is sirloin
steak wrapped in a sort of envelope of eggs scrambled with Parmesan and
thyme. Panettone makes the basis of an ace bread and butter pudding. For
those who prefer sweet and cool there is semifreddo of chocolate with an
almond biscuit base. The short wine list, including dessert wines, offers
some unusual bottles. Finish with grappa.

OPEN: LUNCH: Mon-Fri. DINNER: Mon-Sat. **HOURS:** 12.30-3.00pm and 7.00-
10.30pm. **CREDIT CARDS ACCEPTED:** Access, Visa, Mastercard. **NUMBER OF SEATS:** 35.
SERVICE: Optional. **NEAREST TUBE STATION:** Marble Arch/Paddington.

MAP REF: 11/D

L'Altro

210 Kensington Park Road, W11

071-792 1066/1077 LUNCH £15; DINNER £25-£30

*'Commendable, mainly fish restaurant
in a mainly foul area'*

The fickle, fashionable crowd that flits along Kensington Park Road in
search of supper is looking for something less tangible than satisfying food.
Places remain packed while kitchens take a distinct turn for the worse ('really
filthy' is the appropriate local phrase) then, following some herd impulse,
everyone moves. Only 192 (q.v.) seems to attract faithful customers. At the
northern-most end of the road is L'Altro. This Italian restaurant is tolerably
hip but aspires to meet standards that will make sense to anyone from
outside the locale – to serve pleasant food in a well-mannered, competent

fashion and to do so within a reasonable time limit. The room is decorated as if it were a section of a set for a Rossini opera.

The idea, when L'Altro first opened, was to offer only fish, farinaceous dishes and vegetables. This might have been presumed to attract the curious subset of vegetarians who imagine that fish have no feelings, along with those who simply enjoy eating fish and Mediterranean diet faddists. As well, it would differentiate the restaurant from its older sibling Cibo (q.v.). National antagonism to specialization soon scuppered the plan so now there are a couple of meat or poultry dishes available. But the delicate starters – stuffed courgette flowers or baby artichokes – the various fish roasted or grilled and plainly sauced with olive oil and herbs, and the pasta or rice with shellfish are still really the point of L'Altro. Prices have come down somewhat, without portions becoming perceptibly smaller. Full marks for a wine list where the descriptions help rather than exasperate.

OPEN: Mon-Sat. **HOURS:** 12.00-2.30pm (12.00-3.00pm Fri-Sat) and 7.00-11.00pm (7.00-11.30pm Fri-Sat). **CLOSED:** Christmas Eve, Christmas Day and Boxing Day. **CREDIT CARDS ACCEPTED:** All major cards. **NUMBER OF SEATS:** 35. **SERVICE:** Optional. Wheelchair access. 3 tables outside. **NEAREST TUBE STATION:** Ladbroke Grove. MAP REF: 11/E

Anna's Place

90 Mildmay Park, N1

071-249 9379 £23-£25

'Swedish home cooking and nurturing'

Proprietor Anna Hegarty is known for her motherly concern, her slightly didactic gregariousness. Fortunately for those of us who, for reasons known only to our shrinks, shrink from too much attention in restaurants, her long service in the trade has muted the approach but the menu is still recited to the customers by the staff, including Anna's daughter. From it you would be wise to start with the excellent herrings, gravad lax if you have not figured out the easy-peasy way of making it at home, salt duck with horseradish and follow with biff (beef) Strindberg with its sharp/sour flavours worthy of the titular genesis. Curd cheese in crisply fried pastry is a fitting dessert. Note that the caraway flavoured rolls – worth having – are charged at 40p each. Anna's Place, one of the few Swedish restaurants in town, comes across as a neighbourhood place, an atmosphere intensified when fine weather allows the garden to be used.

OPEN: Tues-Sat. **HOURS:** 12.15-2.15pm and 7.15-11.45pm. **CLOSED:** 2 weeks at Christmas and Easter; 4 weeks in August. **CREDIT CARDS ACCEPTED:** None. **NUMBER OF SEATS:** 42. **SERVICE:** 10%. 5 tables outside in summer. Wheelchair access (but not lavatory), please advise when booking. **NEAREST TUBE STATION:** Highbury & Islington. MAP REF: 8/C2

The Argyll

316 King's Road, SW3

071-352 0025 £28

'An attempt at serious cooking in a street not known for it'

Anand Sastry – a name I've sometimes thought must be an anagram – made a name for himself as chef at a country house hotel, Woolley Grange in Bradford-on-Avon. Something of the characteristics engendered by that dread phrase 'country house hotel' seem to stick to his cooking in the King's Road despite palpable efforts to be modern and city slick. He has taken to serving some dishes (not soups) in shallow soup plates, a move that reinforces a certain vapidity present in them. Notes from one meal chosen from a menu that changes in part each day: 'Roasted celeriac parcels of snails and mushrooms are a mixture of egg and mushroom wrapped in the thin sheets of celeriac with a few chewy snails dotted around the periphery of the dish.' It is an interesting concept but not one that really comes off. Better is another parcel, this time of foie gras inside ravioli served on a bed of creamy lentils, but somewhat overwhelmed by its sweet, buttery sauce. A fine use of unexpected sweetness is the purée of sweetcorn under the ballotine of chicken (undercooked) stuffed with another eggy mixture and surrounded with a mustard seed sauce. A too exuberant use of capers spoils panfried skate with potato and shallot 'dressing'. Much seems to come from the school of too-clever-by-half cooking. It is a shame because Sastry's obvious skills and indeed feeling for food come across in items as simple as truly well-cooked and imaginative vegetables – a selection is served – and the dessert of lemon tart accompanied by a meringue lemon curd sandwich but sadly also by a daft and otiose vodka and celery sorbet. The premises play a significant part in the appeal of the restaurant. They are large and simply decorated with an ad hoc quality to the collection of tables and chairs. On fine days the doors fold back to the street which remains one of the more amusing thoroughfares to observe, particularly if Chelsea sweeties are on their way to Po-Na-Na, the small tented bar in The Argyll's basement. Staff are infected with country house manners in the sense that there is an attitude of 'of course this is not really what I do for a living' and a concomitant inefficiency. To drink interestingly you must spend, which makes for a bill in excess of reasonable expectations.

A SHORT WINE LIST, but one which makes good use of the four points of the compass: there's Oregon Pinot Noir (from Cameron, no vintage cited, at £19) to compare with Burgundy (try Mouton's Vieilles Vignes Givry 1989 at £24); Cabernet Sauvignon from Argentina (Weinert's flavoury 1983 at £18.50) to compare with Bordeaux (the much fresher 1990 de Sours at £19); and Canadian Chardonnay (Hillebrand's slender 1990 at £25) to compare with Chablis (Durup, £23.50). Prices start highish, at £11.50, and stage a lark's ascent from there.

OPEN: LUNCH: Tues-Sat. DINNER: Mon-Sat. **HOURS:** 12.15-2.30pm and 7.00-10.45pm. **CLOSED:** Bank Holidays. **CREDIT CARDS ACCEPTED:** AmEx, Visa, Diner's Club, Mastercard. **NUMBER OF SEATS:** 58. **SERVICE:** Optional. **SET PRICE LUNCH:** £8.50 (two courses), £10 (3 courses). **NEAREST TUBE STATION:** Sloane Square.

MAP REF: 14/C3

Arts Theatre Cafe

6-7 Great Newport Street, WC2

071-497 8014 £15

'A gem in the West End'

The phrase Arts Theatre Cafe might conjure visions of a folk-music, smoke-filled space serving stuffed baked potatoes to out-of-work actors. It is not like that at all. Italian food of The River Cafe/Cibo/Riva school – soon to be as much a London cuisine as was its fake Neopolitan predecessor in the sixties – is exceptionally well-prepared and served in a pleasant if spartan cream-painted room decorated with black and white prints from the Photographer's Gallery upstairs. The menu changes weekly but always features substantial soups and imaginative pastas, plus there is a daily pasta and fresh fish special. There are well-thought-through garnishes to crostini and bruschetta – e.g. Sicilian sweet and sour vegetables (caponata) with baked goat's cheese. Meat and fish are grilled and served with interesting vegetables – e.g. Swiss chard with pancetta, spicy Puy lentils. Grilled chicken and pork meat balls seasoned with lemon and Parmesan and served with cannellini is a nice one if you can get it. Vegetarians can graze here happily with their own daily dish as well as several appropriate menu items. Well-detailed wines from most of the Italian regions are offered. The one drawback to the cafe is the presence of the audience surging in during the theatre intervals. Not since school have you longed so fervently for the bell.

AN EXEMPLARY LITTLE twenty-wine Italian wine list, full of uncompromising reds and – more impressively – some non-neutral Italian whites, like Teruzzi e Puthod's Vernaccia (£12.50), Enofriulia's Tocai Friuliano (£14) and the Greco di Majo Norante (£17.50). There's real Lambrusco, intelligent notes and only the marmaladey Bukkuram over £17.50 (it's worth it).

OPEN: **LUNCH:** Mon-Fri. **DINNER:** Mon-Sat. **HOURS:** 12.00pm-12.00am (6.00pm-12.00am Sat). **CLOSED:** Christmas, Easter and Bank Holidays. **CREDIT CARDS ACCEPTED:** None. **NUMBER OF SEATS:** 35. **SERVICE:** 10%. **SET PRICE LUNCH AND DINNER:** £11.50. **NEAREST TUBE STATION:** Leicester Square. MAP REF: 12/C3

Les Associés

172 Park Road, N8

081-348 8944 £27

'Burgundian food in Crouch End'

Chef Gilles Charvet and his two associates are from Burgundy and the dishes offered in this small (eight tables) cosy, authentically kitschily decorated place are exactly those you might expect to find in a restaurant of that fertile area – although with the way restaurants are going in France you might do better staying in Crouch End. If French means to you dishes like fish soup, snails, frogs' legs, blanquettes, confits and côte de boeuf your assumptions will here be vindicated (subject to seasonal menus plus daily specials, most of them centred around fish). There is a liking for presenting first courses in pastry – feuilletés of this and that, say snails and spinach or leeks and foie gras – but there is a more interesting tendency, that of making a chartreuse. This classic but seldom used technique braises vegetables with a main ingredient in a mould which is turned out onto the plate. Lamb and aubergines are married in this way. The fashion for mixing meat with fish, as in chicken stuffed with scallop or beef fillet with langoustine is one you can only pray will pass. Desserts are best approached through the plate featuring a selection. In the wholly French wine list it would seem disloyal to stray outside burgundies. Lunch offers soups, salads and assemblies of cheese or charcuterie. The assumption when you book for the evening is that you are there for the duration.

Open: Lunch: Wed-Fri. **Dinner:** Tue-Sat. **Hours:** 12.30-2.00pm and 7.30-10.00pm. **Closed:** Christmas, Easter and August. **Credit cards accepted:** Visa, Access. **Number of seats:** 36. **Service:** Optional. **Set price lunch:** £15.95. Wheelchair access (but not lavatory). **Nearest tube station:** Finsbury Park.

MAP REF: 8/B2

Au Jardin des Gourmets

5 Greek Street, W1

071-437 1816   £35

'The wines in the garden are lovely'

This long-established Soho restaurant is a place to plan a treat centred upon a serious bottle of wine. Sensibly, among the main courses there are dishes to share – carré d'agneau, côte de boeuf grillé and poulet de grain rôti – which is not only a romantic way of dining but also removes the problem of finding a bottle to match different foods. A glass of sauternes or champagne with the foie gras en aigre doux to start and a dessert soufflé of the day ordered at the outset completes the pleasure. Should you want to spend less money on food the fine wine list can also be summoned in the ground floor bistro called Salle à Manger, but service there tends to let down both the kitchen and the cellar.

THE LONDON GOURMET, as defined by what's on offer in the Jardin, remains deeply wedded to the red wines of Burgundy and below, and to Bordeaux with a bit of age on it (the most widely listed vintage is 1966). For this, you pay – though less than you might. Drinking Beychevelle '66 here rather than at Le Gavroche will save you £160.12 per bottle, and £266 on Latour '66. For less exalted drinking, the list reflects Joseph Berkmann's agency lines fairly closely; he's one of the few merchants to take Provence seriously, while the celebrated liaison with Duboeuf should not obscure some canny buying from elsewhere on the Eastern French axis. There are plenty of halves, and mark-ups are never less than reasonable.

Open: Lunch: Mon-Fri. **Dinner:** Mon-Sat. **Hours:** 12.15-2.30pm and 6.15-11.15pm. **Credit cards accepted:** All major cards. **Number of seats:** 140. **Service:** 15%. **Set price lunch and dinner:** £19.50. No smoking area. Wheelchair access (but not lavatory). Private rooms seat 12, 18 and 50. **Nearest tube station:** Tottenham Court Road/Leicester Square.   MAP REF: 12/C2

Bahn Thai

21a Frith Street, W1

071-437 8504   **£20**

*'Arguably the best Thai food in London
grudgingly served'*

It seems the dream of some hidden power to place a Thai restaurant – or two
– on every London high street plus one on the first floor of every pub.
Considering the growth in the cuisine over about a decade the standard in
general is not bad but veers towards monotonous. Few places excel; in terms
of food Bahn Thai – in its Kensington days one of the earliest Thai
establishments – does. A starter you do not find everywhere is miang gai,
moist, minced chicken and ground peanuts briskly spiced with pepper, garlic
and mint which is eaten rolled in bitter leaves. Dim sum dumplings are
freshly made. The usual hot and sour soups and salads are well prepared but
there are more unusual and colourful dishes. Cracklingly fresh Thai blue
swimming crab is served in the shell with curry paste. A whole green sea
perch is steamed with a chilli, garlic and lemon sauce. Lean and tender
venison is a constituent of a jungle curry. Thai fried salt beef is something to
be tried more for interest than pleasure. Try green papaya salad and water
lily stems with yellow beans. Somewhat hectoring notes on the menu written
by the English owner (married to a Thai woman) will guide you through the
long list. There are lots of suitably English do's and don't's and at times a
holier-than-thou attitude. Still, you needn't read them. Do concentrate
though on the wine list which has been composed with commendable care to
flatter and highlight the food. The premises have recently undergone a
much-needed revamp. A snack is now offered on the ground floor.

ANYONE WHO RISES to a challenge with as much vim as Philip Harris has
brought to the matching of Thai heat and spice with wine deserves a hearing
– or rather a tasting. This would be a good wine list in any restaurant; in an
oriental one, it amazes. The whites are varietally organized, with
Gewürztraminer and Riesling assigned key roles alongside trusty Chard; the
reds simply divide into France and the rest. Everything is intelligently
annotated; few bottles set you back beyond £20, and there are 14 under £10.
If you don't like the Thai wine (at £7.50 per half), you've only got yourself to
blame: the list stages a memorable public execution.

OPEN: Mon-Sun. **HOURS:** 12.00-2.45pm (12.30-2.30pm Sun) and 6.00-11.15pm
(6.30-10.30pm Sun). **CLOSED:** Christmas, Easter and Bank Holidays. **CREDIT CARDS
ACCEPTED:** All major cards. **NUMBER OF SEATS:** 120. **SERVICE:** 12.5% optional.
Wheelchair access (but not ladies' lavatory). Private rooms seat 20, 30 or 50.
NEAREST TUBE STATION: Leicester Square/Tottenham Court Road.

MAP REF: 12/C2

Beauchamp Place

15 Beauchamp Place, SW3

071-589 4252/0984 £25

'Modern food and a wine list to Khoo over'

Formerly Menage à Trois, Beauchamp Place has as a partner chef David Wilby, one of the head chefs when that quintessentially eighties restaurant was flourishing. In the revamped premises he offers a modern menu faithful to the ways cooking in Britain has evolved since the niminy-piminy days of nouvelle cuisine. A Mediterranean influence is firmly in place as is the school of pile the ingredients high and sell them fairly reasonably. In some instances, such as fashioning fishcakes from a kedgeree mixture and surrounding them with a coriander and cumin sauce and homing in on the seldom utilized herring roe, serving it up on a thick slice of soft white toast glazed with hollandaise, Wilby exhibits original thought. Occasionally an emphasis in the cooking is jarring as in overpowering herbs or spices or inept in technique as in hefty pastry underpinning a dessert tart, but more frequently the ideas come off as in, say, confit of potatoes and artichokes served with slack, grainy polenta and a pool of melted Fontina cheese. Main course meat dishes can share sauces with a rather too egalitarian enthusiasm. All dishes are self-contained in terms of accompaniments and as is now the fashion – here idiotically entitled Not Only But Also – some are served in two sizes at two prices. Another partner in Beauchamp Place is Eddie Khoo, responsible for the exciting and reasonably priced wine list, easily as much, if not more, a U.S.P. of the restaurant as the cooking. A wide selection of wines by the glass encourages experimentation as does the restraint in mark-ups. Astute buying on Khoo's part means some prices bear comparison with those you would find at a wine merchant. Those familiar with the look of Menage à Trois will find they barely recognize the place as the same. The restaurant now extends over three storeys and a new glass roof removes some of the basement feel of old. However, a low ceiling in the main restaurant, wooden floorboards and curious metal screens and sculptures Festival of Britain style bring about a restless, jittery atmosphere. In the ground floor bar there is a menu of light dishes, useful to know if plotting a route through the wine list is your aim.

THE RETURN OF THE piratical Eddie Khoo is good news for London's drinkers: few restaurateurs are more obsessively questing about their wine lists. The fifty-odd wines on the 'Restaurant Selection' are all under £20, and include treats like Conterno's 1990 Conca Tre Pile Barbera d'Alba at £17.50 or, more modestly, the massively proportioned Long Gully 1988 Sauvignon Blanc at £9.50 (£2.65 per glass) and Monmorin's Côtes de Thongue Merlot 1990 at £9. But Khoo's enthusiasms are getting the better of him again, and the rest of the list romps excitedly off in other directions – most notably to Burgundy, where you can drink really dangerously, at Premier and Grand Cru level, for £30 or £40.

OPEN: Mon-Sun. **HOURS:** 12.00-3.15pm (12.00-4.00pm Sun) and 7.00pm-12.00am (7.00-10.30pm Sun). **CLOSED:** Christmas Day and Boxing Day. **CREDIT CARDS ACCEPTED:** All major cards. **NUMBER OF SEATS:** 110. **SERVICE:** 12.5% optional. **SET PRICE LUNCH:** £10.50. No smoking area. Private room seats 25. **NEAREST TUBE STATION:** Knightsbridge. MAP REF: 14/C2

Belgo

72 Chalk Farm Road, NW1

071-267 0718   **£22**

*'Rollick along with mussels, chips, beers and
waiters in monks' habits'*

Belgo is one of the restaurant success stories of the early nineties. Alluding
only stylishly through means of wild, modern architecture – metal ducting
writhes over the open kitchen – and design – chairs are fashioned from axe
handles – to the idea of Belgium as the butt of jokes, the owner provides, in
an atmosphere of Rabelaisian excess, quite carefully prepared food. The
menu reaches beyond mussels done eight ways and served in vast quantity to
asparagus, lobster, composed salads and specialities such as endive au gratin,
wild boar sausage and duck in cherry beer sauce. Tellingly, though, the list
of specialities has dwindled since the opening. For many the point of the
place is drinking; choosing from the long list of Belgian beers, bottled and on
tap, sometimes chasing them with frozen schnapps and genevers. Lunchtime
is relatively calm and thus the moment to appreciate the food as more than
ballast.

THIS IS THE PLACE to come in order to see how close beer, refracted through
the phlegmy Belgian imagination, can come to matching wine's subtlety and
variety. And strength: the penetrating Moinette Blonde at 8.5%abv is
typical, while wine-like, tongue-coating Piraat weighs in at a heady
11.5%abv (£8.75 for a 75cl bottle). There are wines for the perverse. Ready-
mixed rounds of four beers (from the total of eighteen) encourage
experiment. Just remember to sip, not gulp.

OPEN: Mon-Sun. **HOURS:** 12.00-3.00pm and 6.00pm-1.00am (12.00pm-1.00am
Sat, 12.00pm-12.00am Sun). **CREDIT CARDS ACCEPTED:** All major cards. **NUMBER OF
SEATS:** 75. **SERVICE:** 15%. **SET PRICE LUNCH AND DINNER:** £8.95. Wheelchair access.
NEAREST TUBE STATION: Chalk Farm.   MAP REF: 10/C

The Belvedere in Holland Park

Off Abbotsbury Road, W8

071-602 1238   **£30-£35**

'For once catering almost as pretty as the park'

Parks and green open spaces generally are part of the pride and joy of
London. It is, however, perhaps a reflection on an indigenous
underestimation of the pleasure to be found in food that it was the case until
recently that catering concessions therein were awarded to large
conglomerates who provided an expensive and shoddy service. The situation
is improving with some little pockets of enterprise such as The Oshobasho
Cafe, appropriately enough vegetarian, in Highgate Woods and slicker
operations such as The Belvedere in Holland Park. Housed in what was
originally the summer ballroom of Holland House, The Belvedere in the past
offered the sort of pretentious food that was understood to be the price you

had to pay for romantic, verdant surroundings complete with a view of peacocks strutting their stuff.

The company who converted the restaurant to its present style and initiated a modern, relatively inexpensive menu devised by chef Jeremy Strode became one more victim of the recession. Johnny Gold, owner of Tramp nightclub, bought The Belvedere from the receivers and has continued to run it for the pleasure rather than the come-uppance of its customers. Strode has left but a fashionable health-conscious menu, presented as one list to divide up as you wish, continues. All the staples of the style are there; lobster ravioli, onion and sun-dried tomato tart, duck confit, risotto with grilled vegetables, fishcakes, panfried fish, grills, steamed pudding, home made ices plus a fairly terse wine list with one or two famous labels for lashing out. On a pretty day, lunch – including Sunday lunch – on the terrace of The Belvedere is one of the best hands London can deal you.

OPEN: LUNCH: Mon-Sun. DINNER: Mon-Sat. **HOURS:** 12.00-3.00pm and 7.00-11.00pm (6.00-11.00pm summer only). **CLOSED:** Christmas Day, Boxing Day and New Year's Day. **CREDIT CARDS ACCEPTED:** All major cards. **NUMBER OF SEATS:** 120. **SERVICE:** Optional. 6 tables outside. Wheelchair access (but not lavatory). **NEAREST TUBE STATION:** Holland Park.   MAP REF: 11/F

Bertorelli's

44a Floral Street WC2

071-836 1868   **£23 (CAFE £13)**

'Opposite the Opera House, so useful in the aria'

Groupe Chez Gerard Ltd, the owners of Bertorelli's, made a sensible move in employing Maddalena Bonino, previously cooking at 192 Kensington Park Road, to run the brigade of a dozen chefs. However, the difference between cooking for a small trendy wine bar/restaurant and bashing out 400 meals a day in a large bustling establishment in the heart of tourist land leads to an occasional blurring of what ought to be her effect. Sometimes ideas are more thrilling than the outcome as in pearl barley in place of cracked wheat to make a version of tabbouleh. Soups can be institutional rather than vivacious. Quantities as in the mussels with forchietta can be less than bountiful. But on the whole the modernizing of what was a fairly conventional list is all to the good, incorporating as it does the grilled breads and vegetables, flavoured oils, salsas, salads, polenta and sun-dried tomatoes emblematic of the approach. As well as food that is lighter on its feet, there is the provision of a downstairs cafe where quick and simple meals can be taken. Service, even when stretched to the limits, stays sunny. Some of the waitresses who look as if once they were serving bowls of osso bucco to Bloomsbury publishers now cheerfully hand over rocket salads to TV commercials directors.

OPEN: Mon-Sat. **HOURS:** 12.00-3.00pm and 5.45-11.30pm. **CLOSED:** Christmas Day and New Year's Day. **CREDIT CARDS ACCEPTED:** Access, Visa, AmEx, Diner's Club, SCP. **NUMBER OF SEATS:** 80 in Restaurant, 50 in Cafe. **SERVICE:** 12.5%. No smoking area. Wheelchair access. **NEAREST TUBE STATION:** Covent Garden. MAP REF: 12/D3

Beth's

3a Downshire Hill, NW3

071-435 3544 £25

'Where my sister cooks'

Including Beth's as one of my twenty favourite London restaurants may seem like sheer nepotism – and perhaps to some extent it is – but the popularity of this place that has replaced Keats' in Downshire Hill is undeniable. Hampstead and its environs desperately needed a sympathetic restaurant du quartier and in Beth's it has found it. My sister Beth Coventry's previous cooking job was at Green's Restaurant and Oyster Bar (q.v.) and some of the traditional English dishes perfected there – steak and kidney pudding, fishcakes made of smoked haddock and cod, crème brulée, treacle tart – feature on the menu but are matched with lighter, more modern assemblies. The inventive hot and cold soups, ceviche, seared swordfish with an oriental vinaigrette, grilled chicken with salsa and grilled fresh peaches with mascarpone are all popular items. The set-price lunch is a bargain and a draw. The wine list compiled by James Rogers (q.v. Newton's in the same part-ownership) is an exemplary one for a reasonably priced restaurant and it carries the bonus of a wide range of wines by the glass. What had become a pair of tired rooms has been transformed by designer Geoff Laurence with a daring but unerring use of colour and texture into a witty and romantic environment. Believe me, my children and my cousins and my aunts are not enough to keep my sister's place thriving – and it is.

OPEN: Mon-Sun. **HOURS:** 12.30-3.00pm and 7.00-11.30pm (12.00-10.30pm Sun). **CLOSED:** 2 days at Easter and 2 days at Christmas. **CREDIT CARDS ACCEPTED:** Access, AmEx, Visa. **NUMBER OF SEATS:** 50. **SERVICE:** Optional. **SET PRICE LUNCH:** £7.50 (2 courses) and £8.50 (3 courses, Sun only). Wheelchair access – 1 step (but not lavatory). 4 tables outside. **NEAREST TUBE STATION:** Hampstead/Belsize Park. MAP REF: 10/A

Bibendum Restaurant and Oyster Bar

Michelin House, 81 Fulham Road, SW3

RESTAURANT: 071-581 5817 **RESTAURANT: £60**
OYSTER BAR: 071-589 1480 **OYSTER BAR: £25**

'My choice of a desert island restaurant'

Playing on the idea of those desert island questions; if I were asked to which restaurant I would be happiest to be exiled, given that one must of necessity eat there every day twice a day, it would be Bibendum. Of course the imaginary despot or benefactor who sent me would be the one who paid the bills, for the complaints that come up about Bibendum are rarely about Simon Hopkinson's cooking, nearly always about the cost. Sky-high prices are all the harder to take when the aim of noble simplicity is not fulfilled – as just occasionally it is not – and you are left unable even to admire time spent constructing scales for a piece of fish out of slices of potato or whatever other nouvelle nonsensorie you may have encountered elsewhere. Hopkinson and his partner and mentor Sir Terence Conran – and presumably the roly-poly Michelin man who looks on from the windows of what was the Michelin building – value straightforward goodness and also tradition. Thus the oft-changing menu has items as uncomplicated and as tried and true as Baltic herrings à la crème, escargots de Bourgogne, deep-fried fillet of lemon sole, tartare sauce, roast poulet de Bresse with tarragon (served for two), fillet steak au poivre. However, should you choose from this part of the list, say, steak au poivre it will probably be the best steak au poivre you have ever had. Unlike most chefs ever anxious to graze in pastures new, Hopkinson is happy to cook certain dishes again and again until something near perfection is achieved. Another interest of his is Oriental spicing. Thai mussels or a crab dressed with coriander, fish sauce, garlic, sugar, lime juice and chilli and Szechuan duck salad are typical dishes. And another interest is a precise reworking of something made horrible by mass manufacturing, as in the first course of Russian salad, a mixture which when tipped out of a tin is beastly, when fastidiously made, delightful. The influence of Italy is not neglected. Bibendum is one of the few places in London where you can often find bollito misto con salsa verde and the yellow fingers of polenta have crept in here too. Desserts maintain the quest for excellence. The crème brulée is superb, quite extraordinarily creamy, and the Pithiviers au chocolat a work of art. The high, light first floor dining room is as stylish as you would expect from the owner of The Conran Shop but some of the tables for two are cramped and lack any privacy. Complaints have reached me about the management's unwillingness to promise a larger or better table when booked far in advance. Service is unfailingly civil and these days has few lapses.

The Bibendum oyster bar on the ground floor has a short but interesting menu and if raw crustacea are not on your agenda there are appealing salads and omelettes. Avoid peak times when you are made to queue like a naughty schoolchild on the far side of the entrance hall.

THERE IS NO MORE complete wine list in London than this one. Those sitting down for an old-fashioned, self-funded night out can enjoy half-a-litre of Beaujolais-Villages for £9.25. Esotericists can revel in Vajra's electrifyingly strange Freisa (£25.50) or Bonny Doon's improbably pleasing Ca'del Solo Malvasia (£19.95). Both clarets and Burgundies are sure-footed, with real historical depth; you'll find London's most richly textured collection of Alsace wine here, and Rhônes are almost as good; the Italians are better than at most Italian restaurants. German wines are taken seriously, as are New Zealand reds; Western Australia and California both get a sympathetic ear. Finally, sweet-wine enthusiasts will find an enormous range on offer here, including eight (and three ports) by the glass. It's a shame the prices are as high as they are: the cheapest of the fourteen Gewürztraminers is £26.50, but it *is* Zind-Humbrecht's Herrenweg '89, and things just get better and older from there. Time to throw caution to the wind.

RESTAURANT: OPEN: Mon-Sun. HOURS: 12.30-2.30pm (12.30-3.00pm Sat) and 7.00-11.30pm (7.00-10.30pm Sun). NUMBER OF SEATS: 72. SERVICE: 15%. SET PRICE LUNCH: £25. OYSTER BAR: OPEN: Mon-Sun. HOURS: 12.00-11.00pm (12.00-10.30pm Sun). NUMBER OF SEATS: 45. SERVICE: 12.5%. CLOSED: Easter Monday, 24th-27th December. CREDIT CARDS ACCEPTED: Visa, Mastercard. Wheelchair access. NEAREST TUBE STATION: South Kensington. MAP REF: 14/B3

Bice

13 Albemarle Street, W1

071-409 1011   **£30**

'As my companion observed, "You can't franchise chic"'

The original Bice opened in Milan in 1926. There are now Bice restaurants in Paris, Tokyo, various American cities and, since the summer of 1993, London. London is the first time basement premises have been used and I would venture that it will be the last. Somehow no amount of design – and there is a palpable amount – in this windowless space manages to convey smartness or individuality. The food is prodigiously expensive and ironically London has become so sophisticated in Italian food, notably at The River Cafe and to some extent at The Halkin, that it comes across as just dullness for your money. Pastas are better than the mostly assembled (as opposed to cooked) first courses and far better than the main courses. At the time of writing, Bice had just opened and it is hoped that this rival in price and address to Cecconi's will improve. It would be a valuable addition to the area.

OPEN: LUNCH: Mon-Fri. DINNER: Mon-Sat. **HOURS:** 12.00-3.00pm and 7.00-11.30pm. **CREDIT CARDS ACCEPTED:** All major cards. **NUMBER OF SEATS:** 110. **SERVICE:** Optional, £1.50 cover charge. No smoking area. Wheelchair access. **NEAREST TUBE STATION:** Green Park/Piccadilly Circus.   MAP REF: 12/B3

Billboard Cafe

222 Kilburn High Road, NW6

071-328 1374   **£18-£25**

'Mildly groovy hangout in a fairly bleak stretch'

A spell in California inspired the original partners – two cute guys, one Glaswegian, the other Greek Cypriot – in this lively enterprise close to the Tricycle Theatre. Now only Stelios B. Lambis remains. As you might guess the menu is Cal-Ital; the bresaola, bruschetta, salads, pastas and grills formula no longer seems innovative but continues to satisfy and in this area becomes something of an oasis. The American style weekend brunch is popular, the occasional live music appealing if you enjoy noise bouncing off bare, spare surroundings.

OPEN: LUNCH: Sat-Sun. DINNER: Mon-Sat. **HOURS:** 12.00-3.00pm and 6.30pm-12.45am. **CLOSED:** Bank Holidays. **CREDIT CARDS ACCEPTED:** Access, Visa, Mastercard, Switch. **NUMBER OF SEATS:** 65. **SERVICE:** 10%. **SET PRICE BRUNCH:** £6.25. **SET PRICE DINNER:** £10 or £15. Wheelchair access (but not lavatory). Main room may be hired privately. **NEAREST TUBE STATION:** Kilburn/Kilburn Park.   MAP REF: 10/B

Bistrot Bruno

63 Frith Street, W1

071-734 4545   **£25**

'Some of the most inventive cooking in London'

When you talk to Michelin-starred chefs they invariably confide that what they would really like to do is run a big brasserie. It would seem that they tire of offering luxury ingredients to a clientele often at their fancy restaurants for all the wrong reasons. Bruno Loubet, chef of the starred Four Seasons Restaurant (q.v.), has acted on the urge and become consultant to Bistrot Bruno – a name that leads many to suppose that he has more of a role than consultant – sited in what was previously Pierre Condou's Soho fish restaurant L'Hippocampe. Condou remains involved.

One of Loubet's talents is for rehabilitating neglected or scorned ingredients. Thus, on an ever-changing menu, barley is used as an accompaniment to boudin. The possibilities of pumpkin beyond providing a lantern are mined. The neck of lamb called scrag end, usually perceived as too humble for a restaurant, is transformed into a fricassée. He has also beaten the English at their own games of chutneys and pickles, most successfully in the piccalilli, which is spread on puff pastry and topped with scallops. As if he has been constrained in his hotel-cooking mode, at the bistro he lets rip with the modest raw materials, inventively and buoyantly spicing and matching them. Shimmeringly fresh mackerel is grilled on a skewer and served with a sparky relish made from tomato and courgette. The woodsy nature of both chestnuts and mushrooms is capitalized upon in a soup that combines the two. Sardines are used to fill ravioli or as the basis of a first course salad with a lime dressing. Loubet also deploys ingredients in unexpected ways, as in transmuting smoked herring into a sauce and pairing it with sweet fresh trout on sour cabbage. Desserts maintain the pace of invention but not always to their benefit. Quite the best is the uncompromising chocolate tartelette, cooked-off to order, served with coffee cream. Aside from champagne, the most expensive wine on a list that takes its inspiration from all of Europe – not just France – and the New World is £20 and you can drink well at about half that price.

The instant popularity of Bistrot Bruno has, naturally enough, led to extra tables being added in the long narrow rather drably decorated room. Eating there can be literally cheek by jowl. There have been reports of off-hand service and sometimes when the cat's away the mice don't get it together nearly so well. At the time of writing there are plans for expansion to an address north of Cambridge Circus.

OPEN: LUNCH: Mon-Fri. **DINNER:** Mon-Sat. **HOURS:** 12.15-2.30pm and 6.15-11.30pm. **CLOSED:** Christmas to New Year. **CREDIT CARDS ACCEPTED:** All major cards. **NUMBER OF SEATS:** 48. **SERVICE:** Optional. **NEAREST TUBE STATION:** Piccadilly Circus/Leicester Square.   MAP REF: 12/C2

Bistrot 190

190 Queen's Gate, SW7

071-581 5666 £23

*'Where chef Antony Worrall Thompson
first plumped for rusticity'*

Bistrot 190, in the front room of The Gore Hotel and attached via a bar to
the Restaurateurs Club 190, offers a reasonably priced list of eclectic dishes.
Ampersands scattered through the text point to flavours and textures
mixing, matching and sometimes engaging in hand-to-hand combat.
Chorizo tapa comes with onion marmalade, chilli & polenta. Thai noodles
support shrimps, spring onions, shiitaki mushrooms & bok choy. Panfried
haggis meets parsnip and barley risotto & caramelized apples. Chargrilled
squid dices with salsas, arugula & frites. Salmon is surrounded with spinach,
chargrilled aubergines, garlic potatoes & oregano dressing. You get the idea?
Some combinations, now also created by chef Chris Millar, come off better
than others but there is an apparent energy overall that is appealing. The
wines are chosen by a series of suppliers. All are served by the small pitcher
as well as by the bottle; a sound innovation. A no-bookings policy in tandem
with the popularity of the place can make for chaotic service, sometimes to
the extent of spoiling your outing.

OPEN: Mon-Sun. **HOURS:** 7.00am-12.30am (7.00am-11.30pm Sun). **CLOSED:**
3 days at Christmas. **CREDIT CARDS ACCEPTED:** AmEx, Access, Visa, Diner's Club.
NUMBER OF SEATS: 55. **SERVICE:** Optional. **SET PRICE LUNCH:** £7.50 (£13.50 Sun).
Private room seats 22. **NEAREST TUBE STATION:** Gloucester Road. MAP REF: 14/A1

Blakes

33 Roland Gardens, SW7

071-370 6701 £75

'Not the place to dine your bank manager'

The restaurant at Blakes Hotel, designed by the raving beauty Anouska
Hempel Weinberg, has remained defiantly glitzy and moneyed as if to
convey that the ups and downs of the real world do not penetrate here.
There is something to be said for the stance but not when it results in salads
such as tomato and basil or cucumber and dill being priced at £9.75. The
chef who opened Blakes is the much-acclaimed Shaun Hill, now chef and a
partner at Gidleigh Park hotel in Devon. He devised for Blakes one of
London's first eclectic collection of dishes, long before the days when most
menus required an atlas to hand. From being avant-garde the style now looks
static. Chicken tikka, Szechuan duck and Gyuniku (beef) teriyaki with satay
remain constants. Perhaps they have become like Mum's cooking to the
jetsetters who fetch up here. Others wishing to indulge in tabletop travelling
can visit France (foie gras des Landes), Italy (carpaccio con Parmigiano),
Scotland (oak-smoked Scottish salmon), England (Cannon of English lamb

in a mint wrap) and Le Gavroche (Soufflé Suissesse). The cooking is on the whole competent but seems done by a committee rather than an individual. Wine prices maintain the cavalier attitude to your bank balance displayed by the menu. Blakes espouses a certain brand of glamour. It is the Janet Reger of restaurants; for expensive fun sometimes. Incidentally, the restaurant provides a notably stylish breakfast.

OPEN: Mon-Sun. **HOURS:** 7.30-10.30am, 12.30-2.30pm and 7.30-11.30pm. **CREDIT CARDS ACCEPTED:** All major cards. **NUMBER OF SEATS:** 40. **SERVICE:** 15%. Wheelchair access (but not lavatory). Private room seats 22. **NEAREST TUBE STATION:** South Kensington/ Gloucester Road. MAP REF: 14/A3

Blue Elephant

4-6 Fulham Broadway, SW6

071-385 6595 £30-£35

'What is called an eating-out experience'

Some normally intrepid diners admit to a feeling of unease on entering the Blue Elephant's many-splendoured premises. For them it is a bit too overwhelmingly tropical, arousing fears of setting off innocently for supper but finding oneself instead on the stage of a musical set in South East Asia. There are little streams spanned by bridges, bits of quaint dwellings and a forest of palms. There is also the intention of re-creating authentic Thai cuisine with staff and ingredients airlifted from the home country.

This restaurant was one of the progenitors of the great Thai boom and went through a period when its success ran away with it: the room was enlarged, the staff seemed over-stretched and prices went up and up. Now it operates at a more sedate pace and the waiters and waitresses have time to exert some of the famous Thai charm. Just make sure it does not lure you into ordering excessively because too many tempting little £5-£6 starters can easily push the bill skywards.

Both the scope and the quality of the Blue Elephant's menu are commendable. Street snacks from Bangkok, fiery stews and grills from the provinces and elaborate garnishes of carved vegetables in the courtly style all co-exist and a new range of interesting vegetarian dishes has recently been added. A £1.50 cover charge, the habit of leaving credit card slips open after the 15% service charge has been added and the crazy sales pitch of the wine list get the thumbs down: 'Of course you can always spoil yourself with the redcurrant flavours and strong tangy Pinot Noir' it suggests, going on to list a £38 Nuits Saint George and a £74 Clos de Vougeot.

OPEN: LUNCH: Sun-Fri. DINNER: Mon-Sun. **HOURS:** 12.00-2.30pm and 7.00pm-12.30am (7.00-10.30pm Sun). **CREDIT CARDS ACCEPTED:** Visa, AmEx, Diner's Club, Eurocard. **NUMBER OF SEATS:** 230. **SERVICE:** 15%. **SET PRICE LUNCH:** £19.50. **SET PRICE DINNER:** £25 and £28. Wheelchair access. **NEAREST TUBE STATION:** Fulham Broadway. MAP REF: 8/B3

Blue Print Cafe

Design Museum,
Butler's Wharf, SE1

071-378 7031   **£30**

'Food fitting for a design museum'

With the development of the Conran catering complex (q.v. Le Pont de la
Tour) a few steps upstream, the more minimalist Blue Print Cafe above the
Design Museum has become a sort of petty officers' mess to the cruise liner-
inspired design of the larger place. Nothing seems to have suffered by the
comparison; if anything the cooking has grown in confidence and, for
alertness and amiable manners, the waiters here might be preferred.
Bookings seem to be buoyant, with the men in City suits who take lunch or
early dinner being leavened after 8.30pm or at the weekends by more normal
human beings. The look of the Blue Print Cafe is upliftingly light and
bright, with deft touches of colour and reflections from the river, and from
the glass and mirrors the proprietor loves to use. A balcony with thirty-two
seats runs the length of the room looking out on to the Thames, and in
summertime competition to secure a table outside is fierce. The food is in
harmony with the decor, being light and bright, and inspired by the far away
shores of the Mediterranean and Pacific rather than the grey waters of
Limehouse Reach. Piedmontese peppers, Caesar salads, dishes of pasta with
olives and of rabbit with artichoke are fashionable and familiar, but here
pared down and presented unfussily so that even cynics can see the point
(putting cream in a gazpacho was a clumsy exception). The menu changes
every day. Usually there are several types of fish simply cooked and then
served with a jazzy element – salsa or lime, ginger and coriander butter.
Traditional fish and chips are often offered. The wine list is short and to the
point: fair prices and good choices.

OPEN: LUNCH: Mon-Sun. DINNER: Mon-Sat. **HOURS:** 12.00-3.00pm (12.00-3.30pm
Sun) and 7.00-11.00pm. **CLOSED:** Good Friday and Christmas. **CREDIT CARDS
ACCEPTED:** All major cards. **NUMBER OF SEATS:** 85. **SERVICE:** 15%. Wheelchair access.
17 tables outside. **NEAREST TUBE STATION:** Tower Hill/London Bridge.

MAP REF: 8/C2

Bodali

78 Highbury Park, N5

071-704 0741   **£15-£18 (Bring your own wine)**

*'Out of the ordinary Indian; Gujerati
home-style food'*

The phrases 'home cooking' and 'Indian restaurant' rarely go hand in hand
since the Indian restaurant repertoire that has evolved in this country is
totally unlike any domestic tradition. However, this small, insignificant-

looking establishment offers Gujerati home cooking of a refreshingly high standard. Even the chutneys and pickles seem made in-house, not spooned out of huge catering jars. Dishes of the day are listed on a blackboard. In my experience, none disappoint. Spicing is particular to each main ingredient, as in fillets of tilapia (a fresh water fish) coated with coriander, cloves and garlic before grilling, and fresh methi (fenugreek leaves) used to flavour chicken. Vegetables are well-handled. Try the potato and chick-pea and also red kidney bean curry. Be prepared for long waits when Bodali is crowded and go armed with your own wine or beer.

OPEN: Mon-Sat. **HOURS:** 12.00-2.00pm (from 1994) and 6.00-11.00pm. **CLOSED:** Most Bank Holidays and last 3 weeks in August. **CREDIT CARDS ACCEPTED:** None. **NUMBER OF SEATS:** 26. **SERVICE:** Optional, £1.50 cover charge. **SET PRICE LUNCH:** From £4.50. Wheelchair access (but not lavatory). **NEAREST TUBE STATION:** Finsbury Park/Arsenal.   MAP REF: 8/C2

Bombay Brasserie

Courtfield Road
(opposite Gloucester Road Tube), SW7

071-370 4040 or 071-373 0971   **£29**

'A concept and decor grander than the food'

A rash of special set price deals on offer, usually centred around the buffet lunch, suggests that trade needs boosting at this still most beautiful of all Indian restaurants in London. Reasons for its decline, if that is the case, cannot necessarily be laid at the door of the recession. Uneven standards in the food, small portions presented in unsuitable fancy hotel china, slow or sullen service unless you are known to them could be the faults that need remedying. When the Bombay Brasserie opened eleven years ago it opened up to many a realization of the regionality of Indian food, the differences between, say, the meat-centred tradition of the North, the fiery spicing for shellfish and use of pork by the Christian community of Goa, the black peppery dishes of Kerala in the South. Bombay street snacks were woven into the first course and fish coated in mint chutney steamed in banana leaves as is the Parsi custom. It is a pity that standards seem to have slipped. Perhaps some socks will soon be pulled up. The interior retains its sweep of grandeur and its movie set evocation of the days of the British Raj. A table in the conservatory and some judicious choosing from the menu can still serve up a London treat. Wines and beers are marked up with far too great an enthusiasm.

OPEN: Mon-Sun. **HOURS:** 12.30-3.00pm and 7.30pm-12.00am. **CLOSED:** 26th and 27th December. **CREDIT CARDS ACCEPTED:** Diner's Club, Access, Visa. **NUMBER OF SEATS:** 175. **SERVICE:** Optional. **SET PRICE LUNCH:** £13.95 (buffet lunches). Wheelchair access. **NEAREST TUBE STATION:** Gloucester Road.   MAP REF: 14/A2

Bonjour Vietnam

593-599 Fulham Road, SW6

071-385 7603   **£15-£20**

'And Good Evening Teppanyaki San'

Where have all the yuppies gone, long time passing? Gone to Fulham every one. And some are eating at Bonjour Vietnam. The ground floor restaurant decorated with a clever eye for colour by designer Geoff Laurence offers a long Oriental menu with Vietnamese specialities. As Vietnamese restaurants tend to be concentrated in Soho or Peckham, this is of note in SW6. A typical Vietnamese meal would begin with – or consist mainly of – pho, a noodle soup to which herbs, pickled vegetables, chilli, lime and caramelized onion should all add their bit, as do slices of meat and poultry. A less than emphatic pho – as served here – can be boosted with judicious amounts of the dipping sauces. These also come into play with the various wrapped items that should be included in an order. A legacy from the French presence in Vietnam is a hokey but delicious dish of beef and French fries where the potatoes lose their crispness to the savoury gravy. Among the vegetable dishes, beans with crushed garlic and charcoal-grilled aubergines with lime stand out. The clientele appreciate the long fish-tank bar and its range of cocktails and designer beers. Downstairs, signalled by a large papier-mâché prawn, is Teppanyaki San, a room of teppanyaki grills complete with machete wielding chefs. Meat and seafood is grilled on the hot plates. Sashimi to start is not overpriced at £5.50 which is also the price of the Tokyo Express lunch box.

OPEN: Mon-Sun. **HOURS:** 12.00-2.30pm and 6.00-11.30pm (12.30-11.15pm Sun). **CLOSED:** Christmas. **CREDIT CARDS ACCEPTED:** All major cards. **NUMBER OF SEATS:** 160. **SERVICE:** 10%. **SET PRICE LUNCH:** £6.50. **SET PRICE DINNER:** From £12.50. Wheelchair access. Private room seats 20. **NEAREST TUBE STATION:** Fulham Broadway.   MAP REF: 8/B2

Boyd's Restaurant

135 Kensington Church Street, W8

071-727 5452   **£35**

'Vinaigrette rien'

Boyd Gilmour has shortened his restaurant's name. It used to be called Boyd's Glass Garden, which described the interior perfectly. Rattan chairs, pot plants and a curving glass roof turn the oblong room into a pretty conservatory, a rather more relaxing, romantic place than either Clarke's across the road or Kensington Place down the street. His food is matchingly light, and modern, sometimes delicate, sometimes pared down almost to plainness. There is a definitive liking for oil dressings (which are beautifully done), herbs and citrus flavours. An orange and walnut vinaigrette for asparagus sounds fussy but is in fact subtle; the fish of the day came with a lovely basil vinaigrette. The staff are always affable but are sometimes just too over-stretched – probably the result of the cost-cutting regimen which has brought prices here down. They keep a good cheese board and serve appealing versions of popular puddings such as chocolate terrine and crème brulée. All the details please: the quality of the bread, the specially made biscuits to go with the cheese, chocolate truffles that arrive with the coffee.

THIS WINE LIST never touches down long anywhere, but the selections (Klein Constantia's big-boned Sauvignon Blanc 1989 at £14.50, Kistler's silk-stocking 1989 Dutton Ranch Chardonnay at £31.80, or Cape Mentelle's punchy 1988 Shiraz at £18.85) show a sure touch. There's a good half-bottle and spirit range; only the collection of six Boyd-Cantenacs, something of an also-ran among the crus classés, looks self-indulgent.

OPEN: Mon-Sat. **HOURS:** 12.30-2.30pm and 7.00-11.00pm. **CLOSED:** Christmas Day and Boxing Day. **CREDIT CARDS ACCEPTED:** Access, AmEx, Diner's Club, Visa. **NUMBER OF SEATS:** 40. **SERVICE:** Optional. **SET PRICE LUNCH:** £14 (3 courses). **NEAREST TUBE STATION:** Notting Hill Gate.   MAP REF: 8/B2

The Brackenbury

129-131 Brackenbury Road, W6

081-748 0107   **£20**

*'A paragon among modern restaurants with
modest prices and vivid food'*

The Brackenbury qualifies as a local restaurant by being locked within a maze of one way streets, though people from all over London find it worth the voyage. It is an uplifting place, both in terms of the atmosphere and the impression that the chef/proprietor is cooking the food he likes best and finding a ready market for it. Sometimes this is old school French, sometimes new wave Cal-Ital, occasionally there are Spanish influences. Whatever the mood, the daily changing menu is put together with an intelligent palate so there are rarely great dissonances between the starters and second courses. Most dishes have a couple of true, strong flavours rather than being complex ensembles, and the portions are big. What could be better than to lunch on chilled asparagus soup made with pounds of asparagus followed by a meaty capon with roasted garlic and aioli? Perhaps to find that the two have only cost you £9.75. Kate Robinson runs the dining room (really two rooms) in a friendly manner. If the attention of the staff peters out towards the end of long meals that means there is no rush to get you out of the restaurant. The puddings are rich, the coffee strong and the wine list is further evidence of good taste combined with a desire to give value. Wines from the new and old worlds are mostly priced between £10-£16 a bottle and much of the list is also available by the glass, as are fino sherry and dessert wine. Equally impressive, the Brackenbury serves excellent ginger beer.

OPEN: LUNCH: Tues-Fri, Sun. **DINNER:** Mon-Sat. **HOURS:** 12.30-2.45pm and 7.00-10.45pm. **CLOSED:** Bank Holidays and 7 days over Christmas. **CREDIT CARDS ACCEPTED:** Access, Visa, AmEx, Switch, Connect. **NUMBER OF SEATS:** 55. **SERVICE:** Optional. Wheelchair access (but not lavatory). 5 tables outside. **NEAREST TUBE STATION:** Hammersmith.   MAP REF: 8/B2

Brady's

513 Old York Road, SW18

081-877 9599   **£14**

'A recent chip off the old block'

A trip to Brady's settled the question of fish and chips' rehabilitation completely. Here close-cropped men in city shirts meet to discuss mutual acquaintances called Jeremy over a slap-up fish supper. Brady's is a new venture, but one that emulates the best traditions. It serves huge chips and a small choice of the best fish: cod, haddock and plaice in a light, even coating of batter. The portions are not as big as those doled out in older establishments but prices are trimmed accordingly and the preparation is close to perfect. All skin is removed from the fried fish, a controversial refinement, and a decent brand of ketchup is used, which is a distinct improvement on the thin, vinegary sauce provided by many famous specialists. The mushy peas are, in fact, a sweet tasting pea purée. There is vinegar on the clothless tables and a choice of half a dozen sauces, prettily set out in French jam jars. The room is pleasant and practical, if rather cramped, the only cod element being the giant plaster fish heads. As an alternative to fried fish there is grilled lemon sole or tuna, preceded by sensible starters of shrimps and smoked cods' roe pâté and rounded off by those who have worked up a good appetite with a hard day's brokerage, by treacle tart or apple crumble.

OPEN: LUNCH: Sat. DINNER: Mon-Sat. HOURS: 12.30-2.30pm and 7.00-10.45pm. CLOSED: Bank Holidays, 1 week in August and Christmas. CREDIT CARDS ACCEPTED: None. NUMBER OF SEATS: 38. SERVICE: 10%. Wheelchair access. NEAREST BR STATION: Wandsworth Town.   MAP REF: 8/B3

Brasserie du Marché aux Puces

349 Portobello Road, W10

081-968 5828   **£22**

'Very few fleas (Fr. Puces) on this smart, far north Kensington restaurant'

Another brasserie done out in the classic brown and beige livery, this one surprises with its fashionable food and rather serious approach. The tables make a right angle turn around a long bar and windows on two sides look out on to the tail end of Portobello Market – a lively scene when the sun is shining and the market is busy (Fridays and Saturdays) but dull on winter's nights. There is a short, appealing wine list with tolerable mark-ups and a similarly short menu that changes every week. Mousses of exotic vegetables, fish with oriental seasonings, smoked meats and fashionable carbohydrates are characteristic ingredients: asparagus, salsify and Parmesan; smoked lamb with celeriac rémoulade; guinea fowl, lentils and zampone. The buying is good but at the time of writing execution is inconsistent. The brunch menu on Sundays is simpler and full of things that are satisfying any time of day (it is offered between 11am-4pm). Just how useful the main menu is during the long brasserie business hours perplexes: you need to be awfully trendy to take tabbouleh with artichokes as an afternoon snack.

OPEN: LUNCH: Mon-Sun. DINNER: Mon-Sat. **HOURS:** 10.00am-11.00pm (11.00am-4.00pm Sun). **CLOSED:** Bank Holidays. **CREDIT CARDS ACCEPTED:** None. **NUMBER OF SEATS:** 36. **SERVICE:** Optional. **SET PRICE LUNCH:** £9.95. Wheelchair access (but not lavatory). 7 tables outside. Private room seats 35. **NEAREST TUBE STATION:** Ladbroke Grove.   MAP REF: 8/B2

Brasserie Faubourg

28 Queenstown Road, SW8

071-622 6245   **£25**

*'Part of the Gallic colonization of
Queenstown Road'*

Brasserie Faubourg in Queenstown Road is representative of the small neighbourhood restaurant – more bistro than brasserie – that underpins the more glamorous top dressing of the restaurant business. Redecorated this year in lemon yellow and grey with tables clothed in pale blue, French posters, Perrier advertisements and a print from the illustrated *A Year in Provence* make the point, in case you fail to have taken it, that this is a corner of France in Clapham. It is run in the time-honoured French manner with husband in the kitchen, wife front of house. M. François Closset previously cooked at Mon Plaisir. The lunch menu at £9.50 is a bargain, especially as straying from it onto the à la carte does not seem to result in financial penalties. There is probably an old Breton saying along the lines of 'You can judge a bistro by its fish soup'. If so, Brasserie Faubourg comes out well. Identical garnish of a surprisingly fiddly nature – a dab of potato gratin, a blob of purée, a bundle of French beans tied with a spring onion – and the same mahogany veneer of a sauce can make some main courses seem almost interchangeable but the taste is good enough in that way you used to be able to count upon in France. Some dishes seem guilelessly old-fashioned. Here may rest the last vegetable terrine with tomato coulis and breast of duck with raspberry sauce in London. I rather hope so anyway. The dessert speciality is the Limousin upside-down pear cake, le gargouyot, served warm. The wine list is short and simple.

OPEN: LUNCH: Tue-Fri. DINNER: Mon-Sat. **HOURS:** 12.00-2.30pm and 7.00-11.00pm. **CLOSED:** 2 weeks in August and Christmas Day. **CREDIT CARDS ACCEPTED:** Access, Visa, AmEx. **NUMBER OF SEATS:** 34. **SERVICE:** Optional. **SET PRICE LUNCH:** £9.50. Wheelchair access (but not lavatory). **NEAREST TUBE STATION:** Clapham Common.   MAP REF: 8/B3

Brixtonian Backayard

4 Neals Yard,
Covent Garden, WC2

071-240 2769 **£25**

*'The only Caribbean restaurant in
the West End'*

Self-styled as a rhum shop, roti bar and restaurant, Backayard, a branch of
the Brixtonian in Brixton, is something of an oddity in Covent Garden. The
look is almost as dramatic as a set at the nearby Opera House, the ground
floor bar done out in hot-country colours and bleached wood, the first floor
balcony restaurant furnished with the obsolete grandeur of an old plantation
house. The roti bar provides the original snack of Trinidad, soft flat bread
wrapped round curried meat, the restaurant a monthly changing menu
deriving its dishes from the various islands of the Caribbean. They call it
Cuisine Antillaise – the world's melting pot kitchen. Unfortunately the
thought that what might come out of it will be somewhat dilute can prove to
be true. Spicing is timid and sometimes in being genteel they miss the point
of what is essentially rough and ready food. However, there is consolation to
be found in the array of rums and the cocktails based on them. Live
entertainment is a strong selling point. A friend told me he sat through
nearly the whole of an amateur rendition of *Carmen* one lunchtime while
eating crisply fried prawn and potato cakes.

OPEN: LUNCH: Mon-Sun. DINNER: Mon-Sat. **HOURS:** 12.00pm-12.00am (11.00am-
5.00pm Sun). **CREDIT CARDS ACCEPTED:** AmEx, Mastercard, Visa. **NUMBER OF SEATS:**
30. **SERVICE:** 12.5%. **SET PRICE DINNER:** £15.95 (2 courses), £19.95 (3 courses). No
smoking in restaurant. 6 tables outside. Private room seats 35. **NEAREST TUBE
STATION:** Covent Garden/Leicester Square. MAP REF: 12/C2

Bu-San Korean Restaurant

43 Holloway Road,
Highbury Corner, N7

071-607 8264 **£20**

'Neighbourhood Korean with aspirations'

A friendly, family-run small restaurant, Bu-San attracts a loyal following of
Islington and Holloway folk and flourishes while trendier enterprises nearer
to The Angel come and go. The owner and chef is from Korea but has a
penchant for preparing raw fish in the Japanese manner in addition to a long
list of his native dishes. His wife runs the simply decorated dining room in
which their (well-behaved) children are sometimes seen. The grand total of
soups, appetizers, fish, meat, noodle and vegetable dishes on the dinner

menu is ninety, therefore it is sensible for non-specialists to seek help so that they get a meal with contrasting textures and ingredients. Impetuous ordering may bring too many things in rich, garlicky sauce. The Korean version of steak tartare, Yook Hoe, the sesame-marinaded beef called Bul Go Gi which is cooked at the table, or a rich, main course shellfish soup He Mul Chap Tang Chi Ge are satisfying choices. Bu-San's set menus are also a good thing and not, as is the case in most Chinese restaurants, a selection of the tamest items. They also help keep the bill in line with the expectations that the simple surroundings set up.

OPEN: LUNCH: Mon-Fri. DINNER: Mon-Sun. **HOURS:** 12.00-2.30pm and 6.00-11.00pm. **CLOSED:** Christmas Day, Boxing Day and New Year's Day. **CREDIT CARDS ACCEPTED:** Visa, Mastercard, Eurocard. **NUMBER OF SEATS:** 50. **SERVICE:** 10%. **SET PRICE LUNCH:** £4.50-£6.50. **SET PRICE DINNER:** £27.95-£45.50. Wheelchair access. **NEAREST TUBE STATION:** Highbury & Islington.   MAP REF: 8/C2

Le Cadre

10 Priory Road, N8

081-348 0606   £18-£23

*'As indicated a French setting.
In Crouch End'*

The words Pris (sic) Fixe, with an acute accent on the e, heading one of the menus at Le Cadre are fairly meaningless when translated. They do however convey that this bistro near Alexandra Palace is trying most terribly, terribly hard to be French. The frontage, the maps and posters, even the lettering for the name, screech bistro. It is the Francophile approach of being more French than the French and in so doing missing some of the point. However, the small establishment is sympa, useful in the area and some of the dishes come off well. The fixed price list, more expensive for three courses on Fridays and Saturdays than earlier in the week, features standard froggie fare; some examples, fish soup, moules marinières, crudités (over elaborate), terrine, daube de boeuf, civet of rabbit, escalope de veau. The à la carte offers slightly more complex assemblies using more expensive ingredients. With a modest wine your bill will not shock. I note that prices have stayed fairly static since first I visited four years ago.

OPEN: LUNCH: Mon-Fri. DINNER: Mon-Sat. **HOURS:** 12.00-2.30pm and 7.00-11.00pm. **CLOSED:** Bank Holidays and 27th-30th December. **CREDIT CARDS ACCEPTED:** Access, Visa, Diner's Club, AmEx. **NUMBER OF SEATS:** 50. **SET PRICE LUNCH:** £10.50 or £12.50. **SET PRICE DINNER:** £10.50 or £15.50. No smoking area by arrangement. Wheelchair access (but not lavatory). 4 tables outside. **NEAREST TUBE STATION:** Highgate/Turnpike Lane.   MAP REF: 8/B2

Café des Arts

82 Hampstead High Street, NW3

071-435 3608 **£20**

*'Thoroughly modern food in a seventeenth-
century domestic interior'*

The menu of this pine-panelled cafe/restaurant housed in three rooms of a
listed building – formerly the long-running Fagin's – is perhaps too similar
for its own good to its near neighbour Caffe Graffiti, or, to be fair, vice versa
since Café des Arts opened first. It is that eclectic Mediterranean-influenced
list which now runs the risk of seeming clichéd but is nevertheless healthy
and tempting. Grilling is applied to vegetables, including radicchio, as well
as to fish, meat and merguez sausages. There is tuna tataki, salads, stir-fries
and a daily different pasta. Many items may be ordered in two sizes, at two
prices. The kitchen and waiting staff are all female and on sale is Kulta, a
beer brewed by women. I have experienced decidedly uneven standards of
cooking, presumably depending on whether or not head chef Sally Holme is
at the stove. Art on the walls is for sale.

OPEN: Mon-Sun. **HOURS:** 12.00-11.30pm (12.00-11.00pm Sun). **CLOSED:**
Christmas Day, Boxing Day and New Year's Day. **CREDIT CARDS ACCEPTED:** All major
cards. **NUMBER OF SEATS:** 65. **SERVICE:** 12.5%. **SET PRICE LUNCH:** £12.95 (Sun only).
Wheelchair access (1 step). 4 tables outside. **NEAREST TUBE STATION:** Hampstead.

MAP REF: 10/A

Le Café du Marché

22 Charterhouse Mews,
Charterhouse Square, EC1

071-608 1609 **£35**

*'An almost convincing French bistro off one
of London's hidden squares'*

Charterhouse Square is one of the delightful pockets London is so good at
providing. Sandwiched between the urban concreteness of the Barbican and
timewarp Smithfield (near the soon-to-be-vandalized Bart's Hospital), the
area is a mixture of Bohemian and business, something that could be said to
characterize the clientele of Café du Marché set in a passageway just off the
north end of the square. Both the ground floor and first floor – 'Le Grenier'
– pack the tables in tightly and at lunchtime the move pays off (as far as the
owners are concerned). Menus are set price and offer French provincial
cooking which sometimes teeters on being inept. At the prices charged this
can be hard to take. Go for the tried and true dishes such as la soupe de
poissons and côte de boeuf sauce Béarnaise and leave ideas like grilled guinea
fowl with a sauce of mussels to others. It is the romanticism of the location
and the restaurant itself – candlelight leaps and gutters in the evenings –
rather than the food which seems the point of the place.

OPEN: LUNCH: Mon-Fri. DINNER: Mon-Sat. **HOURS:** 12.00-2.30pm and 6.00-10.00pm (7.00pm-10.00pm in Le Grenier). **CLOSED:** Easter, Christmas and New Year. **CREDIT CARDS ACCEPTED:** Access, Visa, Switch. **NUMBER OF SEATS:** 70 in restaurant, 50 in Le Grenier: **SERVICE:** 15% optional. **SET PRICE LUNCH AND DINNER:** £19.00. Wheelchair access (but not lavatory). Private room seats 66. **NEAREST TUBE STATION:** Barbican. MAP REF: 8/C2

Cafe Fish

39 Panton Street, SW1

071-930 3999 £18-£25

'Fish and vegetarian dishes on some scale'

A location off Leicester Square close to the cinemas and theatres gives Cafe Fish a brisk trade. People seem to flow in and out of a crowded room furnished with fish prints and turquoise panels. Blackboards listing fifty dishes reach right up to the ceiling but a spell spent straining the neck to study them turns out to be wasted because the printed menu is almost exactly the same. There is raw fish (oysters, plateau de fruit de mer), smoked fish, fried fish (battered haddock with chips, plaice meunière, fishcakes), grilled fish (sword fish, shark kebabs) and elaborated fish (monkfish with celeriac, roast potatoes and basil sauce, trout baked in paper with shredded vegetables and lemon grass). The more complex recipes and the imaginative vegetarian list – aubergine sausage is the only sort of sausage served – are an indication of the head chef Andrew Magson's pedigree: he trained at Inigo Jones and then was jointly in charge of a critically admired veg and fish restaurant called Burt's, now defunct. It is an ambitious range for a restaurant with a fast turn around to attempt and the result is rather a curate's egg. Simplest dishes are not necessarily the safest bets: bouillabaisse is pleasing, though nothing like as powerful as the Marseillais make it, while kedgeree contained under-cooked rice over-aromatized with fenugreek. Service is smart and the predominantly white wine list is almost as good as the boasts on the blackboard.

ALSO AT: 16 St Barnabas Street, SW1 (071-730 2572).

OPEN: RESTAURANT: LUNCH: Mon-Fri. DINNER: Mon-Sat. WINE BAR: Mon-Sat. **HOURS:** RESTAURANT: 12.00-3.00pm and 5.45-11.30pm. WINE BAR: 11.00am-11.00pm. **CLOSED:** Christmas Day and Boxing Day. **CREDIT CARDS ACCEPTED:** All major cards except Switch. **NUMBER OF SEATS:** 90. **SERVICE:** 12.5%. No smoking area. Wheelchair access (but not lavatory). 4 tables outside. **NEAREST TUBE STATION:** Leicester Square/Piccadilly Circus. MAP REF: 12/D3

Café Flo

334 Upper Street, N1

071-226 7916   **£15**

*'French cafe chain that is a cut above
the competition'*

Flo's creators (she is a thoroughly made up girl) have chosen a vaguely Art
Nouveau appearance for the logo and posters which brighten this little
empire. In large sites open all day a fairly traditional French bistro menu
is served; Bayonne ham, terrines, fish soup, salades tièdes, moules, chicken
with tarragon, steak Béarnaise and chips, omelettes and (on request)
baguettes made into sandwiches. Deep-fried potato skins, a vegetarian
'strudel' and fishcakes explain the qualification. The two-course menu
(L'Idée Flo) – a soup or salad followed by steak, fried fish or omelette, all
served with chips, and then coffee – is notably good value. Quality is not
slipshod; good cheese and ham go into the omelettes, the salad dressing is not
crass and the fries deserve the description French. What you 'gain'
(financially) on the food you might lose to the wine list.

ALSO AT: 205/207 Haverstock Hill, NW3 (071-435 6744).
51 St Martin's Lane, WC2 (071-836 8289).
149 Kew Road, Richmond, Surrey (081-940 8289).
127/129 Kensington Church Street, W8 (071-727 8142).
676 Fulham Road, SW6 (071-371 9673).

OPEN: Mon-Sun. **HOURS:** 9.00am-11.30pm (9.00am-10.30pm Sat-Sun). **CLOSED:**
2/3 days at Christmas. **CREDIT CARDS ACCEPTED:** Access, Diner's Club, Visa.
NUMBER OF SEATS: 76. **SERVICE:** Optional. **SET PRICE LUNCH AND DINNER:** £5.95
(2 courses, Mon-Fri lunch only), £6.95 (2 courses) and £11.50 (2 courses).
No smoking area. Wheelchair access (but not lavatory). 3 tables outside.
NEAREST TUBE STATION: Angel.   MAP REF: 10/A

Cafe Lazeez

93/95 Old Brompton Road, SW7

071-581 9993   **£20-£25**

*'An earnest attempt to make Indian slick
and of the moment'*

This rather unalluringly named place is gamely trying to fill a restaurant gap
– chic and casual Indian. In this they succeed much better than have other
themed ventures such as the ill-fated Chittagong Charlie, but you cannot
help feeling that in South Kensington, however smiling and polite the
welcome, however carefully spiced the frontier burger, it is not really what is
wanted. (A fast-food Chinese operation bit the dust at the same address.)
However, if you like your snacks fired up with chilli – and who doesn't? –

I can recommend the Indian Welsh rarebit, officer's chops, prawns karachi and the daily changing dal dish. Upstairs the menu and decor is designed for longer lingering than in the modern out-of-Rick Mather school of design on the ground floor.

SHORT, TO THE POINT, enthusiastically annotated, this purposeful little wine list manages to offer something for everyone without letting the excitement slip. Challenge your taste buds with Huët's '87 Clos de Bourg (£18) and your prejudices with the 1991 Saintsbury Pinot Noir (£18.50).

OPEN: Mon-Sun. **HOURS:** 11.00am-1.00am (11.00am-11.00pm Sun). **CREDIT CARDS ACCEPTED:** AmEx, Visa, Mastercard, Diner's Club. **NUMBER OF SEATS:** 140. **SERVICE:** 10%. **SET PRICE LUNCH AND DINNER:** £9.95 (Sunday buffet only). No smoking area. Wheelchair access. 8 tables outside. Private room seats 50. **NEAREST TUBE STATION:** South Kensington/Gloucester Road.   MAP REF: 14/A3

Cafe Pacifico

5 Langley Street, WC2

071-379 7728   **£16**

*'A Tex-Mex bar and restaurant with more
than a hint of the Alamo'*

Tex-Mex cooking can be said in many cases – particularly those occurring in London – to be the kitchen's lowest common denominator. Spicy minced meat, re-fried beans, chilli-spiked tomato sauce, grated cheese, mushed avocado, chopped salad, maize pancakes; all is fairly cheap but if allowed to be mixed haphazardly anything but cheerful. The trick is to order precisely and be aware of what is crisp – tacos, nachos and tostadas – and what is floppy – burritos and enchiladas. Fajitas – grilled strips of meat – are reasonably clean-cut and there is the diversion of assembling each mouthful somewhat differently through use of garnish and wrap. Of course after enough tequilas or jugs of margaritas everything will blur anyway. This seems to be the approach of many of the customers who render the large, agreeably undesigned place raucous. Lunch is much quieter. A designer beer with a wedge of lime in the bottle is the correct accessory at the bar.

OPEN: Mon-Sun. **HOURS:** 12.00-11.45pm (12.00-10.45pm Sun). **CLOSED:** Christmas Day and Boxing Day. **CREDIT CARDS ACCEPTED:** Visa, Mastercard, AmEx. **NUMBER OF SEATS:** 120. **SERVICE:** 12.5%. **SET PRICE LUNCH:** £3.95. No smoking area. Wheelchair access. **NEAREST TUBE STATION:** Covent Garden.   MAP REF: 12/C2

Café Rouge

390 Kings Road, SW3

071-352 2226   **£22**

'Faux-French but useful'

It is unlikely that Londoners will not be familiar with the jolly, faked-up brasserie style of Café Rouge group. The red and yellow decor, newspapers for budding boulevardiers to browse through and serving of light meals and drinks all through the day seem very promising. However there are some question marks over authenticity and quality. Why is it not possible to have a proper café au lait and a decent-sized croissant in the morning? Cappuccino and a bantam weight croissant amount to a trop petit déjeuner. Even more deplorable, why was there a rubber band in the watercress soup? The waitress said 'That is not the first time' then removed the soup from the table but not from the bill until prompted. Mistakes such as these demote Les Cafés Rouges from valuable to merely useful places. Menus always read well – plates of charcuterie, classic soups and salads, steak-frites – but the results are pretty ordinary, a fair enough adjustment between quality and price which is – also in fairness – becoming increasingly typical in France. Some Cafés seem to have brighter staff and slightly better standards than others (the Kensington Park Road branch is not recommended). Quality control which approached the diligence applied to portion size would bring about an improvement.

Branches too numerous to list. Please check the telephone directory for details.

OPEN: Mon-Sun. **HOURS:** 10.00am-11.30pm (10.00am-10.30pm Sun). **CLOSED:** Please check with individual branches. **CREDIT CARDS ACCEPTED:** All major cards. **NUMBER OF SEATS:** 55. **SERVICE:** Optional. Wheelchair access (but not lavatory). **NEAREST TUBE STATION:** Sloane Square.

Cafe Royal Brasserie & Grill Room

68 Regent Street, W1

071-437 9090   **BRASSERIE £24; GRILL ROOM £40-45**

'Where Oscar Wilde dropped bon mots so can you'

The truly successful element in the revamping of the decor of the historic Grill Room is that you hardly know it has happened. The extraordinary gilt and plush rococo interior with its cheeky ceiling paintings, cherubs and caryatids looks a little fresher but retains the turn-of-the-century glamour and magnetism. Or it does anyway after you have forgotten your walk through the lobby with its noticeboard of dinner dances and masonic functions. Chef Herbert Berger has been brought in to revivify the menu which he has successfully done, although I would like to see a few old-fashioned classics offered, such as tournedos Rossini, ris de veau financière; dishes in keeping with the surroundings. To suit modern appetites there are salades tièdes, some Oriental spicing, vegetable tagliatelle, flavoured oils used as sauces, fruit coulis and other light touches. Sharing a roasted rack of lamb or a rib of beef with bone marrow and red wine sauce strikes me as the appropriate way to enjoy the Grill Room. The wine list is improving and the service, led by a new manager, has improved. Londoners must now embrace the Cafe Royal and not leave it to tourists.

The brasserie, with its important bar, has an inventive eclectic menu with main courses such as confit of duck with lentils, bangers 'n' mash with roast parsnips, braised knuckle of lamb with roasted garlic, smoked haddock with green cabbage and English mustard sauce that are more than competently prepared. What is totally out of keeping with the ethos of a brasserie is the pricing structure, encouraging you to choose a set price two or three course meal. However, they have recently relented, also offering dishes priced individually. The wine list is sensibly divided by price with several choices at each figure and many served by the glass. Service is with a smile.

OPEN: Mon-Sat. **HOURS:** BRASSERIE: 12.00-3.00pm and 6.00-11.00pm. GRILL ROOM: 12.00-2.30pm and 6.00-11.45pm. **CLOSED:** Telephone for advice. **CREDIT CARDS ACCEPTED:** All major cards. **NUMBER OF SEATS:** 100 in Brasserie, 80 in Grill Room. **SET PRICE LUNCH:** BRASSERIE: £14.75 (2 courses); £17.75 (3 courses). GRILL ROOM: £19.50. **SET PRICE DINNER:** BRASSERIE: £14.75 (2 courses); £17.75 (3 courses). GRILL ROOM: £28. Brasserie available for private hire, seats 80-150. Grill Room available for private hire, seats 80. Wheelchair access. **NEAREST TUBE STATION:** Piccadilly Circus. MAP REF:12/B3

Caffe Graffiti

71 Hampstead High Street, NW3

071-431 7579 **£18**

'One of the better bets in Hampstead'

Owned by the brother of the dry cleaner I use – as I discovered when picking up a skirt – this small Mediterranean cafe has a higher standard of cooking than you might – in Hampstead – reasonably expect. The specials on the blackboard, including fresh fish, tend to be more interesting than the à la carte choices, but from those I can recommend salad of lentils and aubergines on spinach, gnocchi with salmon and black olives and calf's liver with polenta. Food is cooked to order by the chef who comes from Marseilles where his mother has a bistro. Evening has the longer menu but you may just snack at Caffe Graffiti, ciabatta bread being used as a base for various toppings.

OPEN: Mon-Sun. **HOURS:** 12.00-10.50pm (12.00-10.20pm Sun). **CLOSED:** Christmas Day and Boxing Day. **CREDIT CARDS ACCEPTED:** Visa, AmEx, Diner's Club. **NUMBER OF SEATS:** 32. **SERVICE:** 12.5%. **SET PRICE LUNCH:** £6.95. 10 seats outside. **NEAREST TUBE STATION:** Hampstead. MAP REF: 10/A

Calabash

The Africa Centre,
38 King Street, WC2

071-836 1976   **£15**

*'Something different in Covent Garden –
African home cooking'*

The Africa Centre houses in Calabash a cross between a junior common room, a refectory and a fully-fledged restaurant. It is rarely full but the clientele attracted is invariably diverting. Service is at the pace of Central Africa rather than Central London, operating very well as a definition of laid-back. The menu changes regularly to feature the dishes of various countries such as Ghana, Senegal, Sierra Leone, Nigeria and also Morocco. Vegetarians and lovers of spicy food are always well looked after. Not only the lacunae in service but the nature of the food points to dishes being cooked to order and by someone who understands domesticity. Wines from Africa are robust enough to deal with the food but beer might be the better accompaniment.

OPEN: LUNCH: Mon-Fri. DINNER: Mon-Sat. **HOURS:** 12.30-3.00pm and 6.00pm-12.00am. **CLOSED:** Bank Holidays. **CREDIT CARDS ACCEPTED:** All major cards. **NUMBER OF SEATS:** 80. **SERVICE:** 10%. No smoking area. **NEAREST TUBE STATION:** Covent Garden/Leicester Square/Charing Cross.   MAP REF: 12/D3

Camden Brasserie

216 Camden High Street, NW1

071-482 2114   **£18**

'Chips worth a detour'

Camden Brasserie is a long-running success based on a sensible formula, once innovative but now oft repeated; interesting salads, some of them warm – e.g. eel with chorizo and aged vinegar – a home made pasta dish and chargrilled brochettes, sausages, meat and fish served with exemplary chips or in the case of the Toulouse sausages, sweet potato mash. Meat is carefully selected and well hung. Prices are not outlandish. The owners remain very much involved. The Underground Cafe in the basement next door (no. 124), serving a modern Italian menu, is under the same competent ownership (071-482 0010).

OPEN: Mon-Sun. **HOURS:** 12.00-3.00pm (12.30-3.30pm Sun) and 6.00-11.30pm (5.00-10.30pm Sun). **CLOSED:** Christmas Day, Boxing Day, New Year's Eve dinner and New Year's Day. **CREDIT CARDS ACCEPTED:** Visa, Mastercard, Switch. **NUMBER OF SEATS:** 80. **SERVICE:** Optional. Wheelchair access (but not lavatory). **NEAREST TUBE STATION:** Camden Town.   MAP REF: 10/C

The Canal Brasserie

222 Kensal Road, W10

081-960 2732 £15

'One of London's more recherché waterside inns'

The terrible pun of calling an old factory on the Grand Union Canal 'Canalot Studios' gives fair warning of the weird decor within: Spiderman leaps through a window and a lift disguised as a mediaeval turret rides up and down. You enter by stepping through a door within a door to find a pretty fountain, behind which is the whitewashed yard full of plants with tables set out during warm weather, and then into the bar and dining room hung with abstract paintings. People from the film and recording studios come here, especially for lunch. The kitchen has changed chefs frequently, but the last two visits have found confident and sensible modern cooking and real care taken with ingredients. The air-cured ham from Waberthwaite used with quails' eggs and lettuce leaves in a very satisfactory salad is an example of clever buying. Influences on the reasonably priced, daily selection include Thai (fishcakes and curry), Middle Eastern (falafels and couscous), the inevitable Italianate dishes and 'Pomfret and pommes frites', the perfect dish for a polyglot menu. A rarer item was Afrikaans cream pudding, syrupy sponge which had been soaked with cream and baked – enough to prevent any local Lancelot from singing 'Tirra lirra'.

OPEN: LUNCH: Mon-Fri. DINNER: Wed-Fri. **HOURS:** 9.30am-3.00pm and 7.00pm-1am (7.00pm-2.00am Fri). **CLOSED:** Most Bank Holidays. **CREDIT CARDS ACCEPTED:** All major cards. **NUMBER OF SEATS:** 60. **SERVICE:** 12.5%. Wheelchair access. 20 seats outside. **NEAREST TUBE STATION:** Ladbroke Grove/Westbourne Park.

MAP REF: 8/B2

The Canteen

Chelsea Harbour, SW10

071-351 7330 £35

'On form probably the best cooking you can find at this price'

This recently opened, successful big restaurant is the result of a partnership between Michael Caine who is a film star and chef Marco Pierre White who merely thinks that he is one. The Canteen is located in an American-style leisure and apartment complex on the river at Chelsea. A surreal design was a sage response to echoing malls and underground car parks and David Collins – also responsible for the looks of La Tante Claire, Harvey's and The Square – has had fun with the theme of playing cards with their overtones of gambling. There are a few tables from which you can see boats bobbing in the marina – not the case with all the restaurants in Chelsea Harbour. Chelsea girls and boys, a sprinkling of show business and the shifting crowd that follow restaurant fashions tend to eat here late or for lunch at weekends. Chefs Steven Terry and Tim Hughes have worked with Marco at Harvey's and whilst The Canteen cooking is by no means just bargain basement versions of starry-eyed dishes, derivations can be observed and appreciated and details in garnishing, vegetables and saucing are sometimes those of a classic kitchen. This is not what gets called a brasserie operation.

Proof of that is in first courses of vichyssoise of oysters with caviar chantilly, parfait of chicken livers and foie gras with toasted brioche, risotto of (squid) ink served with roast calamari (the last two kissing cousins of Harvey's dishes) and main courses of tranche of salmon with roasted asparagus, a crab crust and shellfish sauce and roast wood pigeon with pommes Anna, buttered spinach and fumet of red wine. When The Canteen is teeming as it often is – customers have not been slow to understand the value in this transaction – ingredients that require precise, last-minute cooking may be mishandled. There are simple dishes – watercress soup with poached egg, cod 'n' chips sauce Tartare, grilled lobster with garlic butter and herb salad, roast rabbit with bacon, petit pois and mustard sauce – for when something straightforward is required. Desserts are of a high standard. When there is no brooding proprietorial presence in the dining room the service is pleasant but not always swift. At the time of writing Marco Pierre White is planning to transform Harvey's in Wandsworth into an operation similar to The Canteen called The Bistro. This leaves us The Restaurant which is mooted as a joint venture with the Forte-owned Hyde Park Hotel.

MOST OF THE ENTRIES on this densely typed sixty-wine list play safe. France offers good things (from Zind-Humbrecht, Sauzet, Druet or Dujac), but none a keen new name. With the cheapest bottles at £12, mark-ups are grasping: the Koonunga Hill Chardonnay, in retail at £4.99, is £17.50 here: some canteen.

OPEN: Mon-Sun. **HOURS:** 12.30-3.00pm (12.30-3.30pm Sun) and 6.30pm-12.00am (7.30-10.45pm Sun). **CLOSED:** Christmas. **CREDIT CARDS ACCEPTED:** Access, Visa. **NUMBER OF SEATS:** 140. **SERVICE:** Optional. Wheelchair access. **NEAREST TUBE STATION:** Fulham Broadway.   MAP REF: 8/B3

La Capannina

24 Romilly Street, W1

071-437 2473 or 071-734 9630   **£25**

'An old Soho Italian with casalinga cooking'

In restaurant terms, or indeed any other, there is not much of old Soho left which makes La Capannina the more precious. Established for more than thirty years its homespun Italian dishes seem not the rare find they once were but items such as osso bucco, oxtail braised in Barolo and cotechino with lentils are still competently prepared and banged down with all the brio you expect. Eat from the daily typewritten menu and go for lunch, when the film and advertising business crowd in, rather than dinner.

OPEN: LUNCH: Mon-Fri. DINNER: Mon-Sat. **HOURS:** 12.00-2.30pm and 6.00-11.15pm. **CLOSED:** Bank Holidays. **CREDIT CARDS ACCEPTED:** AmEx, Diner's Club, Visa, Access. **NUMBER OF SEATS:** 80. **SERVICE:** Optional. No smoking area. Private room seats 25. **NEAREST TUBE STATION:** Leicester Square/Piccadilly Circus.
                                                            MAP REF: 12/C2

Capital Hotel

22-24 Basil Street, SW3

071-589 5171   LUNCH £35 ; DINNER £40

'Small and perfectly formed hotel dining'

From the start, over twenty years ago, David Levin, owner of the Capital, has ensured that his small Knightsbridge hotel is as well known for the restaurant as for the stylishness and comfort of the rooms. His current chef is Philip Britten, whose most formative training was under Nico Ladenis. Britten has retained the Michelin star that for many years has twinkled over the Capital. His cooking style is, on paper, deceptively simple. Dishes are expressed unpretentiously but frequently carry subtle depths and wise pairings of flavour and texture. Thus a sole and tomato soufflé is complemented by an onion soubise. Lobster is 'twinned' with potatoes flavoured with mint. A salad of chicken livers sports beetroot and endive and is dressed with mushroom oil. These dishes are first courses quoted from a set price three course menu at £25 inclusive. This deal is offered both at lunchtime – when there is also a menu at £21.50 – and in the evening. In the evening there is also an à la carte list with the prices of dishes expressed as supplements on a basic price of £25 for three courses. Confusing? Only a bit. I have had meals at the Capital where you could plot the progress on graph paper as a U-shaped curve, with the main course pedestrian compared to the starter and supremely good dessert. The florentines, when served as part of the petits fours with coffee, send the line right off the top of the chart. Service is assiduous and the welcome to the hotel by the lobby staff notably enthusiastic. The wine list has gravitas and a useful section of half-bottles for the careful luncher. In his unstoppable way David Levin has now acquired a vineyard and his own production, inevitably called Le Vin du Levin, a Sauvignon blanc from the Loire, is on sale here, at his next door wine bar Le Metro and doubtless by the case to you, should you so wish. The view into the kitchen, which is a feature of the dining room should be matched by less frowsty decor.

THIS IS A WELL-ORGANIZED and clearly laid-out wine list, but only claret lovers will be excited by it, and even they should remember to empty the piggy bank before setting out. Most of the kit on offer is old and classé, therefore expensive (in absolute rather than relative terms: Ducru-Beaucaillou '62 here is £70 including service; at Pont de la Tour it's £100, to which you add 15% service). Burgundy keeps its end up in the same sort of way (though with less dust on the bottles), but the rest seems little more than an afterthought.

OPEN: Mon-Sun. **HOURS:** 12.00-2.30pm and 7.00-11.15pm. **CREDIT CARDS ACCEPTED:** Visa, Access, Mastercard, AmEx. **NUMBER OF SEATS:** 48. **SERVICE:** Optional. **SET PRICE LUNCH:** £21.50 and £25. **SET PRICE DINNER:** £25. Wheelchair access. Private room seats 22. **NEAREST TUBE STATION:** Knightsbridge.   MAP REF: 14/C1

Le Caprice

Arlington Street, SW1

071-629 2239   **£35-£40**

'See and be seen with good food and slick service'

Christopher Corbin and Jeremy King are an odd couple. Formerly managers at, respectively, Joe Allen and Langan's Brasserie they have developed into arguably the best restaurateurs in London – they also own The Ivy – with a loyal following amongst the glitterati. Le Caprice and The Ivy have always been associated with showbiz but just one of Corbin and King's talents is to make the atmosphere at both the restaurants egalitarian. If you can get a table at Le Caprice, which it must be said is easier since the recession took a firm grip, you will get the same courteous, efficient treatment as does – oh, who shall we say these days – Kate Moss? The definition of famous has changed since the era of the original Caprice. The look of the place is decidedly Eighties with a hard-edged, brittle definition of glamour and pics by David Bailey, a collection that becomes ever more fascinating with passing years. The menu is a shrewd list of dishes with appeal to those who eat out a great deal. Such people value simplicity but also often harbour retrogressive tendencies where food is concerned and think wistfully of the nursery. Pork sausages with mash, salmon fishcake, deep-fried cod with pea purée and chips and the dessert of drop scone, banana ice cream and maple syrup appeal to the latter. The former order tomato and basil galette, dressed Cornish crab, grilled squid, tuna, poussin or rabbit and cappuccino brulée (clever conceit). Pastas and risottos are well-made. Chips come in two sizes, thin and fat, unlike the customers who tend to be of the former persuasion. The standard of cooking is higher than average, and equally importantly, consistent. Every day dishes of the day are added to stave off boredom on both sides of the swing door. Wines have been given as much careful consideration as the food. I go to Le Caprice when I want to feel all is right with the world.

OPEN: Mon-Sun. **HOURS:** 12.00-3.00pm (12.00-3.30pm Sun) and 6.00pm-12.00am. **CLOSED:** Dinner Christmas Eve to lunch 2nd January. **CREDIT CARDS ACCEPTED:** All major cards. **NUMBER OF SEATS:** 75. **SERVICE:** Optional. Wheelchair access (but not lavatory). **NEAREST TUBE STATION:** Green Park.   MAP REF: 12/B4

Caravan Serai

50 Paddington Street, W1

071-935 1208   **£19**

'Afghan food pitches its tent in Marylebone (and Putney)'

Afghan cooking can be illuminatingly compared with Nepalese in its filled pasta dumplings, with Northern Indian in the emphasis on meat and the clay oven as a cooking vessel and with Persian in the use of tart fruit in sauces and the importance attached to rice. On the long menu offered here where some dishes are described as highly recommended it begs the question of how they feel about the others. But, in any case, to get the sense of the cuisine, include in your first courses either ashak or mantu, both lamb-stuffed pastas (vegetarian versions available) the former including leek and, perhaps, dalda, a kebab of minced lamb served with spiced lentils. From the main courses consider gosala gaak, a dish based on veal with a sauce flavoured with cherries, ground seeds and olive oil and the house recommendation of poorshuda, stuffed poussin cooked in a lightly spiced sauce and as a vegetable, subzi, spinach cooked with leeks and peppers. Whatever you choose, have as accompaniments kabuli or narengh chalaw, basmati rice dishes flavoured with fruits and almonds and also nan bread, preferably nan seree with garlic. The decor is hung about with ethnic artifacts. The service can be rather abrupt. Incidentally, if a visit to Caravan Serai or its brother restaurant Buzkash in Putney (4 Chelverton Road SW15, 081-788 0599) engenders an interest in Afghan cooking, look out for an excellent recipe book called *A Pinch of Salt* by Rahima Amini (Quartet Books). Afghan food is excellent for parties and picnics.

OPEN: Mon-Sun. **HOURS:** 12.00-3.00pm and 6.00-11.00pm (6.00-11.30pm Sat-Sun). **CLOSED:** Christmas Eve, Christmas Day and Boxing Day. **CREDIT CARDS ACCEPTED:** Access, AmEx, Barclaycard. **NUMBER OF SEATS:** 56. **SERVICE:** 10%. **SET PRICE LUNCH:** £9.95. No smoking area. Private room seats 16. **NEAREST TUBE STATION:** Baker Street.   MAP REF: 12/A1

Caruso Ristorante Italiano

585 Fulham Road, SW6

071-381 3422   **£25**

'Most main courses under a tenor'

This insalubrious corner of Fulham fields a surprising number of restaurants – the flashiest being Blue Elephant – and the big frontages of some might divert your eyes away from the discreet entrance to Caruso, a new-wave Italian restaurant in some filial relationship to Bacco in South Kensington. The agreeably plainly furnished premises benefit from a conservatory and a small garden at the back. Were you to emulate our hero, who sang not only for his supper but apparently for three-hour lunches too, some time should be spent on the pasta course. Although home made pasta is no novelty these days the stuff here is notably well-made. I can recommend the tagliolini di mare. There is a pasta of the day and they will happily match your favourite sauce to your favourite noodle shape. Try truffled grilled kidneys with polenta to start. From a winter menu, main courses of the chef's mixed grill of fish, mashed garlic sausage with spinach and sauteed potatoes and osso bucco alla Milanese served with couscous stand out. Prices are reasonable, the service proficient.

OPEN: LUNCH: Mon-Fri. DINNER: Mon-Sat. **HOURS:** 12.00-2.30pm and 6.30-11.30pm. **CREDIT CARDS ACCEPTED:** All major cards. **NUMBER OF SEATS:** 80. **SERVICE:** 12%. **SET PRICE LUNCH:** £12. No smoking area. Wheelchair access (but not lavatory). Private room seats 20. **NEAREST TUBE STATION:** Fulham Broadway.

MAP REF: 8/B2

Casale Franco

134-137 Upper Street, N1

071-226 8994 £20

'A warehouse of Italian food'

There is a professional friendliness about the waiters here which strikes me as sometimes being tinged with contempt. The modern Italian food is delivered with an air of 'Here you are suckers'. Perhaps given the restaurant's popularity and an evening no-bookings policy, people are so grateful to get a table that they don't complain about a detail such as cold grilled vegetables. However, some of the cooking is fine, as in spicy Italian sausages and cuttlefish cooked in its ink. The pizzas with their thin volcanic crusts are a reason in themselves to visit. They are not served at lunchtimes. The premises are a two-storey high-tech conversion of a factory reached down a discreet alley not far from the Almeida Theatre. On fine days when the car repair workshop opposite has shut up shop, the courtyard is utilized.

OPEN: LUNCH: Fri-Sun. DINNER: Tue-Sun. **HOURS:** 12.30-2.30pm and 6.30-11.30pm (6.30-11.00pm Sun). **CLOSED:** 1 week at Christmas and 2 weeks end of August. **CREDIT CARDS ACCEPTED:** Visa, Mastercard, Switch. **NUMBER OF SEATS:** 120. **SERVICE:** 10% for tables over 5. Wheelchair access (but not lavatory). 10-15 tables outside. **NEAREST TUBE STATION:** Angel/Highbury & Islington. MAP REF: 8/C2

The Causerie

Claridge's Hotel, Brook Street, W1

071-629 8860 £29

'A corner that will be forever, we hope, England'

For one price (£16) you can have the 'Smorgasbord' with a glass of Dubonnet, beer, cider, fruit juice, squash or other minerals. For £1 more you can drink a glass of sherry, gin and tonic, vin rosé, vin blanc sec or Hock, Bordeaux rouge or kir. For an additional £1.50 you can kick off your trawl of the buffet with a schnapps, dry martini, Manhattan, whisky sour, negroni or Pimms No. l. The drinks say nearly all about this quirky, time-warp corner of a grand hotel that is much favoured by aristocratic ladies and gents but deserves wider appreciation. The buffet is carefully composed and the impeccable manners of the staff make several circumnavigations to achieve 'good value' quite in order. In addition to the salads, pâtés, smoked fish and so forth there are hot dishes of the day. There is also – at a high price – an à la carte, but opting for that would be missing the point of this vignette from a certain sector of English society. Supper is served pre- and post-theatre.

OPEN: LUNCH: Mon-Sat. DINNER: Mon-Fri. **HOURS:** 12.00-3.00pm and 5.00-11.00pm. **CLOSED:** Easter, Christmas Day and Boxing Day. **CREDIT CARDS ACCEPTED:** All major cards. **NUMBER OF SEATS:** 40. **SERVICE:** Optional. **SET PRICE LUNCH:** From £16. **SET PRICE DINNER:** £23.50. Wheelchair access. **NEAREST TUBE STATION:** Bond Street. MAP REF: 12/A3

Caviar Kaspia

18/18a Bruton Place, W1

071-493 2612 £35

'For when you want to eat caviar in public'

You reach the restaurant Kaspia through the shop which sells caviar and other expensive delicacies. In the same family ownership as the shop, salle de dégustation and restaurant at 17 place de la Madeleine in Paris, Kaspia in Bruton Place does its best to emulate the original. But the illuminated glass-fronted cases displaying lacquered boxes and china from the imperial collection simply convey hotel lobby. Obviously you go to Kaspia to eat caviar, even if only 50g of salmon eggs with baked potato at £8.95. The arrival of a new chef, Annabelle Job, has added a few specials presented separately from the list of sturgeon eggs, smoked fish and shellfish salads. The press release calls these specials White Russian Cuisine, but looking at salmon mousse, gravad lax and fishcakes it would seem an empty phrase. Bortsch is thin. Smoked eel fillets are too soft. Pirojki is one flaky pastry pie filled with minced meat. Blinis are the flat, anaemic variety rather than the buckwheat-dark, yeast-raised kind – both are traditional.

The most economical way to deal with Kaspia is through the set price menus inclusive of tax and service which start at £27 unless you find, as can happen, that pressed caviar is not available. There is good patisserie for dessert. Service is well-led by Patrick Bellville but he is in charge of a most eccentric waiter who seems to view a meal as an exam you must pass – and within the time limit. Kaspia, for obvious reasons, is a very particular place that attracts a rather picturesque elderly clientele and rich, discreet ladies who lunch. There is a good selection of vodkas.

OPEN: Mon-Sat. **HOURS:** 12.00-3.00pm and 7.00-11.30pm. **CREDIT CARDS ACCEPTED:** Access, Mastercard, AmEx, Diner's Club. **NUMBER OF SEATS:** 52. **SERVICE:** 15%. **SET PRICE LUNCH:** £20. **SET PRICE DINNER:** £27. Wheelchair access (but not lavatory). Private room seats 12. **NEAREST TUBE STATION:** Green Park.

MAP REF: 12/A3

Cheneston's

1 Kensington Court, W8

071-917 1200 £35

'One of the more curious, but likeable,
developments in hotel dining'

The Milestone is a Kensington hotel recently restored by a Kuwaiti family to a pristine state of high Victoriana. Cheneston's (the restaurant), referring to the original name for Kensington, has one half of the dining room sited in what was formerly an oratory. Seated in this dignified splendour the Pacific Rim menu, prepared by American chef Marvin Wood, comes across as weirdly idiosyncratic. It is what you least expect but might find to be a surprise of a diverting kind. Dishes such as lobster red pepper chilli chowder, Asian carpaccio with raw root noodles, oat-crumbed brook trout with black bean sauce and peppered greens, spiced rib-eye steak with sweet potato lime purée, crispy spinach and gingersnap gravy, iced coconut parfait with Kahlua-soaked peaches are doubtless some of the reasons the hotel has attracted as guests a rather unlikely rabble of pop stars. The demands of such a clientele are also well met by the snack menu in The Park Lounge served throughout the day and until late; somewhere new to keep in mind in that slightly dowdy part of town.

OPEN: Mon-Sun. **HOURS:** 7.00-10.30am (7.30-11.00am Sun), 12.30-2.30pm and 7.30-11.00pm (7.30-10.30pm Sun). **CREDIT CARDS ACCEPTED:** All major cards. **NUMBER OF SEATS:** 30. **SET PRICE LUNCH AND DINNER:** £15.50-£18.50. Private room seats 20. **NEAREST TUBE STATION:** High Street Kensington.   MAP REF: 11/F

Chez Gerard

8 Charlotte Street, W1

071-636 4975   **£26**

'The steak/frites formula well executed'

There have been various attempts over the years to perfect the meal of steak and chips and surround it with a distillation of Gallic élan. The Chez Gerard restaurants, now owned by the folk who bring you Cafe Fish, Bertorelli's, Soho Soho and Chutney Mary, do a workmanlike job. The meat is good quality, the French fries, slender, crisp and plentiful. It would seem perverse to choose other dishes or to ignore the well-stocked, usually well-kept cheeseboard. The wine list is balanced and fairly priced. It is wise to book not only to be sure of a table but to check if there are any special deals in operation. Chez Gerard in Charlotte Street has undergone radical refurbishment and is as sleek and modern as the others are mock-Montmartre.

ALSO AT: 119 Chancery Lane, WC2 (071-405 0290).
31 Dover Street, W1 (071-499 8171).

CHARLOTTE STREET: OPEN: LUNCH: Mon-Fri, Sun. DINNER: Mon-Sun. **HOURS:** 12.30-2.30pm and 6.30-11.00pm. **CREDIT CARDS ACCEPTED:** All major cards. **NUMBER OF SEATS:** 95. **SERVICE:** 12.5%. **SET PRICE DINNER:** £15 (and Sat lunch). No smoking area. 13 seats outside. Private room seats 50, evenings only. **NEAREST TUBE STATION:** Tottenham Court Road.   MAP REF: 12/B1, 12/B3, 8/C2

Chez Moi

1 Addison Avenue, W11

071-603 8267   **£35**

'Long-established genteel restaurant with some tearaway food'

Proprietors Richard Walton and Colin Smith, chef and front of house, have
been partners in this restaurant since 1967. They came together to Holland
Park after working relatively briefly at Robert Carrier's Islington restaurant.
One or two dishes created by the chap who brought together food and
glamour in the late fifties, early sixties still feature on the menu. However,
what is surprising and beguiling about Chez Moi – cosily old-fashioned in
terms of decor and formal service – is the modernity of the food in the very
best sense of the word. Wide reading and a willingness to learn from the
various chefs he has employed keep Walton's dishes abreast of every trend.
Dedication and a life mainly lived above the shop means that high standards
are consistently maintained. The menu is divided in two parts entitled Chez
Moi Traditionnel on the left and Quelque Chose de Different on the right. If
one of the more experimental dishes on the right behaves itself and is well
received it stands a chance of being transferred. One such is 'oursins' Chez
Moi, deep-fried angel hair pasta forming the spines and diced prawns and
scallops the flesh of that menace to bathers. As clever as it is, even brighter is
the idea of pairing it with mostarda de fruta. Coquille Saint Jacques minute
et sa ballotine Japonaise is a spirited and more or less successful attempt at a
nori-rolled sticky rice cylinder studded with smoked salmon, avocado and
cucumber accompanying some griddled marinated scallops. A little
incendiary bomb of wasabi (Japanese horseradish) can zap the unsuspecting
diner (and wine drinker). An understanding of Thai spicing is apparent in
sa-teh de volaille Thailandaise. Many regulars visit Chez Moi for the
superlative lamb dishes. A rack comes with garlic and mint or with a crumb
and herb coating bound with vividly hot mustard. Fish dishes veer towards
the complex and creamy although there is the offer of steamed John Dory or
smoked salmon. Vegetables, such as purée of carrot flavoured with orange or
cabbage with bacon and shallots, are prepared with care and attention.

   Petit pot au chocolat has done twenty-seven years on the menu. Other
desserts vary but try tarte au citron should it be offered. The good value set
lunch is when Walton tries out dishes and he says it is the cooking he most
enjoys. The wine list, compiled by manager Philippe Bruyer, is not showy
but is a thoughtful selection which he discusses knowledgeably. Chez Moi is
one of the restaurants to pass the Michael Winner test. You'll find him at the
table tucked away at the back of the right-hand room.

PERHAPS THIS WINE LIST would benefit from the adventurousness which
creeps in around the edges of the menu; yet what it does, it does well: sound,
mature claret and burgundy. I can still taste my half of Dauzac '83; not cheap
(at £15.50), yet ripe and rich enough to suggest I was penny-pinching to
scruple over its cost.

OPEN: LUNCH: Mon-Fri. **DINNER:** Mon-Sat. **HOURS:** 12.30-2.00pm and 7.00-
11.00pm. **CLOSED:** Bank Holidays. **CREDIT CARDS ACCEPTED:** All major cards. **NUMBER
OF SEATS:** 45. **SERVICE:** Optional. **SET PRICE LUNCH:** £14. Wheelchair access (but not
lavatory). **NEAREST TUBE STATION:** Holland Park.   MAP REF: 11/F

China Court

Swiss Centre,
10 Wardour Street, W1

071-434 0108   **£10-£20**

'At time of writing one of the better bets in Chinatown'

Given the restlessness of Chinese chefs and the fragility sometimes of Chinese restaurant ownership, recommending a Chinatown restaurant in a guide published a few months after writing is a chancy affair. However, there is a considerable amount of investment obvious in the decor of China Court which, it could be argued, gives some hope for stability. The dim sum, most priced at £1.50, are excellent. If you are inclined towards the mysterious and slippery ask for translations of the items in Chinese characters. Outside dumpling hours – usually ending at about 5pm – the main menu also repays study. Spare ribs are better than usually done. Egg foo yung with crab meat, a dish not offered everywhere, is beautifully prepared. Pork chops in ginger and spring onion is a likeable crisp dish; sweet and sour pork for the grown-ups. Lobster seems reasonably priced until the creature arrives with parts apparently missing, a sad case of a physically handicapped lobster. Service has a lack of charm now not so universal in Chinatown. Piped music plays relentlessly. Remember you are there for the food.

OPEN: Mon-Sun. **HOURS:** 11.45am-11.30pm (11.00am-11.00pm Sun). **CREDIT CARDS ACCEPTED:** All major cards except Diner's Club. **NUMBER OF SEATS:** 450. **SERVICE:** Optional. **SET PRICE DINNER:** £6.50. Private room seats 20. **NEAREST TUBE STATION:** Leicester Square.   MAP REF: 12/C3

Chinon

25 Richmond Way, W14

071-602 4082   **£35 (£15 at the bar)**

*'At last the estimable cooking of Jonathan Hayes
sees the light of day'*

When a wine bar near Shepherd's Bush called The Triangle went into receivership, the next door restaurant Chinon snapped up the premises and divided their operation into ground floor bar, open for lunch and dinner, and downstairs restaurant, evenings only. Both parts look out onto a terrace and overgrown garden beyond and on a fine day light pours onto an operation that before seemed always shrouded in gloom. The menus at lunch and dinner share some dishes although a main course during the day may become a starter at night. At all times the cooking is thoughtful and creative with meticulous attention paid to the sort of detail that makes a difference. Salad Chinon, which varies according to what is available, shows the resourcefulness of a market gardener with different sprouted seeds and grains as well as radish thinnings mixed into the rocket and other green leaves, green beans and chives acting as a base for salami, smoked pork loin, and shaving of Parmesan. Stuffed pepper – usually a moment to be wary – is a whole red pepper carefully skinned, filled from a small hole in the top with a delicious mixture of aubergine, melted mozzarella, herbs and breadcrumbs. Surrounding it is a necklace of interwoven stalks of water asparagus. A wing of roasted skate scattered with peppers comes with a mound of carefully cooked pale green cabbage leaves enclosing some mashed potato. On the accompanying salad are slender rings of fried squid next to curls of julienned cucumber. A quail is boned, larded with bacon and roasted, served under a sheet of fine pasta with an enticingly sparse number of lentils in a creamy sauce. Although on the ground floor you sit at bare marble-topped tables (but with a large linen napkin for your knees) this is by no means wine bar food. The wines are a singular assortment but offer enough variety. The service doubtless means well but relates to customers in a peculiarly defensive way.

OPEN: LUNCH: (Bar only): Mon-Fri. DINNER: Mon-Sat. **HOURS:** 12.30-2.30pm and 6.00-10.45pm. **CLOSED:** Bank Holidays. **CREDIT CARDS ACCEPTED:** All major cards, except Diner's Club. **NUMBER OF SEATS:** 30 (15 at bar). **SERVICE:** 12.5%. Wheelchair access (but not lavatory). 6 tables outside. **NEAREST TUBE STATION:** Olympia/Shepherd's Bush.   MAP REF: 11/F

Chopstix Xchange

1314-1316 High Road,
Whetstone, N20

081-343 7335   LUNCH £8; DINNER £14

'A generous-spirited Oriental buffet'

The Zen restaurant group has decided that one way forward in this recessionary world is to offer buffet-style Oriental food at a fixed price with none of the mystification of long menus. This first spacious, colourful outlet in Whetstone – formerly the Chinese restaurant Ma & Pa – has proved a success. Unlike many self-service operations, there is no stigma attached to piling the (generously-sized) plates high and eating cheaply. With time customers will presumably realize that several discriminating trips to the hot plates and bain-maries deliver a more satisfactory meal than does a pile-up. This is particularly true given the various styles of dishes; Chinese, Japanese, Vietnamese and Malaysian and their different tolerances of canteen-style presentation. A bonus to the deal is the special of the day – for example Peking duck – prepared throughout the service and handed round the restaurant by waiting staff. The set price varies according to the day and time, becoming more expensive towards the weekend. Chopstix Xchange is far from a gourmet experience but infinitely more appealing and diverting than most fast food.

OPEN: Mon-Sun. **HOURS:** 12.00-3.00pm and 6.00-11.00pm (12.00-10.45pm Sun). **CREDIT CARDS ACCEPTED:** Access, Visa. **NUMBER OF SEATS:** 130. **SERVICE:** Optional. **SET PRICE LUNCH:** £4.80 (buffet). **SET PRICE DINNER:** £10.80 (buffet). Wheelchair access (1 step). Private room seats 10. **NEAREST TUBE STATION:** Totteridge & Whetstone.   MAP REF: 8/B1

Christopher's American Grill

18 Wellington Street, WC2

071-240 4222 £35-£40

'American food for sophisticates'

The eponymous Christopher is Christopher Gilmour who discovered his liking for the food served in American steak houses such as Palm when working as a commodity broker in Chicago. Much about the menu echoes the concerns, some might say obsessions, of mainline American eating. There are large Maine lobsters (3lbs), large steaks (New York strip can be served at 14oz), grilled breast of chicken served with red pepper salsa and shoestring fries and a hamburger. First courses include clam chowder and Caesar salad and the dessert list is not sniffy about offering cheesecake and Häagen-Dazs ice creams. However, the resemblance ends there. The premises, a converted neo-Renaissance nineteenth-century building that once housed a casino, bear all the hallmarks of an interior designer having been hard at work. The most successful element is the winding stone staircase where opera is played giving you the feeling that you are on the stairway to heaven.

Not all the food in the first floor restaurant provided by chef Adrian Searing, who has worked in New York, can be defined as ambrosial. Standards are uneven with over-seasoning and over-cooking sometimes a fault but when it is good it is very, very good as in a definitive carpaccio, lobster guacamole (a dish of the day that should transfer to the carte), spicy crab cakes with red pepper mayo and rocket and a pig's trotter stuffed with sweetbreads and served with mash that at £14 stands comparison with that of Pierre Koffmann's at Tante Claire for £24 although, it must be said, it comes minus the morilles. Some of the vegetables priced separately are well worth ordering; creamed spinach, tobacco onions and celeriac mash.

Christopher's, down from the opera house, attracts a smart crowd and there is often a face present that you can put a name to. Perhaps the least American-inspired element is the service which sometimes seems to be just going through the motions of affability or efficiency. But if you were to divide the after-theatre dining world into Orso people and Christopher's people, I would be of the latter persuasion.

OPEN: LUNCH: Sun-Fri. DINNER: Mon-Sat. **HOURS:** 12.00-3.00pm (11.30am-3.00pm Sun) and 6.00-11.30pm. **CLOSED:** Bank Holidays. **CREDIT CARDS ACCEPTED:** All major cards. **NUMBER OF SEATS:** 110. **SERVICE:** Optional. **SET PRICE DINNER:** £15-£19. Private room seats 32. **NEAREST TUBE STATION:** Covent Garden.

MAP REF: 12/D3

Chutney Mary

535 Kings Road, SW10

071-351 3113   **£35**

*'One of the more delicious results of the
British presence in India'*

You've seen the movies (*Passage to India, Heat and Dust* to name two).
You've watched the TV series (*The Jewel in the Crown* to name one). Now eat
the food. Chutney Mary is the first restaurant in London, and it is claimed
the world, to serve (intentionally) Anglo-Indian food. This cuisine which
has some of its roots in the presence in India of the English-owned East India
Company since the seventeenth century should not simply be dismissed as a
bastardization of indigenous traditions. Many dishes have evolved particular
to the various communities of mixed English and Indian descent. The fact
that these were for the most part Christian communities was an influence on
the cooking since Hindu or Muslim dietary restrictions were not in force.
Chutney Mary – the term is a not wholly admiring one that used to be
applied to Indian women too keen to ape Western ways – is the creation of
two Indian sisters. They have researched the subject thoroughly, including
recipes from Maharajahs' palaces famous for their banquets, strictly regional
specialities and even their own experiences of Indian boarding school food.
    Chefs have been brought directly from India. Prices more in keeping with
a 'Western' restaurant tend to steer customers into ordering a two or three
course meal rather than dishes to share although a range of first courses
taking in items such as Goan crab cakes, dumplings in yogurt, seekh kebabs
from Lucknow, and fiery Madras prawns makes good communal grazing.
There are mainstream Indian dishes but prepared with unusual care, for
example, almond chicken korma where the sauce is based on ground
almonds plus ground melon and poppy seeds and flavoured with rose
petals.There are various fish specialities and a chicken dish called Country
Captain irresistible to anyone who grew up on totally inauthentic curries
which nevertheless have a charm all their own. Chutney Mary prepare the
best bhindi (okra) ever. An effort has been made to match wines to the food,
the New World bottles scoring well. Service can be uneven, sometimes
chaotic. Indian artefacts amidst hotel foyer decor and a conservatory
addition help to give character to a space that is part of a post-modern toy-
town development.

OPEN: Mon-Sun. **HOURS:** 12.30-2.30pm (12.30-3.30pm Sun) and 7.00-11.15pm
(7.00-10.00pm Sun). **CREDIT CARDS ACCEPTED:** All major cards. **NUMBER OF SEATS:**
150. **SERVICE:** 12.5%. **SET PRICE LUNCH:**   £13. No smoking area. **NEAREST TUBE**
STATION: Fulham Broadway.   MAP REF: 14/B4

Chutneys

124 Drummond Street, NW1

071-387 6077   **£10**

'Indian vegetarian with style'

Some Indian vegetarian restaurants have a bleak, do-gooder atmosphere that makes you dwell on everything you have ever read about the action of fibre in the intestine. Chutneys, an offspring of a group that has restaurants in Bombay and LA, is not like this. It is cheerful and even quite slickly designed. The menu pinpoints the areas of the sub-continent from where the various dishes originate and it is possible to combine the West, Madras, Gujerat and Bombay to create a meal surprising in its complexity given the deliberately limited range of ingredients. Do not omit the special poori, spheres of fried dough filled with potatoes and sev, moistened with yogurt and flavoured with sweet and sour sauces. Potatoes figure importantly, sometimes mashed, mixed with lentils and deep-fried. Tamarind chutney is a sparky accompaniment. The dosa and uttapam are well-made. If you like sweet, creamy Indian desserts, variations on rice pudding, ice cream and yogurt you will be happy here. In tatty Drummond Street, a sort of little India, Chutneys stands out. The buffet lunch, a way to explore the cuisine, is a bargain.

OPEN: Mon-Sun. **HOURS:** 12.00-2.45pm and 6.00-11.30pm (12.00-10.30pm Sun). **CLOSED:** 1 week at Christmas. **CREDIT CARDS ACCEPTED:** Access, Visa. **NUMBER OF TABLES:** 70. **SERVICE:** 10%. **SET PRICE LUNCH:** £3.95. **SET PRICE DINNER:** £4.95-£5.95. Wheelchair access. Private room seats 60. **NEAREST TUBE STATION:** Euston Square.
MAP REF: 8/B2

Cibo

3 Russell Gardens, W14

071-371 6271/2085   **LUNCH £15; DINNER £25-£30**

*'Exhibitionist art and modern Italian
food close to Olympia'*

During the first flush of its popularity tables were packed into Cibo so tightly that every move seemed to require a fellow customer to breathe in and shift their chair. Cibo was part of the Italian restaurant Renaissance opening after The River Cafe and before Riva. Now it has become a more leisurely place, serving much the same food to a loyal local following. Once your face is known this is an effortlessly friendly restaurant where the owner Gino Taddei is generous with his grappa (a mixed blessing). It is also one where the antipasti and pasta courses are skilfully made, developing clear flavours from two or three ingredients. Unusual recipes and rare ingredients such as the cardoon are a sign of Cibo's commitment. Pasta with game or shellfish and various risotto have been outstanding. But the main courses, especially slow-cooked ones, do not always possess the same clarity. The memory of a murky fish stew still lingers. The menu changes weekly and now includes a good value set lunch. Critical types say that it is time the three dimensional artwork was removed.

OPEN: LUNCH: Sun-Fri. DINNER: Mon-Sun. **HOURS:** 12.00-2.30pm (12.30-3.30pm Sun) and 7.00-11.00pm (7.00-11.30pm Sat). **CLOSED:** Christmas Eve, Christmas Day and Boxing Day. **CREDIT CARDS ACCEPTED:** All major cards. **NUMBER OF SEATS:** 45. **SERVICE:** Optional. **SET PRICE LUNCH:** £10. Wheelchair access (but not lavatory). Private rooms seat 12 or 16. **NEAREST TUBE STATION:** Olympia/Shepherd's Bush.

MAP REF: 11/F

Clarke's

124 Kensington Church Street, W8

071-221 9225   **LUNCH £30; DINNER £50**

*'Some say Ms Clarke is the best interpreter
in London of Californian cooking'*

My feeling about eating at Clarke's in the evening is this; if you do not want to give people a choice of what they eat, then throw dinner parties. This is not to say that Sally Clarke does not produce spiffing food. She does, but, to my mind, part of the pleasure of eating out is scrutinizing what is on other plates; feeling jubilant or feeling jealous. A more venal side of me dwells on how very cost effective is the ploy – precise ordering, minimal wastage – and yet prices are high. One good reason that they are is that ingredients are first rate. They are also well-deployed but sometimes the effect seems little more than a grill plus salad, even if the meat or fish has been marinated and the salad does sport rare leaves and an imaginative dressing. The accoutrements such as breads, chutneys, relishes, flavoured oils and the well-chosen cheeses are excellent. Many of these items can be bought at the shop next door. Despite her sojourn in California, and the effect it has had on her cooking, in the dessert course Sally Clarke shows her Englishness. As with many domestic dinners in this country it is invariably an upbeat part of the meal. Lunch, which is somewhat cheaper, offers a small choice in each course of the menu. The wine list is impressive, strong on Italy and California and there is the bonus of several wines being offered by the glass.

CLARKE'S IS A GOOD place to drink in glassfuls. You could start with pungent Don Zoilo Fino (£3) or a honeyed Pineau des Charentes (£4); carry on with a glass of the earthy Domaine Limbardie 1992 (£2.50); see down dessert with a glass of Cauhapé's 1990 Jurançon Vendange Tardive (£4); and bolster coffee with an Oregon apple brandy (£4.50) or Bonny Doon's haunting Prunus (£4.50). If you must have whole bottles of things, make the most of the nifty Californian sections, where varietal pluralism, engendered by the likes of Qupé, Jade Mountain and Bonny Doon, is everywhere evident.

OPEN: Mon-Fri. **HOURS:** 12.30-2.00pm and 7.00-10.00pm. **CLOSED:** 2 weeks in summer, 10 days at Christmas and 4 days at Easter. **CREDIT CARDS ACCEPTED:** Access, Visa. **NUMBER OF SEATS:** 90. **SERVICE:** Optional. **SET PRICE LUNCH:** £22 or £26. **SET PRICE DINNER:** £37. No smoking area. Wheelchair access (but not lavatory). **NEAREST TUBE STATION:** Notting Hill Gate.   MAP REF: 11/F

Connaught Hotel

Carlos Place, W1

071-499 7070   **£42**

'An historic monument of a restaurant'

Publishing an article in the *Evening Standard* about the Connaught and its chef Michel Bourdin we came up against the hotel's highly developed sense of exclusivity and discretion. No, we couldn't photograph in the dining room, nor in the Grill Room. We would be allowed to photograph the front porch. Nobody eats in the porch we pointed out but it took more than that snappy riposte finally to get a snap of Bourdin in his renovated kitchen (opened by his heroine the Queen Mother) and in a corner of the dining room. This attitude, whilst irritating, is to some extent justified. The Connaught, in terms of service and, indeed, menus, is trapped in a timewarp. There is nowhere else like it in London and in these days of imitation and homogenization that is a valuable quality. The style of food is grand hotel with a mixture of traditional English dishes – mostly inflexibly served as dishes of the day, Monday steak and kidney, Tuesday Irish stew, Wednesday roast beef with Yorkshire pudding and so on – and classic French. Before the Connaught, Bourdin spent ten years at Maxim in Paris under the watchful eye of the late Monsieur Vaudable.

Not only the prodigious cost of a meal but the way our sensibilities and preferences concerning food have developed and moved on can make eating at the Connaught sometimes not the glorious event you hope for. Seasoning can be lacklustre, sauces clumsy and an item like a quenelle not the tethered soufflé you anticipated. In season, game is a wise choice, as are the roasts, supplied by loyal and high class suppliers, trundled on the trolley at any time of year. Oeuf en gelée Stendhal and one of the signature dishes, croustade d'oeufs de caille Maintenon, are first courses I like. To mark the fact that you are near a kitchen with an army of commis order those magical spheres, soufflé potatoes, and a dessert such as crêpe soufflé. Bourdin is anxious to introduce more English dishes onto the menus and is using the new rather shocking concession of £25 set price menus – even the Connaught can suffer from recessions – as a vehicle. The smaller Grill Room, a greeny gilded feminine answer to the masculine panelled clubbiness of the dining room, is an intimate place where you imagine certain families put their children down for a table at birth. Service in both areas is professional, formal and stratified in a manner that exists in few other establishments. The wine list is conservative, prizing the virtues of age beyond the fleeting novelties of the moment. There are no bargains but some famous bottles and some priceless ports.

NOTHING ABOUT THE Connaught could ever be described as 'showy', and the wine list certainly isn't going to ruffle the old gents' decorum. Champagne, Bordeaux and Burgundy are all fairly though not fanatically represented, and a modest sense of history lends the selections gravitas. Hocks and Moselles (like the Erdener Treppchen Riesling Kabinett 1989 from Dr Loosen, £15.50) reflect the good taste of a former age. But the real reason for coming here is to drink a small glass (one-third gill) of Cockburn's 1935 port (£8.35), or one of the Cama de Lobos Solera 1864 madeira (£6.10). Thus the world is rectified; thus the shades assuaged.

OPEN: RESTAURANT: Mon-Sun. GRILL ROOM: Mon-Fri. **HOURS:** RESTAURANT: 12.30-2.00pm and 6.30-10.30pm. GRILL ROOM: 12.30-2.00pm and 6.00-10.30pm. **CLOSED:** GRILL ROOM: Bank Holidays. **CREDIT CARDS ACCEPTED:** All major cards. **NUMBER OF SEATS:** 75 in Restaurant, 35 in Grill Room. **SERVICE:** 15%. **SET PRICE LUNCH:** £25-£30. **SET PRICE DINNER:** £35 (Grill Room only). Wheelchair access (but not ladies' lavatory). Private rooms seat 10-22. **NEAREST TUBE STATION:** Bond Street.

MAP REF: 12/A3

La Copita

63 Askew Road, W12

081-743 1289   £10

'One of the earlier and better tapas bars'

This small tapas bar opened before that phrase began to instil dread and boredom and a closedown of the tastebuds. The wide range of little dishes (about thirty) are carefully prepared and varied enough to keep the appetite ticking over. There are some items that seem relatively unusual e.g. pepes – potato, onion and chorizo cooked together; calabacines fritos – deep-fried courgettes with aioli; merluza con cilantro – hake cooked in fresh coriander sauce. Paella can be ordered for two to four persons, or presumably more if organized in advance. To satisfy the English desire to make a meal of everything, there are desserts including ice creams imported from Majorca and a list of Spanish dessert wines.

OPEN: LUNCH: Wed-Fri. DINNER: Mon-Sat. **HOURS:** 12.30-3.00pm and 6.00pm-12.00am. **CLOSED:** Bank Holidays. **CREDIT CARDS ACCEPTED:** Visa, AmEx. **NUMBER OF SEATS:** 60. **SERVICE:** Optional. **SET PRICE LUNCH:** £5.95. **SET PRICE DINNER:** £7.50. Wheelchair access (but not lavatory). Private room seats 30. **NEAREST TUBE STATION:** Shepherds Bush/Goldhawk Road.

MAP REF: 8/B2

The Criterion

224 Piccadilly, W1

071-925 0909   £20

'London's shimmering centrepiece in need of a more seductive style'

The Criterion, originally opened in the 1870s, should be a London restaurant landmark. It is in Piccadilly Circus opposite where Eros soars. Owned by Forte plc since 1949, for the last year it has been run as a joint venture between Forte and American theme restaurateur Bob Payton. In the heart of another capital city and under different ownership you would imagine chairs, tables and umbrellas outside, dashing waiters darting through crowds, aperitifs, assignations, romance; a real cafe scene. Local government restrictions and English attitudes may prevent the above, but the decision to have no signage, no view in through the windows and a revolving door obscuring the interior defies rather than encourages customers to enter. Should they do so they would be dazzled and delighted by the glittering interior resembling a Byzantine station concourse. The initial decision to have no bar area for just a drink means that The Criterion has not developed casual use in the way that would be fitting for somewhere at the centre of theatreland. A new decision means you may now drink and eat light food on the Terrace at the back after 6pm. Afternoon tea is another development. The sandwiches peer out from a heap of salad leaves. Although Brian Baker, formerly Michelin-starred chef at Hambleton Hall, is now in charge of the kitchen the menu has changed little from the Italian/American list devised by the original American chefs. The food is basically competently done; a decent Caesar salad, flavourful rib-eye steak with crisp fries, adequate pasta as in penne with rock shrimp but there are occasions where it goes horribly wrong as in something called crispy risotto fritter with roasted vegetables – more like leftover fried rice pudding with ratatouille and reminiscent of an earlier aberration, fried spaghetti. Perhaps Baker's talents and ideas will be allowed to percolate through as time goes on. Service is toned-down American, friendly enough but with irritating habits; coffee brought before dessert and unrequested bills brought to the table even when the place is virtually empty.

OPEN: Mon-Sun. **HOURS:** 12.00-11.30pm (12.00-10.30pm Sun). **CLOSED:** Christmas Eve, Christmas Day, Boxing Day and New Year's Eve. **CREDIT CARDS ACCEPTED:** All major cards. **NUMBER OF SEATS:** 160. **SERVICE:** Optional. **SET PRICE LUNCH AND DINNER:** £15 (2 course) or £20 (3 course) for parties over 8. Wheelchair access. Private room seats 70. **NEAREST TUBE STATION:** Piccadilly Circus. MAP REF: 12/B4

Daphne's

112 Draycott Avenue, SW3

071-589 4257   **£35**

'An old Chelsea girl given a glamorous face lift'

Chef at the revamped, relaunched Daphne's in South Kensington is Edward Baines who at twenty-four possesses a long culinary c.v. He has apparently worked at the Dorchester, at hotels in the South of France, in private service in Tuscany, at The River Cafe, Bibendum, Emporio Armani and latterly Est in Soho. He must be a quick learner. In preparation for Daphne's he did a stint at a catering college in Milan. Were you to infer that his menu would be fundamentally what has become known as modern Italian, you would be right. To a regular restaurantgoer it does not, at first glance, how shall we say, induce shivers of anticipation. However, as with all the other Italian restaurants of SW1 and SW3 the point is not altogether the food but the atmosphere in which it is eaten and who with. As a good looker, Daphne's, now owned by Finnish-born, Danish-bred Mogens Tholstrup, is up there among the best. The premises, unrecognizable from the previous incarnation, sport a plant-filled glazed backyard and a set of rooms decorated in singed umber punctuated by small squares of dull gold. Flagstones and tiles as floor contribute to the noise level and to the sub-palatine feel. The restaurant is thronged by the tribe who live to eat out and even the service throws up individuals who can turn heads. Sometimes you might wish they would turn theirs your way. It was while I was eating the cotoletto Milanese – escalopes of veal dusted with breadcrumbs, fried and scattered with capers – that the realization came to me that here is the trat. de nos jours; San Frediano strained through The Conran Shop. We are most of us these days familiar with mozzarella, and grilled vegetables, bruschetta, carpaccio, risotto, sea bass, confit and chargrilled steak just as once we knew inside out our antipasto del chef, petto di pollo sorpresa, saltimbocca alla Romana and arancia Positano. The old formula was popular and so is the new. Tested and approved are sauté of wild mushrooms with grilled polenta, cheese and mushroom soufflé, panzanella, spaghettini with clams, risotto with porcini, soft-shell crab, herb encrusted rack of lamb cooked pink and the side order of artichoke mash. The dessert of crostata with apples is the Italian version of a French tarte fine aux pommes, a circle of puff pastry overlaid with thin slices of apple and sugar cooked fiercely and to order. There are soufflés; chocolate, Grand Marnier or lemon. The wine list has some good and not unfairly priced Italian bottles. Daphne's is glamorous, an epithet you can apply to surprisingly few restaurants.

OPEN: Mon-Sun. **HOURS:** 12.00-3.00pm (11.00am-4.00pm Sun) and 7.00-11.50pm. **CREDIT CARDS ACCEPTED:** Diner's Club, AmEx, Visa, Access. **NUMBER OF SEATS:** 120. **SERVICE:** 12.5%. Wheelchair access (but not lavatory). 60 seats outside. **NEAREST TUBE STATION:** South Kensington.   MAP REF: 14/C3

Deals

Harbour Yard,
Chelsea Harbour, SW10

071-352 5887   £20

'Minor royals offer ribs and spring rolls'

The marriage of Viscount Linley may well bring into news focus again his catering venture in partnership with fellow aristo Lord Lichfield and restaurateur Eddie Lim. Once the only restaurant outlet to crack the curse of Chelsea Harbour, the first of the small group sited in that soulless development might be seeing some of its customers growing up and defecting to The Canteen opposite. Deals in a series of witlessly titled sections – such as No Big Deal, Raw Deals, Dealsburgers, Side Deals, Sweet Deals – offers food to tempt a childish palate albeit a cosmopolitan one happy to include satay, chilli con carne, coleslaw and chocolate mud with vanilla ice cream in the same order. It is what sometimes gets called 'a fun concept', one to which Sloanes respond enthusiastically. As you might expect, there is good use made of wood in the decor. The West End branch attracts a different, more workaday crowd.

ALSO AT: 14-16 Foubert's Place W1 (071-287 1001).

OPEN: Mon-Sun. **HOURS:** 12.00-11.00pm (12.00-11.30pm Fri-Sat. 12.00-10.00pm Sun). **CLOSED:** Christmas Day, Boxing Day and New Year's Day. **CREDIT CARDS ACCEPTED:** AmEx, Access, Visa, Diner's Club. **NUMBER OF SEATS:** 170. **SERVICE:** 12.5%. Wheelchair access (limited access to lavatory). 10 tables outside. Private area seats 16. **NEAREST TUBE STATION:** Fulham Broadway.   MAP REF: 8/B3

Del Buongustaio

283 Putney Bridge Road, SW15

081-780 9361   **£24**

'A delightful learning curve in Italian food'

This second venture of the Italian/Australian team who brought you the resoundingly successful Osteria Antica Bologna in Clapham has a heartier, more countrified menu centred on a section fittingly entitled Soddisfazioni, and a somewhat more sophisticated look. The extent of the changes from one day to the next throughout the whole menu points to responsiveness and impressive knowledge in the kitchen. This is a restaurant where you could behave like an Italian in Italy and go every day for your lunch and/or dinner (there is a set price two-course lunch). And an Italian, familiar with various regions, would recognize the dishes – not always the case in London's Italian restaurants – and think fondly of mamma. Some cooking modes not often encountered flourish here, e.g. sformato, a savoury pudding usually baked in a bain-marie and torta di verdure, a traditional pie made here with fresh artichokes, spinach, rice and Parmesan in the way it is done in Cessole in Piedmont. Pastas are good and interestingly sauced and filled. Among the main courses there is always an enlightened vegetarian dish, an unobvious fish dish such as skate, red mullet or octopus and a casserole or long-cooked assembly usually bolstered with a purée of potatoes or soft polenta. Desserts tend to be creamy and calorific but unconventional, e.g. sapajean con diplomatico, warm red wine zabaglione with baked egg custard and panettone pudding. A menu degustazione takes you through five courses, some of them served in small quantity. Reflecting the ownership, the wine list is Italian and Australian. It is fascinating, fairly priced and divided in a novel way by mood and style, some of which you may feel attuned to: Young and Innocent or Full, Perfumed and Mature or Elegant and Well-Regarded or Knowledgeable and Dangerous. You might just settle for Wines for The Good Times. Meals at Del Buongustaio are almost invariably exactly that.

OPEN: Mon-Sun. HOURS: 12.00-3.00pm and 6.30-11.30pm. CLOSED: 2 weeks at Christmas, Bank Holidays and Easter. CREDIT CARDS ACCEPTED: Access, Visa, AmEx. NUMBER OF SEATS: 48. SERVICE: Optional. SET PRICE LUNCH: £9.50. SET PRICE DINNER: £19.50. NEAREST TUBE STATION: Putney East/Putney Bridge.   MAP REF: 8/B3

La Delizia

246 Old Brompton Road, SW5

071-373 6085   **£8**

'Some say the best pizzas in town'

Much appreciated by a young, fashionable crowd, these are only arguably the best pizzas in town if you are of the thin-crust-is-good faction. The bases are large (18") and sensibly come not smothered in toppings. Salads and bresaola are there for starters orders if you want to go in for – as the English seem to do – three-course eventing. Pastas are also offered. The Chelsea

Manor address has chiefly al fresco eating and an adventurous wine shop nearby for BYO. The decor in the usually crowded Old Brompton Road premises is coolly stark. The Italian waiters will steal your girlfriend.

ALSO AT: Chelsea Farmers' Market, Sydney Street, SW3 (071-351 6701). 63-65 Chelsea Manor Street, SW3 (071-376 4111).

OPEN: Mon-Sun. **HOURS:** 12.00pm-12.00am. **CLOSED:** Christmas Day and New Year's Day. **CREDIT CARDS ACCEPTED:** None. **NUMBER OF SEATS:** 45. **SERVICE:** Optional. **NEAREST TUBE STATION:** Earls Court. MAP REF: 14/A3, B3, C4

dell'Ugo

56 Frith Street, W1

071-734 8300 £23

'A place to take the pulse of food fashion'

The plenipotentiary chef here is Mr A. Worrall Thompson, a man who can be accused of many things but never of restraint. Unilaterally declaring that design was dead, he had the old Braganza site decorated in a discordant selection of colours and patterns, retaining the murals because they had cost a lot of money. His menu, interpreted by chef Mark Emberton, is remorselessly fashionable, sporting every modish ingredient, but not always in arrangements where they successfully co-operate. From the dazzling array the card presents it is as well carefully to think through the impact of some assemblies that may have one or two flavours or textures too many. Lamb shank with flageolets flavoured with garlic and rosemary is classic. Lamb shank with flageolets etc. and olive-oil mash might just floor you. Composed salads are good and like the grilled vegetables, pastas and risottos are offered at two sizes and two prices. Mussells with steamed greens and a lentil and coriander broth is one of the most successful round-ups of ingredients. Now that the excitement that attended the launch of dell'Ugo has not only worn off but also spun off (see Zoë and watch out for Wozza's hand in the menus of the Palio and Muswell's chains) it becomes clear that, on the whole, tried and true combinations are best. The one-pot dishes inviting a single-course meal also succeed as slow cooking provides a melding of flavours. Breads are delicious, justifying £1.95 for the assortment. Relatively low prices and the informality of dell'Ugo are attractive although the service seems prone to bad patches. The standard wine list is enhanced by the choice of a different wine merchant each month. Originally the ground floor was for drinking and snacks ('consequential nibbles'), the first floor did not take bookings and the top floor was the plushest part, but these distinctions have blurred and the first floor is most consistently busy (and now bookable).

OPEN: Mon-Sat. **HOURS:** CAFE: 11.00am-11.00pm. RESTAURANT: 12.00-3.00pm (not Sat) and 6.30pm-12.30am. **CLOSED:** Bank Holidays, Easter and 4 days at Christmas. **CREDIT CARDS ACCEPTED:** All major cards. **NUMBER OF SEATS:** 190. **SERVICE:** Optional. **SET PRICE LUNCH AND DINNER:** £7.50-£10 (Cafe only). 5 tables outside. Private room seats 16. **NEAREST TUBE STATION:** Leicester Square/Tottenham Court Road. MAP REF: 12/C2

The Dog House

187 Wardour Street, W1

071-434 2116 £26

'Not such a bad place to be sent to'

The name and anarchic decor of this Soho basement restaurant and bar might not instil in you great hopes for the food but the modern menu – brought to you by the same team who gave you First Floor – is carefully cooked, reasonably priced and has on it some nice conceits. Examples are vegetable and barley soup, Arizona cheese beignets with salsa, pappardelle with roast roots and mascarpone, grilled flank steak with sweet red onions and honey and yogurt bavois (sic. presumably bavarois). Loud and sometimes live music is part of the package at Dog House. A dogged, determined banjo player threw me into profound empathy with the cast of *Deliverance*. It helps to be young.

OPEN: LUNCH: Mon-Fri. DINNER: Mon-Sat. **HOURS:** 12.30pm-12.00am (5.30pm-12.00am Sat). **CLOSED:** 24th December to 4th January. **CREDIT CARDS ACCEPTED:** All major cards, except Diner's Club. **NUMBER OF SEATS:** 36. **SERVICE:** Optional. Private rooms seat 6 or 10. **NEAREST TUBE STATION:** Oxford Circus/Tottenham Court Road.

MAP REF: 12/C3

The Grill Room

Dorchester Hotel
53 Park Lane, W1

071-629 8888 LUNCH £30; DINNER £40

*'English food served in gloomy
Iberian splendour'*

Refurbishment at the Dorchester has not deflected the Grill from its aim of providing what is best about British food. This continues to be served in the unlikely setting of what looks like a Moorish guildhall. The menu is a comprehensive list juxtaposing classics in the first course such as smoked salmon and dressed crab with culinary fancies such as glazed Landford goat's cheese with autumn leaves and south-coast scallops with a rose petal vinaigrette. The main courses follow a similar route and just in case you hadn't jumped to this conclusion already, I can attest that it is better to stay with the simpler, unfussed approach. Game in season is extremely well-handled as was revealed by a superb saddle of hare with pears and pan-roasted potatoes. At lunchtimes there is a set price menu that tends to over-emphasize in its choice of dishes that you are ploughing the economical furrow. In addition there is a special for each day, a list that covers most of the traditional English dishes and enables regulars to know what day of the week it is: 'If this is boiled beef it must be Monday'. Trolleys are used to great effect, not only to wheel around roasts but also salads, cheese, breads and desserts. I dare say, if necessary, they would even wheel customers out on one. Wines are expensive. Service is gracious.

A LUMBERING JUGGERNAUT of a wine list, this rambles on for page after page, picking up mossy bits and pieces as it does so. The curious might unearth a 1983 Gaillac 'vin de voile' (i.e. a *flor* wine), though £66 makes the punt a pricey one; the heroically singular Greek Château Carras 1978, all coffee and prunes, is there for £21; while the cheapest wine on the list (£13.50) has changed its nationality without telling the Dorchester – it's now a Croatian Cabernet Sauvignon.

OPEN: Mon-Sun. **HOURS:** 7.00-11.00am, 12.30-2.30pm and 6.00-11.00pm (7.30-11.00am, 12.30-2.30pm and 7.00-10.30pm Sun). **CREDIT CARDS ACCEPTED:** All major cards. **NUMBER OF SEATS:** 80. **SERVICE:** Optional. **SET PRICE LUNCH:** £20. **SET PRICE DINNER:** £28. Wheelchair access. **NEAREST TUBE STATION:** Hyde Park Corner.

MAP REF: 12/A4

Down Mexico Way

25 Swallow Street, W1

071-437 9895 £20

'Better Mexican food than you might expect –
if you can hear yourself eat'

'Better than they deserve' is what middle-aged matrons with a liking for Mexican food (like myself) might think about the menu served here to a raucous young crowd. The management would seem to be, as it were, slamming themselves in the foot by going to some trouble to produce fairly authentic Mexican dishes and importing good Argentian beef but creating a relentlessly noisy environment in which they can be 'enjoyed'. The ground floor of the stately tiled premises that was originally the Spanish restaurant Martinez houses the Late Night Salsa Dancing Bar with a disco and occasional live music. On the first floor is the dining room often prey to large groups and parties. The trick – if you are there not for the beer (or tequila) but the food – is to pick a relatively quiet time. But perhaps I am being foodist in supposing that those who like loud music and tequila slammers would not appreciate the finer points of a *mole*.

OPEN: Mon-Sun. **HOURS:** RESTAURANT: 12.00-11.45pm (12.00-10.30pm Sun). WINE BAR: 12.00pm-3.00am (7.00-10.30pm Sun). **CLOSED:** Christmas Day and Boxing Day. **CREDIT CARDS ACCEPTED:** All major cards. **NUMBER OF SEATS:** 180 in Restaurant, 100 in Wine Bar. **SERVICE:** Optional, 6% commission. Wheelchair access to bar (but not lavatory). **NEAREST TUBE STATION:** Piccadilly Circus.

MAP REF: 12/B3

Downstairs at One-Ninety

190 Queen's Gate, SW7

071-581 5666 **£30**

'A fish restaurant revolution'

Until the unimaginatively named Downstairs at One-Ninety was conceived by Antony Worrall Thompson, fish in restaurants was approached reverentially, almost biblically. Menus were either English-style or French-style and fish & chip shops occupied a separate, lowly place in the social strata. Wozza – as he is sometimes known – decided to run the gamut between fish & chips and lobster, fish sausages and sea bass, taking in crostini, raw crustacea, carpaccio, confit, chowder, chargrills, crab cakes, risotto and Cajun blackened along the way. This is a classless but not a clueless fish restaurant, inhabiting basement premises lightened and brightened since the previous incarnation as a serious 'gourmet' restaurant. Head chef Australian Chris Millar makes his own contributions, often dishes with an Oriental influence such as lobster nori tempura with saffron risotto (something of a mix of metaphors) and Thai scallop cakes with toasted peanut sauce. Even those who consider meals without meat somewhat spineless find pleasure on the menu in items like smoked lobster risotto and corn and crab cakes with sweet red pepper sauce and chilli potatoes. However, there are meat dishes of the day and game in season, for example roast partridge with quince marmalade, sweet potato crisps and thyme jus. Sometimes over-elaboration can be a problem with flavours shuffled and dealt into unwinning hands. Many dishes are served at two prices making appetizers possible entrées and vice versa. Desserts are fittingly indulgent after the sensible start imparting fish oils and barely a calorie . . . . Good would certainly be undone by whisky fudge cake with caramelized oranges and pavlova with banana cream and passion fruit sorbet. Service can be haphazard and sometimes achingly slow. The wine list is an impressive document spanning the world. It repays careful study.

OPEN: Mon-Sat. **HOURS:** 7.00pm-12.00am. **CLOSED:** 2 weeks in August and 1 week at Christmas. **CREDIT CARDS ACCEPTED:** AmEx, Access, Diner's Club, Visa. **NUMBER OF SEATS:** 75. **SERVICE:** Optional. Private room seats 22. **NEAREST TUBE STATION:** Gloucester Road. MAP REF: 14/A1

Dragon Inn

12 Gerrard Street, W1

071-494 0870 **£15**

'For the adventurous eater of Cantonese food'

The Dragon Inn won an *Evening Standard* search for The Best Dim Sum. This was a few years back and something you can be sure of in Chinatown is that almost nothing stays the same for long. However, standards have remained high and any change seems to be in the temperament of the staff.

They are now quite friendly and helpful. If you ask for a translation of a dish printed only in Chinese characters they will tell you the answer rather than tell you how much you won't like it. Indeed if you are an unsqueamish eater attracted by peripheral bits such as fish lips and duck's web, you will find a happy hunting ground here. The Dragon Inn is a popular place for dim sum and also for one-dish meals of barbecued and roasted meats with rice and green vegetables, one of the most cost-effective and satisfying ways to lunch.

OPEN: Mon-Sun. **HOURS:** 12.00-11.45pm (11.00am-11.45pm Sun). **CLOSED:** Christmas. **CREDIT CARDS ACCEPTED:** Visa, Access, AmEx. **NUMBER OF SEATS:** 120. **SERVICE:** 10%. **SET PRICE LUNCH:** £8.50. **SET PRICE DINNER:** £17.50. Wheelchair access (but not lavatory). Private room seats 10. **NEAREST TUBE STATION:** Leicester Square. MAP REF: 12/C3

The Eagle

159 Farringdon Road, EC1

071-837 1353 £12

'The way forward for pubs'

'Up and down the City Road, in and out of The Eagle', could be the song of the *Guardian* hacks who flock here to fraternize with their peers on the *Independent*. Benefiting from a cheap near-end-of-lease deal, Michael Belben and (chef) David Eyre, who had worked at Smith's and Mélange in Covent Garden, took over this spacious pub, decorated it with nothing much and nothing matching, installed an art gallery upstairs and offered simple and good Italian food. This formula has been a great success and spawned others such as The Lansdowne (q.v.). Would that more London pubs follow suit. The small grill/kitchen struggles to deal with the crowds who pack the place at lunchtime but usually pleases customers with rustic soups, grilled vegetables on bread (crostini), steak sandwiches using ciabatta, grilled meats and spiced sausages. There is no compulsion to eat more than one plateful or, indeed, anything; the management is keen to hang on to the ethos of a pub. Wines are reasonable and the blackboard list changes in part regularly.

OPEN: Mon-Fri. **HOURS:** 12.30-2.30pm and 6.30-10.30pm. **CLOSED:** Bank Holidays. **CREDIT CARDS ACCEPTED:** None. **NUMBER OF SEATS:** 50. **SERVICE:** Optional. Wheelchair access (1 step). 4 tables outside. **NEAREST TUBE STATION:** Farringdon.
MAP REF: 8/C2

Efes Kebab House

80 Great Titchfield Street, W1

071-636 1953 £15

'Long-established Turkish place invaluable in the area'

For nearly twenty years Efes Kebab House has served good, reasonably priced Turkish food to people who live or work around Oxford Street: the rag trade, BBC bods and the rich and/or famous who have houses in the quieter streets. No doubt it would benefit shoppers and tourists to make the trek from the main thoroughfare to Great Titchfield Street, but the regulars might not welcome more competition for lunchtime tables. The restaurant begins with a busy grill kitchen, from which a top quality doner and other kebabs can be bought to take-away. What looks like a tiny dining space opens out into a big room, painted pistachio green. Perhaps the meze are not as delicate and varied as could be had in more leisurely places but they are made here, as opposed to being bought in. The dishes from the grill are excellent: good quality lamb skilfully cooked and served in large portions with hot tomato and celery sauce. The staff are sometimes hurried but serious questions about what to order and how things are made will be answered by the courteous manager or the brothers who own Efes.

ALSO AT: Efes II, 175-177 Great Portland Street, W1 (071-436 0600).

OPEN: Mon-Sat. **HOURS:** 12.00-11.30pm. **CREDIT CARDS ACCEPTED:** All major cards. **NUMBER OF SEATS:** 160. **SERVICE:** Optional. **SET PRICE LUNCH AND DINNER:** £14 and £15. Wheelchair access. 10 tables outside. **NEAREST TUBE STATION:** Oxford Circus/Great Portland Street. MAP REF: 12/B1

Emporio Armani Express

191 Brompton Road, SW3

071-823 8818 £23

'Definitive designer food'

There is something rather dreamy about taking lunch in this gallery room suspended above the traffic, where handsome men wearing what appear to be silk pyjamas bring delicate nourishment. The rumour is that the staff are models filling in time. They are particularly kind and willing, which does seem to indicate that they do not belong to the hardened London school of service. Despite the light, modern Italian food and the shapely appeal of the room, there is not usually a press for tables. Perhaps some potential customers are put off by the walk through the Emporio Armani shop and others cannot tear themselves away from the racks. The pleasures of the table are not easily compatible with the dictates of fashion.

OPEN: Mon-Sat. **HOURS:** 10.00am-6.00pm (10.00am-7.00pm Wed). **CLOSED:** Christmas Day and Boxing Day. **CREDIT CARDS ACCEPTED:** All major cards. **NUMBER OF SEATS:** 60. **SERVICE:** Optional. Wheelchair access (assistance provided). **NEAREST TUBE STATION:** Knightsbridge/South Kensington. MAP REF: 14/B2

The Enterprise

35 Walton Street, SW3

071-584 3148   **£20**

'The only pub in town for the ladies who lunch'

The gentrification, Italianization, yuppification and taking in of Thai lodgers on the first floor has distinguished the history of London pubs in the last five years. The Enterprise, significantly, lies more or less half way between Harrods and The Conran Shop. The menu and wine list, with as many choices in champagne (ten) as in white and red, is designed to please the passing trade. Smoked salmon is served with horseradish mousse. Excitable appetites prefer quesadillas with guacamole and salsa and baby new potato skins with soured cream. There are various composed salads, fishcakes, lamb cutlets with a cassis sauce Lord Lucan would not like, sausages and a home made burger, many of these served with chips. Specials are listed on a blackboard. Overall The Enterprise is well-kept, well-heeled and well-run. It closes in the afternoons, presumably for a lie down.

OPEN: Mon-Sat. **HOURS:** 12.30-2.30pm and 7.30-10.30pm. **CLOSED:** Christmas Day, Boxing Day and New Year's Day. **CREDIT CARDS ACCEPTED:** All major cards except Diner's Club. **NUMBER OF SEATS:** 36. **SERVICE:** 10%. Wheelchair access (but not lavatory). 12 tables outside. **NEAREST TUBE STATION:** South Kensington/ Knightsbridge.   MAP REF: 14/C2

Esarn Kheaw

314 Uxbridge Road, W12

081-743 8930   **£25**

'Lose yourself in the Golden Triangle'

A reason for trying to pronounce the name of this Thai restaurant in West London is the Northern Thai specialities offered in addition to a list that may be all too familiar. Northern dishes – pioneered in London at Chiang Mai – have as their proudest possession aspects of charcuterie including a sausage. I have had good examples but I see the note I made when eating at Esarn Kheaw is 'wind-dried Wall's'. Even so, if you think about it, that has a sort of appeal. Tiger Cry is dry-cooked well-spiced beef. Sweet liver Northern style, cooked in thin strips, is not to be missed. And if you can tolerate exploding taste buds order Northern style green papaya salad. Its effects can be muffled by a portion of sticky rice served in a container of bamboo. The Thai love of Artex and log cabin architecture is apparent here. A significant part of the clientele is Thai (good sign). Towards Westerners the waitresses are rather tediously pushy.

OPEN: LUNCH: Mon-Fri. DINNER: Mon-Sun. **HOURS:** 12.00-3.00pm and 6.00-11.00pm. **CLOSED:** Bank Holidays. **CREDIT CARDS ACCEPTED:** All major cards. **NUMBER OF SEATS:** 40. **SERVICE:** Optional. **SET PRICE LUNCH:** £12.50 for two. **NEAREST TUBE STATION:** Shepherds Bush.   MAP REF: 8/B2

L'Escargot Restaurant and Brasserie

48 Greek Street, W1

071-437 2679   **BRASSERIE £25; RESTAURANT £40**

'The snail slithers down yet another new track'

Chefs David Cavalier and Garry Hollihead, who have been brought in by L'Escargot's new owner Jimmy Lahoud, trained together at the Grosvenor House Hotel. They have since more recently worked at establishments – to some small extent their own – where each was awarded a Michelin star. Both places subsequently closed which may or may not be more than a sign of the times but it seems ironic that the brasserie section of L'Escargot comes off so much better than the ambitious, haute-cuisine, more expensive, upstairs restaurant. At the time of writing responsibility for the two parts is shared. Cavalier has remarked that it is fortunate that basically he is happiest cooking meat while Hollihead likes to work with fish. The restaurant menu, priced at £27.50 for three courses but studded with supplements, is terse in description, reminiscent of the style that evolved at the eponymous Cavaliers. This, combined with the modern trend of dishes not having to bear out their title, can lead to surprises. The first course tortellini of langoustines turns out to be a row of the shellfish perched on a bundle of slender asparagus and long ribbons of courgette with one tortelloni placed at each end. Some main courses provide hallucinogen for a trip down gastronomy's memory lane. Their sauces tend to be over-reduced and the otiose garnishes rendered too finicky. Main ingredients are almost equally divided between fish and meat. There is no shrinking from offal as evidenced by tête du porc Joel Robuchon and roast veal kidney and sweetbreads. Desserts keep up the intensity. Caramel miniatures is a parade of small dishes. Chocolate tart is accompanied by vanilla ice cream and orange sorbet.

It is the sort of food that in other circumstances would make me wonder if it is what restaurant customers any more want, but when a short trip down a staircase can deliver simpler, cheaper and, to my mind, infinitely more beguiling meals, it seems particularly out of time and out of place. In the cream-painted, cheerfully decorated brasserie there is evidence of a real understanding of French bistro food. Competence and the requisite generosity are applied to dishes like pot au feu (served for two), belly of pork with Puy lentils, and moules marinières with chips. Salad of pigs' trotters, boudin blanc with apple and onions and oeuf en meurette are all comme il faut. The inverted commas around morue in the dish entitled brandade of 'morue' salad of French beans may account for the bland, gelatinous quality of what turns out to be a scoop of fish mousse. It seems a pity that within a pleasingly consistently French menu they had to insert Caesar salad as a side order. The ground floor is reinstated as a place for media types to schmooze. The wine list, although not as good as in Nick Lander's (and thus Jancis Robinson's) day, has a good range of choices to suit the style.

OPEN: LUNCH: Mon-Fri. DINNER: Mon-Sat. **HOURS:** BRASSERIE: 12.15-2.30pm and 6.00-11.30pm; RESTAURANT: 7.00-11.00pm. **CLOSED:** Christmas and Bank Holidays. **CREDIT CARDS ACCEPTED:** All major cards. **NUMBER OF SEATS:** 80 in Brasserie, 35 in Restaurant: **SERVICE:** Optional. **SET PRICE LUNCH AND DINNER:** £27.50 (Restaurant). No smoking area. Wheelchair access (Brasserie only). Private room seats 25. **NEAREST TUBE STATION:** Leicester Square.   MAP REF: 12/C2

L'Estaminet

14 Garrick Street, WC2

071-379 1432   **£30**

'That rare thing; unfussed French bourgeois food'

Occupying the premises that were formerly Inigo Jones, L'Estaminet (meaning tavern) is not only a welcome shot of restaurant sanity in Covent Garden but an asset generally. The sort of bourgeois French food it offers is these days quite hard to find. Salade de harengs pomme de terre à l'huile, escargots de Bourgogne, saucisson chaud Lyonnais, omelette aux choix, grenadin de veau aux olives, blanc de volaille à l'estragon, côte de boeuf Béarnaise, nougat glacé, oeufs à la neige; this sort of menu with no fashion or frippery to rely upon stands or falls on its competence. On the whole you can count on that and sometimes be pleasantly surprised as in the brochette of mussels with the shellfish interspersed with charred bay leaves. Service, usually with a smile, is unflaggingly French. The wines are not a strong point and tend to err on the side of callow youth. The ground floor now takes full advantage of the corner site. The gothic windows remain but added in are kitsch touches such as copper pans on bare brick walls, slightly gruelling still lifes and repro gas light brackets that serve as a shorthand for the style. In the basement is the wine bar La Tartine where the eponymous open sandwiches and also various assiettes of charcuterie, cheese etc. are served at reasonable prices. Handy to know about for before or after the theatre.

OPEN: Mon-Sat. **HOURS:** 12.00-2.30pm and 6.30-11.30pm. **CLOSED:** Bank Holidays. **CREDIT CARDS ACCEPTED:** All major cards, except Diner's Club. **NUMBER OF SEATS:** 55. **SERVICE:** Optional. No smoking area. Private room seats 30. **NEAREST TUBE STATION:** Leicester Square/Covent Garden.   MAP REF: 12/C3

Feng Shang Floating Restaurant

opp. 15 Prince Albert Road, NW1

071-485 8137   **£30**

'The closest we get in London to Hong Kong's Jumbo'

I have a sentimental liking for Feng Shang. It dates back to the day I first encountered the owner Mr Wong at The Welcome Restaurant in Belsize Park. He was very sweet to my then small children. Having originally taken over a crock of a barge on the canal in Regent's Park and christened it The Gallery Boat he subsequently had built a much more sprauncy affair resembling in small part the Jumbo in Hong Kong harbour. The menu has been upgraded in price as well as ambition but it is a fact of London life that you pay over the odds for watery views and Disneyland structures. On the menu there is the encouraging detail of dishes being described in Chinese characters as well as English, pointing to a slice of Chinese clientele. Maybe they think the pairing of fish and meat with fruit is le dernier cri but it leaves me unimpressed. Try instead grilled dumplings, mou shu pork with its diverting complement of crunchy gelatinous mushrooms, steamed pomegranate chicken where the chopped meat plus vegetables are enclosed in a purse seemingly made from fried egg white and one of the 'zhai' vegetarian dishes in which meat or fish is imitated by savoury wheat gluten. It is more interesting than bean curd. Feng Shang is for when you want a different sort of night out; bobbing on a boat like a Fisher-Price toy.

OPEN: Mon-Sun. **HOURS:** 12.00-3.00pm and 6.00pm-12.00am (12.00pm-12.00am Sat-Sun). **CLOSED:** Easter Sunday and Monday, August Bank Holiday, Christmas Day and Boxing Day. **CREDIT CARDS ACCEPTED:** Access, AmEx, Diner's Club, Visa. **NUMBER OF SEATS:** 120. **SERVICE:** 10%. **SET PRICE DINNER:** £15-£25. Wheelchair access (but not lavatory). **NEAREST TUBE STATION:** Camden Town.

MAP REF: 10/C

The Fifth Floor Restaurant

Harvey Nichols,
Knightsbridge, SW1

071-235 5250   **£35**

*'If shopping drives you to drink the Fifth Floor Bar
is the place to do it'*

The Hong Kong ownership of Harvey Nichols department store considerably upped the ante in their long-standing rivalry with Harrods by opening what, in a riposte to Harrods' famous Food Hall, they refer to as a Food Market. It is on the fifth floor, a challenging distance to carry down your groceries. Overlooking the produce invitingly displayed in the high-tech, airily-glazed super-dupermarket (designed by architect Julyan Wickham) is the seductive bar and restaurant. Flights of fanciful design in the restaurant, such as blue bucket chairs sitting on blue spheres, are balanced by china, cutlery and glass of serious intent. The view on the window side is of the cake decoration architecture of the Hyde Park Hotel. Ladies who lunch are, of course, out in force but the gossip is not of Versace and Moschino and the success, or not, of fruit acids on those fine lines, but of chef Henry Harris's zippy way with black bean soup, his ability to contrast the sweet with the smooth as in onion confit with pork rillettes and grape chutney with terrine of foie gras, his grasp of salads such as the one that pairs merguez sausage with chick-peas and peppers, and his understanding of the honest grub that calms a fevered fashion victim (and also satisfies simply keen eaters who appreciate the restaurant staying open at night and on Sundays); main courses such as Bury black pudding with (notable) mashed potatoes and onion gravy, and braised tripe Madrid style which means with a potent tomato and pepper-based sauce. Harris is ex-Bibendum and has learned from his mentor Simon Hopkinson the importance of intensifying the impact of ingredients rather than lacing together a disparate assembly. His menu is deceptive in its apparent simplicity. The fact that Harris is English is most apparent in the desserts. Steamed puddings, crumbles and burnt cream achieve under his hand a newfound elegance. Butter-yellow thick Jersey cream is the ideal accompaniment, especially to the definitive treacle tart. The wine list is also the stock-taking for the wine shop. There are some classic bottles and vintages but also a wide selection under £20. Wine service is sometimes not up to the list and service in general can be wobbly. Adjacent to the restaurant there is a cafe serving light meals. On a pretty day you can sit outside.

YOU'RE GIVEN THE LITTLE LIST – around thirty-five cliché-free wines from own-label at £9.50 to Léoville-Las-Cases '70 at £75 (it's £190 at Le Gavroche, if that makes you feel any better). Ask, though, for The Big List: a huge, wide-awake range raided from the wine shop shelves and marked up so as not to induce outrage in those who have just shopped there. Sweet wines are particularly good, and the Australians include hard-to-find Shiraz from Château Tahbilk (the '85 at £23) and Henschke's Hill of Grace (the '89 at £30).

OPEN: LUNCH: Mon-Sun. DINNER: Mon-Sat. **HOURS:** 12.00-3.00pm (12.00-3.30pm Sat-Sun) and 6.30-11.30pm. **CLOSED:** Christmas Day and Boxing Day. **CREDIT CARDS ACCEPTED:** All major cards. **NUMBER OF SEATS:** 120. **SERVICE:** 12.5%. **SET PRICE LUNCH AND DINNER:** £16.50-£19.50. Wheelchair access. **NEAREST TUBE STATION:** Knightsbridge.   MAP REF: 14/C1

First Floor
186 Portobello Road, W11

071-243 0072   **£30**

'I know this really cool place along the Portobello Road'

The transformation of 186 Portobello Road from a den of iniquity into touristic bohemia in four years is a paradigm of the area. From a dodgy pub, the first floor of this site was converted initially into a drinking club that was too far ahead of its time then, with a few, deft decorative touches, into a hip happening kind of restaurant which gave the impression of dining in the middle of a set for *The Tempest*. The partnership responsible for that success fell apart (and Peter Cross, one half of it, now has The Dog House in Soho) but the First Floor is once again playing to packed houses under new management. The place seems to have lost some of its edge, though live jazz on Sundays appeals. Now the menu has many more main courses based on big bits of animal protein (rack of lamb with baby veg, fillet of beef with mushroom tagliatelle) and a much longer wine list includes Dom Pérignon. Early middle class colonists of the area hang their heads in shame. Meanwhile many other people ('Do they live here?') are having a good time. In truth some of the mad melées of ingredients offered by departed chefs do not deserve to be mourned, and service is now the slickest in the area. Things like bruschetta with just about everything (roasted peppers, goat's cheese and guacomole) are in keeping with the past but a curious, unmixed Caesar salad that includes bacon and anchovies, the hated lollo rosso lettuce and a crude dressing is not. Crazy, punchy cocktails no longer seem to be offered but the puddings are still good.

THIS IS A GOOD LIST within the £10 to £20 price range. The French wines are fair, but it's those from other countries which entice – like Rosemount's 1989

Semillon (phew, not Chardonnay for a change; £14), the 1990/91 Dry Creek Fumé Blanc (£17), the superb 1990 Barbera d'Alba Pian Romualdo from Prunotto (£18), or David Wynn's blessedly unoaked 1992 Shiraz (£12). The tasting notes are useful and succinct.

OPEN: LUNCH: Mon-Sun. DINNER: Mon-Sat. **HOURS:** 10.00am-3.00pm and 7.30pm-1.00am (11.00-6.00pm Sun). **CLOSED:** Christmas Day and New Year's Day. **CREDIT CARDS ACCEPTED:** All cards except Switch and Diner's Club. **NUMBER OF SEATS:** 100. **SERVICE:** 15%. **SET PRICE DINNER:** £27.50. Private room seats 28. **NEAREST TUBE STATION:** Ladbroke Grove.   MAP REF: 8/B2

Florians

4 Topsfield Parade,
Middle Lane, N8

081-348 8348   **£23**

*'The neighbourhood Italian every
neighbourhood should have'*

Florians wine bar and restaurant in Crouch End is one of the establishments in that oddly named suburb that make people remark, isn't it odd how many good restaurants there are in Crouch End? Opened in 1989 by two chaps who worked at Le Bistroquet in Camden Town and Café Flo, the Italian menu seemed more revolutionary then than perhaps it does today. However, if you live in North London you now don't have to go too far to find smoked venison fillet on rocket, crostone of cuttlefish stewed in its own ink, hare stew with grilled polenta, Italian sausages with canellini beans served with a pesto potato cake, oxtail stew served with truffle-flavoured mashed potatoes, fish pastas and risottos of the day, a wine list that could tutor you in Italian wines and a grappe list that could make you fall over. Some blasé users of Florians say that they don't stray from the bar where Italian snacks are served but it can be worth moving on to a table in what looks like a converted garage with the brickwork painted in lemon yellow, the woodwork in blue/grey. It might be one of those meals where you covet your neighbour's choice but enough of what you order will succeed.

GRAPPA (PLURAL: GRAPPE, and they are very plural here) is the speciality: twenty-two by the glass (£1.90-£3.50), surely meriting sponsorship by Neurofen or Beechams Powders. Six Amari, too, for those with a taste for bitter herbs (my favourite is the Sicilian Averna: £2 per glass). But you need something with your food, and thirty-five well-chosen Italian wines (Capello di Prete '88 at £9.10, for example) oblige. The list outlines their virtues, and prices are fair.

OPEN: Mon-Sun. **HOURS:** RESTAURANT: 12.00-3.00pm and 7.00-11.00pm (7.00-10.30pm Sun). BAR: 12.00-11.00pm (12.00-10.30pm Sun). **CLOSED:** Bank Holidays and Christmas. **CREDIT CARDS ACCEPTED:** Access, Visa. **NUMBER OF SEATS:** 65 in restaurant, 30 in bar. **SERVICE:** Optional. **SET PRICE LUNCH AND DINNER:** £5.95 (bar only). Wheelchair access. 4 tables outside. Private room seats 23. **NEAREST TUBE STATION:** Highgate.   MAP REF: 8/C2

La Fontana

101 Pimlico Road, SW1

071-730 6630/3187 £30-£35

'Serving white truffles in season since 1964'

La Fontana is a long-running Italian show and the first in London to have starred white truffles. The owner, Signor Pavesi, has a passion for this pricey fungus and will go to great lengths to obtain it. Of course wafer-thin slices of white truffle (in season late autumn/early winter) or even a salsa made from its trimmings will add considerably to the cost of what are already relatively exuberantly priced dishes. Out of truffle season concentrate on fresh pastas and risottos and the dishes of the day which almost invariably include a good osso bucco alla Milanese and a 'jugged' dish, e.g. wild duck. Pavesi is one of the old school who likes the show business of gueridon service with its flash in the pan of ignited brandy and the slightly awkward, unequal relationship that it sets up between cook and customer. Decor is cosy and cluttered. The wine list offers some examples of how Italy is now competing in the world market of fine wines – but at a price.

OPEN: Mon-Sun. **HOURS:** 12.00-2.30pm and 7.00-11.30pm. **CLOSED:** Bank Holidays. **CREDIT CARDS ACCEPTED:** All major cards. **NUMBER OF SEATS:** 40. **SERVICE:** Optional. Wheelchair access (but not lavatory). **NEAREST TUBE STATION:** Sloane Square. MAP REF: 14/D3

The Footstool

St John's Church,
Smith Square, SW1

071-222 2779 £20-£25

'Eat in the crypt of St John's, Smith Square'

Of the four restaurants opened by the entrepreneurial Elizabeth Philip MBE to provide sustenance where before it was hard to find – others are at the South Bank, Southwark Street and The Wigmore Hall – the cooking at the Footstool in the crypt of St John's, Smith Square stands out as providing more than just calories. At lunchtime office workers and MPs – a division bell is installed – can enjoy in a slightly boarding school atmosphere carefully cooked dishes which read like those articles in women's magazines about how to do a dinner party but transcend the genre, sometimes simply through the use of good ingredients. Concert-goers in the evenings must make do with the wine bar buffet from which you cannot escape the clammy embrace of quiche.

OPEN: Mon-Fri. **HOURS:** 12.15-2.15pm. **CLOSED:** Alternate Thursdays and Bank Holidays. **CREDIT CARDS ACCEPTED:** AmEx, Access, Visa. **NUMBER OF SEATS:** 55. **SERVICE:** Optional, discretionary 10% for parties of 6 or more. No smoking area. **NEAREST TUBE STATION:** Westminster. MAP REF: 8/C2

Four Seasons Restaurant

Four Seasons Hotel,
Park Lane, W1

071-499 0888   **£47**

'The most interesting hotel dining in London'

The restaurant decor at the Four Seasons is plush hotel but Bruno Loubet's food is not. It is surprising to find such distinctive cooking and cooking of such distinction in this London corner of four thousand beds. The Four Seasons Hotel is brilliantly managed by Ramon Pajares and it was his vision that tempted Loubet away from Le Petit Blanc in Oxford. Although hotel dining imposes some rules concerning perceptions of what is gastronomic luxury (and therefore value for money) Loubet's preoccupation with cuisine de terroir shines through. It is evident in his delices du Sud-Ouest (Loubet hails from Libourne), a selection of rillettes, tartare and foie gras of duck served with mushroom pickles, and in other first courses – on a seasonally changing menu – such as cabbage broth with snail ravioli and his interpretation of a tian, this one made with crisp pastry layered with scallops and courgettes and flavoured with garlic and ginger. In his choice of flavourings and combinations Loubet can be as eclectic and peripatetic as his English peers but there is an interesting twist when the basis is not a lack of tradition (as in England) but French culinary classicism. Thus a carré d'agneau rôti is paired with a little moussaka and the jus flavoured with coriander. Veal sweetbreads are accompanied by a pumpkin risotto. Oven-baked cod comes with a daube of oysters and baby squid in its ink. It is thoughtful, inventive cooking kept well within the bounds of deliciousness. Favoured desserts – not a course to pass up – are chocolate fondant with pistachio ice cream, a tarte Tatin of quince with vanilla ice cream and (irresistible) iced gingerbread with amaretto and prune sauce. Excellent petit fours are served with coffee and just as you are contented and replete more temptation is offered in the form of iced chocolate-coated sorbet. Service is in the grand style but friendly and unsnobbish. For Loubet's diffusion line in food, see entry for Bistrot Bruno.

At the time of going to press the hotel informs us that Loubet will be leaving to concentrate on Bruno Bistrot (q.v.). His probable successor, Jean-Christophe Novelli, is another chef well worth checking out.

IT'S HARD TO FIND any areas in which this list fails to live up to expectations. Blue-blooded classics are most evidently present: there's good historical depth to the clarets (organized by commune; Latour a speciality), and Burgundy, too, is widely listed (with a huge range from Jadot giving the section spine). You want Madiran, Forster Ungeheuer, an Albarino from Rias Baixas in Galicia? They're here, too. The prices, between three and four times retail for the cheaper bottles, are the drawback: you'll need £35 to give yourself any choice.

OPEN: Mon-Sun. **HOURS:** 12.30-3.00pm and 7.00-10.30pm. **CREDIT CARDS ACCEPTED:** All major cards. **NUMBER OF SEATS:** 60. **SERVICE:** Included. **SET PRICE LUNCH:** £25 (Mon-Sat); £28 (Sun). **SET PRICE DINNER:** £40. Wheelchair access. **NEAREST TUBE STATION:** Hyde Park Corner/Green Park.   MAP REF: 12/A4

Foxtrot Oscar

79 Royal Hospital Road, SW3

071-352 7179 or 071-351 1667 £20

*'Where you will find the oldest swingers in town –
and their young girlfriends'*

Foxtrot Oscar is a Chelsea hangout founded as a copy of an American neighbourhood bar and burgerie in 1979. Overgrown public school boys who meet to deplore their Lloyd's losses, hair losses and the quality of the food are the hardcore of custom. You can eat a lean, generous burger, steak and kidney or shepherd's pies, club sandwiches or blinis and feel well-satisfied. What would no doubt be referred to as 'girlie' choices – anything light, modern or featuring a lot of lettuce – are not so reliable. The wine list is sensible, cocktails are professionally mixed and the decor is a cork-tiled, orange-walled period piece. If your face is not known you will miss out on the banter (and insults), and may be put downstairs. However this seems to be a club into which anyone persisting will eventually be welcomed.

OPEN: Mon-Sun. **HOURS:** 12.30-2.30pm (12.30-3.30pm Sat-Sun) and 7.30-11.30pm (7.30-10.30pm Sun). **CLOSED:** 4 days at Christmas. **CREDIT CARDS ACCEPTED:** Access, AmEx, Delta, Switch, Visa. **NUMBER OF SEATS:** 50. **SERVICE:** Optional. Wheelchair access (but not lavatory). Private room seats 35. **NEAREST TUBE STATION:** Sloane Square. MAP REF: 14/D3

The French House Dining Room

49 Dean Street, W1

071-437 2477 £23

'One of the best things to happen to Soho'

Chefs Fergus Henderson and Margot Clayton (now Mr & Mrs) can between them muster a modish list of addresses where they have cooked. It includes 192, First Floor, Smith's and The Globe. At this small, atmospheric restaurant above the famously louche eponymous pub they have developed a style more singular and less eclectic than that work experience might imply. Theirs is robust, old-fashioned food with potent flavours, served in quantities that stop you in your tracks. The dishes they have submitted as typical are rabbit and garlic stew, home made sausages with vegetable stuffed bread and Dorset crab with mayonnaise. Straightforward as those sound, they will be cooked with verve and élan. The short menu changes each day and nearly always includes something unexpected, for example sea urchins or a particularly creative way with offal. Service led by Jon Spiteri is professional; amiable without being matey. Some of the ways in which Soho is developing make you sigh out loud, 'get real'. Here they did.

OPEN: Mon-Sat. **HOURS:** 12.30-11.30pm. **CLOSED:** Christmas Eve and Christmas Day. **CREDIT CARDS ACCEPTED:** AmEx, Diner's Club, Visa. **NUMBER OF SEATS:** 30. **SERVICE:** Optional. **NEAREST TUBE STATION:** Piccadilly Circus. MAP REF: 12/C2

Fung Shing

15 Lisle Street, WC2

071-437 1539 or 071-734 0284   **£25**

'The most reliably good Cantonese
place in Chinatown'

Although more adapted to Western ideas about restaurant interiors than some of its neighbours in Lisle Street, Fung Shing is not so salubrious that you would praise it for anything but the food; it is for those serious about what is on their plate. Always ahead of the pack in pricing, Fung Shing has kept up the lead but at least the money is translated into fine and fresh ingredients. This is a place to find out if you can see the point of abalone marinated in spicy oil with other shellfish or realize how adept are the Chinese at cooking (steaming) sea bass. Include in your order at least one hot-pot dish, such as belly pork with yam, and, to test a variation on the usual barbecue method, steamed spare ribs with sour plum sauce. If that leaves you longing for something hokey add in barbecued beef, strips of meat first crisply fried in batter then soused in a deeply savoury sauce. The Chinese green vegetables can be relied upon to be squeaky-fresh. The concept of a booking seems a fuzzy one to the management but making one might at least ensure that after a wait you are given a table on the (preferable) ground floor. The wine list is probably the most ambitious in the quartier.

OPEN: Mon-Sun. **HOURS:** 12.00-11.30pm. **CLOSED:** Christmas Eve, Christmas Day and Boxing Day. **CREDIT CARDS ACCEPTED:** Access, AmEx, Barclaycard, Diner's Club. **NUMBER OF SEATS:** 80. **SERVICE:** Optional. **SET PRICE LUNCH:** From £11. **SET PRICE DINNER:** From £15. Private room seats 28. **NEAREST TUBE STATION:** Leicester Square/Piccadilly Circus.   MAP REF: 12/C3

Galicia

323 Portobello Road, W10

081-969 3539   **£16**

'Authentically spartan and moody Spanish
restaurant with a busy bar at the front'

North Kensington is home to a large Spanish and Portuguese population and when a fair proportion of them are crowded into Galicia and in a good mood, it is great fun to spend an evening at the bar sipping sherry or a small beer and ordering racions (a more generous serving than tapas) of serrano ham, lean, hot chorizo and tortilla full of potatoes. The caveat is that even when your face is known, for a non-Iberian the welcome is unpredictable – sometimes warm, sometimes as if you had tipped the barman in Irish coin on the last visit. This has to be because the streets outside are swarming with undesirables, not so much drugs dealers (who usually don't take fino) but trustafarians, the rich kids who are ruining the tone of the district. Perhaps also to repel boarders, the calibre of the cooking served from a simple menu in the two-storey dining room is inconsistent. Sometimes the Sunday fabada (a substantial stew that can rival the best cassoulet) has been specially made, at other times it could have come from a tin; an example of pot luck. The shellfish and octopus seared on a hot skillet (a la plancha) are usually good, and to walk into the bar when the tortilla has just come out of the kitchen and is still moist and scrambled inside is serendipity.

OPEN: Tues-Sun. **HOURS:** 12.00-3.00pm and 7.00pm-1.00am. **CREDIT CARDS ACCEPTED:** All major cards. **NUMBER OF SEATS:** 55. **SERVICE:** Optional. **SET PRICE LUNCH:** £6.50. Wheelchair access (but not lavatory). **NEAREST TUBE STATION:** Ladbroke Grove.   MAP REF: 8/B2

Gate of India

68 Church Road, SW13

081-748 6793   **£16**

*'A contender for best local Indian
south of the river'*

Nothing about the look of the Gate of India – a small pink-painted room decorated with some Indian art – or, to a large extent, the menu, indicates that here is anything more than a local curry house. There are one or two signs of enterprise such as the moghlai dishes of khurzi lamb or chicken that can be ordered (for four people) twenty-four hours in advance and the Persian pulaos (disappointing), but the rest of the list you would see in any high street in any town. However, the food reflects careful preparation and, importantly, spicing particular to each dish, something easily apparent in the vegetable selection. The house special of chicken, meat or grilled king prawns cooked in garlic sauce is essential for garlic-lovers; many chopped cloves are rendered by slow cooking gloriously nutty in flavour. Also unusually good is sag gosht, lamb cooked with spinach, featuring lamb without any of that tallow flavour you can get. Kori chicken is chicken tikka cooked with tomatoes and peppers where the original marination and tandoor cooking process add a nice pungency to the sauce. The pulao rice is divertingly spiced. From the list of vegetables try cauliflower, sag bhaji and bhindi bhaji. Another way of approaching the Gate of India is via their Sunday buffet lunch at £6.95 per person. Service is sweet and kind.

OPEN: Mon-Sun. **HOURS:** 12.00-3.00pm and 6.00pm-12.00am. **CREDIT CARDS ACCEPTED:** All major cards. **NUMBER OF SEATS:** 35. **SERVICE:** Optional. **SET PRICE LUNCH:** £6.95 (Sunday buffet). No smoking area on request. **NEAREST TUBE STATION:** Hammersmith.   MAP REF: 8/B3

La Gaulette

53 Cleveland Street, W1

071-580 7608 or 071-323 4210   **£30**

'For exotic fish cooked in a Mauritian manner'

You could catch exotic fish cooked Mauritian style first at Beau Rivage in Kilburn (now closed), then at Chez Liline in Stroud Green and then at La Gaulette in Fitzrovia. Sylvain Ho Wing Cheong, who cooks at the last two and may well have been involved in the first, would seem to be operating a pincer movement with his supply of vacqua, capitain, bourgeois, red snapper and parrot fish, plus lobster, crab, king prawns and vaneau (queenies). La Gaulette, in the shadow of the British Telecom tower, is the more enticing looking of his two restaurants and the one where Sylvain spends more time cooking. The selection of dishes depends to some extent on availability – there is a separate list entitled L'arrivage du jour – but basically it is exotic fish and shellfish cooked in a wide interpretation of Mauritian style, meaning drawing on herbs, chilli, tomatoes, spices, curry powder, ginger and pickled lime for flavourings. Native or familiar fish such as salmon and Dover sole are also offered served grilled, meunière or in a champagne sauce. It is wise to balance a complicated main course with a simple first course – or vice versa – as the sauces can be overwhelming although sometimes too tame with the chilli for my liking. Fruit makes an incursion, in a first course of vaneau au kiwi et à l'orange and in a main course of vacqua meunière à la mangue. I suppose if you like that sort of thing it will be the sort of thing you like. There are various soups and platters of assorted fish – a way of snorkelling around to discover the tropical fish that you favour. Prices are high, militating against ordering a salad or a selection of vegetables at £3.50. Just some rice should do. Unlike most English fish restaurants, La Gaulette is a jolly, sometimes almost uproarious place. The staff are keen.

ALSO AT: Chez Liline, 101 Stroud Green Road, N4 (071-263 6550).

OPEN: LUNCH: Mon-Fri. DINNER: Mon-Sat. **HOURS:** 12.00-3.00pm and 6.30-11.30pm. **CLOSED:** Bank Holidays. **CREDIT CARDS ACCEPTED:** Visa, Mastercard, Access, AmEx, Diner's Club, JCB. **NUMBER OF SEATS:** 40 in Restaurant, 30 in Bistro. **SERVICE:** Optional. **SET PRICE LUNCH AND DINNER:** £16.95. Wheelchair access (but not lavatory). Private room seats 35-40. **NEAREST TUBE STATION:** Goodge Street/Warren Street/Great Portland Street.   MAP REF: 12/B1

Le Gavroche

43 Upper Brook Street, W1

071-408 0881 or 071-499 1826   **Lunch £40 Dinner £70**

'For serious lovers of food and luxury'

In 1982 Le Gavroche was the first restaurant in Britain to be awarded three stars (top rating) in the Michelin Guide. In the 1993 edition Le Gavroche lost a star, a bit of carelessness that may be explained – is explained by proprietor Albert Roux – by the fact that Albert is no longer head chef and has passed the baton onto his son Michel junior. The reasoning seems perfectly plausible and doubtless its correctness is encoded somewhere in the book of Michelin's mysterious ways. The level of comfort, formality and service in the basement premises remains very much three-star and because Michel is the son of his father and has worked with him over a period of years, there is not a great deal of discernible change in the cooking. Many of the dishes for which Le Gavroche has become famous – they forbear from calling them specialities – stay in place. Thus papillote de saumon fumé Claudine and soufflé Suissesse are there to reassure regulars and inculcate the idea in newcomers that life should be sybaritic. It is, however, possible to avoid too much creamy richness, although oddly easier in the à la carte than the fixed-price lunch menus. A relatively delicate meal could start with a sauté of scallops with spices and fried vegetables, move on to Bresse pigeon en vessie accompanied by the nice conceit of two manifestations of celery – root and branch – and finish with exquisite sorbets served from the silver containers in the refrigerated trolley. What might be classified as a development in the cooking and a nod towards fashionability is greater use made of theoretically humble ingredients such as rabbit and ox cheek.

Outside of hotels there are now few restaurants in London serving classic, ambitious French food. The regrettable closure of L'Arlequin means one less and doubtless there is a good deal of truth in what Christian Delteil, chef/proprietor of L'Arlequin, said when he remarked that people now wanted more casual food in more casual surroundings. This leaves Le Gavroche in an even more elevated position than before. To my mind one of the reasons it belongs at the top is the pleasure to be derived from seeing an operation so elegantly, almost faultlessly, run. If you give yourself over to the idea of paying for couture rather than off-the-peg, there is as much reward to be found in the skilled attentive service as there is in dishes fashioned with painstaking care and precision. It is not a place to see and be seen but for private pleasure. What could be termed a 'bargain' is lunch at a price inclusive of canapés, three courses, mineral water, coffee, petit fours, half a bottle of well-chosen wine, tax and service. It is one of the few set-price deals to cost exactly what you anticipate it will. Eating à la carte, you must be prepared to spend a lot but Le Gavroche is the antithesis of the fancy place pictured in a New Yorker cartoon where the waiter says to the customer who has asked for recommendations, 'Sorry, sir, but none of our food is very good. It's the chef's way of punishing the rich.'

THIS IS A SUPERB (and expensive) list for fine French wines. No first growth, for example, is available in less than seven vintages; there are seventeen DRC burgundies, and Pétrus in five vintages, '76 to '85 (though '82 in magnum only at, ahem, £2,625). The half-bottle range is excellent, regional France gets a good look in, as does Germany. But Italy and California run on buzz wines alone (like Tignanello, Sassicaia and Opus One); and the lack of a single bottle of Australian red or New Zealand white is puzzling, to say the least.

OPEN: Mon-Fri. **HOURS:** 12.00-2.00pm and 7.00-11.00pm. **CLOSED:** Bank Holidays, Christmas and New Year. **CREDIT CARDS ACCEPTED:** Access, AmEx, Diner's Club, Eurocard, Mastercard, Visa. **NUMBER OF SEATS:** 60. **SERVICE:** Optional. **SET PRICE LUNCH:** £36. **SET PRICE DINNER:** £42. Private room seats 20. **NEAREST TUBE STATION:** Marble Arch. MAP REF: 12/A3

Gavvers

61-63 Lower Sloane Street, SW1

071-730 5983 £22-£29

*'The original site of Le Gavroche and still Rouxled
by the same company'*

The restructuring of the Roux brothers' empire means the involvement of
Albert and Michel the Elder in Gavvers (on the site of the original Le
Gavroche) is less these days and there is talk of changes at this address. At
the time of writing, the chef is Bruno Valette, a Roux alumnus who has
worked at La Tante Claire, Le Gavroche, Les Trois Plats (now no more) and
Michael's Waterside Inn (run by another old boy) in Santa Barbara,
California. Few Californian influences, however, seep into the French menu
which, with the rise in London of so many good and reasonable places, is not
the great value it was once perceived to be. But it is food which reflects a
thorough, classically-based training which is served in suitably staid, if
rather cramped, surroundings. A set price lunch – the cheapest deal – might
start with millefeuille of salmon with beurre blanc or duck confit and
mushroom salad and move on to navarin of lamb with spring vegetables or
fillet of halibut wrapped with spinach and shrimps. This is representative of
the style. House wines are included in some of the prices. Otherwise there is
a short, completely French list.

OPEN: LUNCH: Mon-Fri. DINNER: Mon-Sat. **HOURS:** 12.00-2.30pm and 6.30-
11.00pm. **CLOSED:** Bank Holidays, Easter Saturday and Christmas week.
CREDIT CARDS ACCEPTED: Access, Diner's Club, Visa. **NUMBER OF SEATS:** 57.
SERVICE: Included. **SET PRICE LUNCH:** £12.50 (2 courses) and £14.75 (3 courses).
SET PRICE DINNER: £19.75. Wheelchair access (but not lavatory). **NEAREST TUBE**
STATION: Sloane Square. MAP REF: 14/D3

The Gay Hussar

2 Greek Street, W1

071-437 0973 £28

*'Established long ago when the name
had only Hungarian connotations'*

The new owners of The Gay Hussar who took over a few years ago when
reasons of health obliged Victor Sassie to sell up have mercifully committed
no vandalism either to the Hungarian food or the decor at this historic Soho
establishment. Indeed, apart from Sassie not being there to bully his
customers into ordering what he thinks would be good for them to have, it
would be hard to pinpoint much difference save for the inevitable hike in
prices. Lunch remains good value and retains its devotees from the worlds of
politics and the arts. Dinner fields a quite different clientele, some of it
regular visitors to London who realize they have discovered a good thing.

Because so few other places offer them, I usually choose dishes such as pressed boar's head, smoked goose with scholet, cold pike with beetroot sauce and the exemplary cucumber salad, quenelles of carp, spiced Hungarian sausage and anything accompanied by beans, lentils, tarhonya (egg barley), kasha or glossed-with-lard red cabbage. Roast duck with apple sauce, a particularly hefty duck with crisp skin, is another favourite. As you might infer this is not a destination for the dieter. It seems to be universally agreed that poppy-seed strudel is the best dessert but dobos torta, a confection of chocolate-filled pastry layers crowned with caramel, has its fans. It seems logical, and is also sensible, to choose a Hungarian wine and perhaps a glass or two of sweet Tokay to finish. The long narrow red-plush, oak-panelled room resembles an old-fashioned railway carriage and such is the disposition of tables it is not unknown for passengers to start chatting to each other.

THIS WINE LIST COMES seasoned with some great quotations; the wines, alas, are less lofty. Hungary is teeming with wine-making talent at present, though you wouldn't know it from the eight squaddies on offer here. Bordeaux (like the '89 Angludet at £29) or the Bulgarian reds (at £12.50) provide the safest choices; and Tokay provides the fittest finish, though it's a shame only one is available by the glass.

OPEN: Mon-Sat. **HOURS:** 12.30-2.30pm and 5.30-11.00pm. **CLOSED:** Bank Holidays. **CREDIT CARDS ACCEPTED:** All major cards. **NUMBER OF SEATS:** 70. **SERVICE:** Optional. **SET PRICE LUNCH:** £15.50. Wheelchair access (but not lavatory). Private room seats 12. **NEAREST TUBE STATION:** Tottenham Court Road.   MAP REF: 12/C2

Geales Fish Restaurant

2 Farmer Street, W8

071-727 7969   £10

'Purveyors of fish, chips and champagne to the gentry'

Complete with beautiful pea green frontage, this fish and chip institution fits the romantic tourist's image of how Olde England ought to be. The appearance is bogus rustic (what, no formica?). There are motherly waitresses, well-educated children scoffing themselves to a standstill, and frying fumes which are not too oppressive. Fried fish in batter here is reliably good and so are the mushy peas, a vain gesture towards fibre, but the chips do not please – they are rarely piping hot or even slightly crisp. Bisque to begin and canteen puddings to end, plus a wine list: through the teeth, around the gums, look out stomach here it comes!

OPEN: Tue-Sat. **HOURS:** 12.00-3.00pm and 6.00-11.00pm. **CLOSED:** 2 weeks at Christmas and 2 weeks end of August. **CREDIT CARDS ACCEPTED:** Access, Visa. **NUMBER OF SEATS:** 100. **SERVICE:** 10% on parties of 5 or more. **SET PRICE LUNCH:** £6.95. Wheelchair access (but not women's lavatory). **NEAREST TUBE STATION:** Notting Hill Gate.   MAP REF: 11/E

Geeta

59 Willesden Lane, NW6

071-624 1713 £10

'Discover the cheap thrill of Southern Indian vegetarian food'

Geeta was one of the pioneers of Southern Indian vegetarian food in London and although there are now many other outlets to judge it against, the standard of cooking remains high and the prices low. The surprisingly varied things you can do with rice, lentil flour and split peas (urad dal) in the shape of dosa, idlis, adai, uttappam, are all available with the fiery soupy mixture based on toovar dal (sambar) to contrast with their mealiness. The vegetables that go into avial, a stew cooked with yogurt, might provide the interesting contrast of sweet potato with bitter gourd. Dry spicy green banana is another vegetable dish to try. For meat eaters there is the usual list plus tandoori dishes but it would be a pity not to explore the basic diet of Tamil Nadu. Surroundings are simple but so is settling your bill.

OPEN: Mon-Sun. **HOURS:** 12.00-2.30pm and 6.00-10.45pm (6.00-11.45pm Fri-Sat). **CLOSED:** Christmas Day. **CREDIT CARDS ACCEPTED:** Access, AmEx, Diner's Club, Visa. **NUMBER OF SEATS:** 90. **SERVICE:** 10%. **SET PRICE LUNCH AND DINNER:** £7 or £8. No smoking area. Wheelchair access. Private room seats 35. **NEAREST TUBE STATION:** Kilburn. MAP REF: 10/B

Gilbert's

2 Exhibition Road, SW7

071-589 8947 LUNCH £23; DINNER £25

'Modest restaurant with big ideas about the wine list'

Julia Chalkley and Ann Wregg share the cooking and service – frightfully National Trust – at Gilbert's, a small restaurant with a somewhat unprepossessing interior near South Kensington station, much appreciated, I noted on one occasion, by staff from the V & A. Since its inception, about five years ago, the menu structure has changed to offer a set price menu of two courses and coffee (with home made fudge) – cheaper at lunch than at dinner – plus extra dishes, three in each course, that carry a supplement, sometimes a surprisingly hefty one. Desserts are all £4.50. The cooking is domestic in the sense that you feel you could trace the dishes back to recipes chosen from the cookery book shelf of any middle class home. Most of the preparation is competent, usually more satisfying in the first courses and desserts than the main course. You are not quite told to finish your vegetables before you can have your pudding but you would want to anyway; they are well-chosen and well-cooked. Most people would say the point of Gilbert's is the wine list and beautiful and/or complex wine is, after all best matched by uncomplicated food. Sadly realities of business have meant that at time of writing the scope of the list has had to be reduced but it remains notable.

FROM START TO FINISH, this is an utterly convincing wine list – though its compiler, Douglas Wregg, has just left Gilbert's and changes may follow. At present the selection is wide-ranging, intelligent, full of stimulation and surprise; the annotations are exemplary; the prices are never greedy. A bottle of Kistler Dutton Ranch '89 followed by Chave's '86 Hermitage, and you'll still go home with change from £55. Just £20 will put superb wines like the flavour-drenched '91 Cloudy Bay Sauvignon Blanc, Fritz Haag's shockingly expressive '88 Brauneberger Juffer-Sonnenuhr Kabinett, the softly massive '89 St Hallett Old Block Shiraz or Graillot's smokey, peppery '90 Crozes-Hermitage in front of you. Good halves; and enticing bin ends from time to time, too.

OPEN: LUNCH: Mon-Fri. DINNER: Mon-Sat. **HOURS:** 12.30-2.00pm and 7.00-10.15pm. **CLOSED:** Bank Holidays. **CREDIT CARDS ACCEPTED:** AmEx, Diner's Club, Mastercard, Visa. **NUMBER OF SEATS:** 32. **SERVICE:** Optional. **SET PRICE LUNCH:** £11.50-£16. **SET PRICE DINNER:** £13.50-£18. No smoking area on request. Wheelchair access (not lavatory). **NEAREST TUBE STATION:** South Kensington.
MAP REF: 14/B2

Gonbei Restaurant

151 King's Cross Road, WC1

071-278 0619   **£15-£20**

*'Make a pick-up in King's Cross, some sushi
or sashimi'*

With more and more cheap and cheerful Japanese places opening – giving a new definition to Raise the Red Lantern; one of those outside an establishment signifies the cheaper robatayaki style of food inside – Gonbei is not quite the treasure it once seemed. It is included in part because of its location in King's Cross, an area known for appetites other than for food. However, the sushi, sashimi, yakitori, tempura and so forth are all competently put together or cooked, the surroundings are simple and the welcome is friendly. As a Westerner you are not, as can happen, made to feel foreign – a gaijin – clumsy and crass.

OPEN: Mon-Sat. **HOURS:** 6.00-11.00pm (6.00-10.30pm Sat). **CLOSED:** Bank Holidays. **CREDIT CARDS ACCEPTED:** Access, Diner's Club, JCB, Visa. **NUMBER OF SEATS:** 27. **SERVICE:** 10%. **SET PRICE DINNER:** £13-£20. **NEAREST TUBE STATION:** King's Cross.
MAP REF: 8/C2

Gopal's of Soho

12 Bateman Street, W1

071-434 1621/0840   **£20**

'An out of the ordinary Indian restaurant with curry house prices'

It seems to be the way that after a flurry of initiative has led to the re-appraisal of particular cuisines, the British diner slinks back to familiar, anglicized versions and so restaurants that were thought of as vanguards become outposts. Those Indian restaurants of the 1980s which tried to convey the variety and subtlety of food on the subcontinent do not seem to have set the high street on fire. Some of the names of dishes pioneered in there have been disseminated, but little of the verve with which they were cooked. Gopal Pittal is one of the upholders of authenticity, a veteran of Lal Quila and The Red Fort who opened his own restaurant in a Soho side street three years ago. The oblong room is fairly plain and rather full of chairs, and the cocktails you may be cajoled into ordering from a special list can be crammed with fruit, but the cooking is clear-headed. Spices and herbs may be discrete or in careful combination. Pungent Goan lamb cooked with vinegar, chicken steamed to tenderness under a huff crust, a copy of Karnataka's famous fish curry, good breads and fragrant Southern coconut rice: the fact that the menu does not change much is not really a criticism when so much is enjoyable. The thalis are generous samplers but do not include Gopal's most unusual specialities.

OPEN: Mon-Sun. **HOURS:** 12.00-3.00pm and 6.00-11.30pm. **CLOSED:** Christmas and Boxing Day. **CREDIT CARDS ACCEPTED:** AmEx, Diner's Club, Access, Visa. **NUMBER OF SEATS:** 50. **SERVICE:** Optional. No smoking area. **NEAREST TUBE STATION:** Leicester Square/Tottenham Court Road/Piccadilly Circus.   MAP REF: 12/C2

Granita

127 Upper Street, N1

071-226 3222   **£22**

'How to run a successful modern local restaurant'

This stark, fundamentally Italian restaurant has been a hit since it opened in the autumn of 1992. The way it has been conceived and put together would make an instructive case history for a course aimed at prospective restaurateurs. The decor is modern to the point of almost vanishing but conveys knowingness and stylishness and, no bad thing, cleanliness. The menu is short, but has enough choice – soup and three other first courses, a pasta dish, four main courses, four desserts and cheese – and changes weekly. The marketing is obviously done in a quotidian manner as popular dishes can run out of an evening. Details such as a tub of unsalted French butter on each table, sultana bread, chocolate coffee beans served with coffee (or one of the selection of teas), and interesting non-alcoholic drinks in addition to the wine list, convey – correctly – that thoughtfulness and caring has been applied. The same virtues are applied in the kitchen to dishes such as – to give you an idea of the style – small pizza with aubergine and sun-dried tomato purée, roasted red pepper with rocket, oregano and a garlic vinaigrette, chargrilled organic salmon, roast chump of lamb with flageolets, floating islands with berry compote. An accolade came from Ruthie Rogers – co-owner of The River Cafe (q.v.) – who mentioned Granita to me saying that she and Richard (the architect Richard Rogers) had wandered in by chance after going to the Almeida Theatre and how great it was. She rather touchingly didn't seem to realize what part both of them have played in restaurants like Granita now being if not commonplace, not so very unusual.

OPEN: LUNCH: Wed-Sun. DINNER: Tues-Sun. **HOURS:** 12.30-2.30pm and 6.30pm-12.00am. **CLOSED:** 10 days at Christmas, 1 week at Easter and last 2 weeks of August. **CREDIT CARDS ACCEPTED:** Access, Visa. **NUMBER OF SEATS:** 62. **SERVICE:** Optional. **SET PRICE LUNCH:** £11.50-£13.50. Wheelchair access (but not lavatory). **NEAREST TUBE STATION:** Highbury & Islington/Angel. MAP REF: 8/C2

Great Nepalese

48 Eversholt Street, NW1

071-388 6737/5935 £14

'The name of the place says it all'

Fortunately the longevity of the Great Nepalese opposite Euston station looks set fair to continue with several sons of the owner – who looks far too young to have produced them – already working in the business. It is, to my mind, quite best source of Nepalese food in central London. Given the range offered it seems hardly worth straying into lists of dishes familiar from other Indian restaurants. First courses to order are masco-bara, (thick, crisp black lentil bread served with curry sauce), mamocha, (dumplings with a filling resembling spicy sausage), and kalezo ra chyau, (chicken livers sauteed with mushrooms and spices). Since few Indian restaurants offer duck, this is an opportunity to try it cooked in the tandoor or curried when it is called hash ko bhutawa.

The Nepalese set at £9.95 provides a blueprint for a Nepalese meal which, along with meat dishes, should include a cold potato assembly incorporating other vegetables, achar (pickle) and the spinach dish called toriko sag. Whatever you decide to order ask for the coriander pickle (dhaniya achar) as a condiment. From the non-Nepalese list of vegetarian dishes two that pleased were mutter panir made with something resembling marrowfat peas and a dry aubergine (brinjal) curry. Lassi or lager is a better bevvie for this sort of food than wine but if you get talking with the beaming Mr Manandhar he may pour you some galvanizing Nepalese rum. The vivid decor is somewhat scruffy but Kumari, the living goddess, portrayed in a large picture, seems not to mind one bit.

OPEN: Mon-Sun. **HOURS:** 12.00-2.45pm (12.00-2.30pm Sat-Sun) and 6.00-11.45pm (6.00-11.30pm Sat-Sun). **CLOSED:** Christmas Day and Boxing Day. **CREDIT CARDS ACCEPTED:** AmEx, Visa, Mastercard, Diner's Club. **NUMBER OF SEATS:** 48. **SERVICE:** 10%. **SET PRICE LUNCH:** £5.50. **SET PRICE DINNER:** £9.95. Wheelchair access (but not lavatory). Private room seats 30. **NEAREST TUBE STATION:** Euston. MAP REF: 8/C2

Greek Valley Restaurant

130 Boundary Road, NW8

071-624 3217   **£16**

'To put you in a good humous'

The fact that Jonathan Meades, restaurant critic of *The Times*, used to live almost next door to Greek Valley helped to shoot the restaurant to prominence – but deservedly. It was not just a case of propinquity being nearly all. However, there is not a, how shall we say?, daunting amount of competition in the category Greek/Cypriot restaurant. This is a family run establishment with Effie efficiently working the usually crowded room and her husband in the kitchen. Most of the items on the menu will be familiar from any taverna in the town but the carefulness of preparation lifts them into a different sphere and there are a few unusual items, viz. grilled red pepper served cold with vinaigrette, sausages made in-house humming with garlic, prawns baked in tomato sauce with feta cheese and the idea of offering a vegetarian version of moussaka, souvlaki and dolmades. Briami is a mixture of vegetables baked with tomatoes, onions, herbs and garlic. This looks like a bid for votes from the vegetarian lobby but in fact reflects Greek home cooking where meat makes a relatively rare appearance. With Greek coffee have another taste of Greek domestic life, a spoonful of glyko (meaning sweet), a home made preserve of fruit. The wine list includes some of the better Greek production such as Chateau Carass and Cava. Incidentally, Meades orders the meze.

OPEN: LUNCH: Mon-Fri. DINNER: Mon-Sat. **HOURS:** 12.00-2.30pm and 6.00pm-12.00am. **CREDIT CARDS ACCEPTED:** Access, Visa. **NUMBER OF SEATS:** 62. **SERVICE:** Optional. **SET PRICE LUNCH:** £7.95. **SET PRICE DINNER:** £7.95 (Mon-Thur). Wheelchair access (but not lavatory). Private room seats 30. **NEAREST TUBE STATION:** St. John's Wood/Maida Vale/Swiss Cottage.   MAP REF: 8/B2

Green Cottage Chinese Restaurant

9 New College Parade, NW3

071-722 5305/7892   **£15**

'Chinatown in Swiss Cottage'

For a while, back in the mid-eighties, Green Cottage had a nearby sister restaurant inventively called Green Cottage II which featured the vegetarian Chinese Buddhist cuisine known as 'zhai' (q.v. Vegetarian Cottage and Feng Shang). The sibling closed but the original Green Cottage now sports a vegetarian list that includes zhai 'duckling' and Buddha's cushion; stewed black moss and mushrooms on Chinese leaves. That it does seems almost ironic since Green Cottage is so good at delivering the Cantonese one-dish meals based on barbecue meat. As you would find in Chinatown, meats are hung up in the window and a chef is deployed to chop them in full view of passers-by. I go to Green Cottage for crispy belly pork, Cantonese duck and what they call soyed mixed meats, an assembly of liver, gizzard, squid and duck wings served on rice and accompanied by Chinese greens. Chow mein is not a term found on many Chinese restaurant menus these days but these noodle assemblies featuring seafood, mixed meats or shredded pork also deliver comfort and fortification. Green Cottage is not a place for a celebratory outing but for a reasonably priced meal honestly made. The premises are slightly gloomy. Service is all right but the waiters are never going to be your best friends.

OPEN: Mon-Sun. **HOURS:** 12.00-11.30pm. **CLOSED:** Christmas Eve, Christmas Day and Boxing Day. **CREDIT CARDS ACCEPTED:** Access, AmEx, Visa. **NUMBER OF SEATS:** 70. **SERVICE:** Included. **SET PRICE DINNER:** £11.50-£15. Wheelchair access (but not lavatory). Private room seats 14. **NEAREST TUBE STATION:** Swiss Cottage/Finchley Road. MAP REF: 10/A

The Greenhouse

27a Hay's Mews, W1

071-499 3331 £35

'Punk chef produces spotted dick'

Gary Rhodes, the Nigel Kennedy of the kitchen, has no doubts about the direction of his vocation. It is to espouse proper English food. In doing so Rhodes has become the scholar of once near-forgotten dishes like braised oxtail, faggots, stews with dumplings, mackerel fishcakes, steamed lemon sponge, jam tart, apple fritters and so forth. Dicing so daringly with folk memories of institutional food can only come off if the standard of cooking remains consistently high which, sad to say given the noble cause, it does not. Perhaps these dishes died out originally because they are not particularly rewarding to prepare regularly. To say so now seems almost unpatriotic which may account for the – to my mind – recent overstated acclaim for The Greenhouse. In addition the at-first-glance reasonable prices are scuppered by cover charge, vegetables priced separately, expensive coffee and a not particularly cheap or interesting wine list. However, apart from the memories of merrie Englande there are other, more pleasing dishes; smoked eel kedgeree, sauteed foie gras with grape chutney, panfried cod with cabbage and wild mushrooms, steak Béarnaise, roasted chicken, crème brulée and cappucino mousse. Of interest is the Sunday lunch menu built round various roasts, and Sunday supper which pioneers the sensible idea of serving a cooked breakfast as well as items such as home made beans on toast, eggs Benedict, macaroni cheese with leeks, spotted dick and Knickerbocker Glory. Given the potential of the restaurant site in a Mayfair mews, the design both of the interior and the staff uniforms is inexplicably awful. I suspect it is thought to fulfil tourist expectations of cute lil' ol' England.

OPEN: LUNCH: Mon-Fri, Sun. DINNER: Mon-Sun. **HOURS:** 12.00-2.30pm (12.00-3.00pm Sun) and 7.00-11.00pm (7.30-11.00pm Sat, 6.00-10.00pm Sun). **CLOSED:** Christmas Eve to 2nd January. **CREDIT CARDS ACCEPTED:** All major cards. **NUMBERS OF SEATS:** 100. **SERVICE:** Optional, £1 cover charge. **NEAREST TUBE STATION:** Green Park. MAP REF: 12/A3

Green's Restaurant & Oyster Bar

Marsham Court, SW1

071-834 9552   **£32**

'Upper-class English food'

I try to be upfront and honest when I review restaurants. I have praised Green's in the past and taken great care to stress my connection with the place; that my sister Beth Coventry (now at Beth's q.v.) was chef. Some gossip came back to me a while ago: somebody said to someone who said to me, 'You know why Fay Maschler is so complimentary to Green's, don't you? Well, her husband is Simon Parker Bowles' (the proprietor). I don't suppose this little anecdote concerning hearsay will make his brother Andrew feel one whit better.

Green's is one of the surprisingly few places to try to distil what is good about Englishness when applied to food. The menu is divided into a list of standards and dishes of the day. The former offers what you might suppose – oysters in season, smoked fishes, caviar, lobster cocktail, grilled sole, lamb cutlets and steak – but also has some signature dishes in Queensberry's cod's roe pâté, smoked salmon and scrambled egg with blinis, spicy Raj fishcakes and fresh salmon fishcakes, kippers with poached eggs and bangers and mash. Daily specialities taken from one day's list included cream of cauliflower and cheese soup with chives, smoked duck breast with horseradish cream, shepherd's pie, baked fillet of turbot with scallops and a shrimp sauce. Nursery puddings are always on offer. They appeal to the sector of the clientele who think back longingly to nanny – but also to others. Although the clubby wood-panelled Green's attracts the upper classes and the racing fraternity – a sort of toff 'n' turf – you also find ladies lunching and wide boys at the bar; a little slice of England really.

OPEN: Mon-Fri. **HOURS:** RESTAURANT: 12.30-2.45pm and 6.00-11.00pm. **BAR:** 12.00am-3.00pm and 6.00-11.00pm. **CLOSED:** Easter, Christmas Day, Boxing Day and New Year's Day. **CREDIT CARDS ACCEPTED:** AmEx, Access, Barclaycard, Diner's Club. **NUMBER OF SEATS:** 60 in Restaurant, 20 in Bar. **SERVICE:** Optional. Private room seats 34. **NEAREST TUBE STATION:** Pimlico/Westminster.

MAP REF: 12/B4

Grill St Quentin

3 Yeomans Row, SW3

071-581 8377   **£28**

'Not really like La Coupole but trying'

These surprisingly extensive basement premises reached via a handsome staircase have been decorated seemingly with an eye to the revamped La Coupole in Paris. The turquoise and gilt-smudged supporting pillars are reminiscent anyway. Large restaurants (the Grill seats 140) have a charm of their own. Here it is reinforced by the agreeable plainness of decor and the vistas of white clothed tables radiating out from a handsome central waiters' station. Sadly corporate ownership – in this case The Savoy Group – seems to dilute the possible impact and prevents the place from taking off and being if not as glam as Quaglino's, at least not far off. The French menu, which has rather too great a similarity to that of the Restaurant St Quentin, is adequately well-prepared but that is all. To get the best out of Grill St Quentin, order oysters or a plateau de fruits de mer or a lobster of crab mayonnaise – all stylishly served – and follow with steak and the good but not spectacular chips, or the dish of the day from the trolley. The section plats cuisiné is innocent of the sort of assemblies I think should be offered: cassoulet, daube de boeuf, pot au feu, garbure, and somehow one feels this kitchen would not be up to making them. What is very nice is the matter of factness of surroundings large enough usually to accommodate spur-of-the-moment medium-priced eating out.

OPEN: Mon-Sun. **HOURS:** 12.00-3.00pm (12.00-3.30pm Sun) and 6.30-11.30pm (6.30-10.30pm Sun). **CREDIT CARDS ACCEPTED:** All major cards. **NUMBER OF SEATS:** 140. **SERVICE:** 12.5%. **SET PRICE LUNCH:** £13.50. **NEAREST TUBE STATION:** South Kensington.   MAP REF: 14/C2

The Room at the Halcyon Hotel

129 Holland Park, W11

071-221 5411   **£30**

'Modern food for jaded palates'

This smart Holland Park hotel has seen a high turnover in chefs for its basement restaurant with terrace but the style of cooking – perhaps best summed up as modern English – has remained pretty constant. It is a pity that much improved decor with its junking of the indoor trellis-work has coincided with cooking that is somewhat spineless. It must be difficult for hotels which attract guests of the 'I'll just have mineral water and eat a few vegetables' type to persevere with enthusiasm in the kitchen but cooking must be predicated on the chance of gourmands showing up. The latter would be disappointed by the cautious amount of chargrilled monkfish and the vapidity of its red pepper sauce. They would query the wisdom of first steaming then frying pieces of duck, a process that rendered what meat there was overdone and tasteless but still fatty. They would aver that lemon tart should not be made by pouring a lemon curd mixture into a pastry shell. However better reports have been given of more straightforward items such as steak and chips and grilled calf's liver with mashed potatoes and roasted garlic. Service is young and anxious to please but someone failed to please me with the choice of intrusive music. The terrace looking up on the grand mansions of Holland Park is a place to bear in mind for sunny days and warm evenings.

OPEN: BREAKFAST: Mon-Sun. LUNCH: Sun-Fri. DINNER: Mon-Sun. **HOURS:** 7.00-11.00am, 12.00-2.30pm (12.00-4.00pm Sun) and 7.00-10.30pm (7.00-11.00pm Sat, 7.00-10.00pm Sun). **CLOSED:** Bank Holidays. **CREDIT CARDS ACCEPTED:** All major cards. **NUMBER OF SEATS:** 40. **SERVICE:** 15%. **SET PRICE LUNCH:** £12.95. Wheelchair access with assistance. 8 tables outside. Private room seats 10. **NEAREST TUBE STATION:** Holland Park.   MAP REF: 11/F

The Halkin

5-6 Halkin Street, SW1

071-333 1234   LUNCH £33; DINNER £40

'Where the chic meet to eat discreetly'

The sleek uncluttered design of this relatively new Belgravia hotel is a sight for eyes made tired by gazing on metres of mixed and matched chintz and plump little cushions, the usual response from hotel designers. Its restaurant keeps up the momentum by offering sleek uncluttered food designed by Gualtiero Marchesi, a three-star Michelin chef from Milan who has marketed himself as a product or, as he puts it, Le Idee di Gualtiero Marchesi. What this boils down to – although his cooking does not depend on intense reductions – is food of subtle simplicity which sometimes delights or sometimes disappoints in such a manner that the emperor seems to be wearing next to nothing. This can be because a simple roast has been mistimed (undercooked) whereupon the bold lack of much garnish just reinforces the fault, or insufficient seasoning leaves a dish too bland to be enjoyable. However, understatement can also pay off. A kidney roasted in its own suet to just the right degree served thinly sliced alongside a potato cake is masterly. The risottos seem almost foolproof although their presentation as a one grain-deep cover of rice on a big plate means they must be eaten fast if warm food is to your liking. A dish that is a success and as such seems a constant on the menus is open ravioli with scallops. Although the à la carte justifies the high prices with the use of foie gras, black truffles and bottarga, I prefer the economy, in all senses of the word, of the set price menu which has plenty of choice in each course. Were I to choose three courses it would be a salad, perhaps one of sole with ginger, followed by a pasta, say, sweetbread and artichoke ravioli, followed by eel with balsamic vinegar or veal cutlet in breadcrumbs with a small salad; a Milanese speciality. The Italian wine list is excellent but shows no mercy towards your pocket. Service in the calm room is discreet and the diners often provide colour and display.

OPEN: BREAKFAST: Mon-Sat. LUNCH: Mon-Fri. DINNER: Mon-Sat. **HOURS:** 7.00-11.00am, 12.30-2.30pm and 7.30-10.30pm. **CREDIT CARDS ACCEPTED:** All major cards. **NUMBER OF SEATS:** 50. **SERVICE:** Optional. **SET PRICE LUNCH:** £18-£24.50. **SET PRICE DINNER:** £24.50-£28.50. Wheelchair access. Private room seats 26. **NEAREST TUBE STATION:** Hyde Park Corner.   MAP REF: 14/D1

Harbour City Chinese Restaurant

46 Gerrard Street, W1

071-439 7859   **£18**

'Even the set meals are described in Chinese characters as well as English'

If you are a true fan of Cantonese food, as opposed to someone who occasionally fancies going out for a Chinese, go to Harbour City in Chinatown and concentrate either on the dim sum (of necessity during the day) with special reference to the list entitled Exotic or study the parts of the à la carte list headed Chef's Special Selection and Special Authentic Cantonese Hot-Pot. From this last true aficionados of the role of gelatinous textures in Chinese food could pick braised duck web with fish lips in oyster sauce. Anyone would appreciate what is called braised beef goulash (with fat) and braised lamb goulash (with fat) with bean paste. Another restaurant writer has compared these casseroles with those at Le Gavroche and should you agree with him, it almost goes without saying, you will be quids in. They do have wonderful melting meat and sonorous sauces. Star anise, which may not be in the larder at Le Gavroche, is one key to their success. Eel with garlic and crab with ginger and spring onion mixed with vermicelli are other fine hot-pots. What might strike you as daring dishes can be matched with more familiar items from the main list.

Some unusual dim sum to try are baked miniature roast pork pie which has superlative pastry, shark's fin dumpling, chicken feet in Shy Maiden sauce served cold with raw carrot, steamed cockles in curry sauce, crabmeat and coriander dumpling and deep-fried or steamed milk and egg bun. Buoyed up with that you might then consider pig skin and turnip in soup but certainly a noodle assembly. Service in Harbour City is uncommonly polite and the seating is spacious.

OPEN: Mon-Sun. **HOURS:** 12.00-11.30pm (12.00pm-12.00am Fri-Sat; 11.00am-11.00pm Sun). **CLOSED:** Christmas Eve and Christmas Day. **CREDIT CARDS ACCEPTED:** AmEx, Diner's Club, JCB, Mastercard, Visa. **NUMBER OF SEATS:** 160. **SERVICE:** 10%. **SET PRICE DINNER:** From £10.50. Wheelchair access (but not lavatory). Private rooms seat 40 and 50. **NEAREST TUBE STATION:** Leicester Square/Piccadilly Circus.

MAP REF: 12/C3

Hard Rock Cafe

150 Old Park Lane, W1

071-629 0382   **£17**

'The queue itself is a tourist attraction'

Seen by knowing Londoners to be a very bridge and tunnel or, worse still, a tourist attraction, the fact is the Hard Rock does a damn fine burger. Queues form from midday to join the 240 or so inside – downstairs is Siberia – who are assaulted with almost unbearably loud old and new wave rock while choosing from the predictable American menu of burgers, ribs, sandwiches, steaks, salads and sundaes all of which are consistently competently prepared. Service is from long-serving experienced waitresses – no out of work actresses or bimbos here – and is friendly and skilled. The rock memorabilia continues to fascinate even after all these (over twenty) years. I possess a Gold Hard Rock card which means I can zoom to the head of the queue. Nyah nyah na nyah na.

OPEN: Mon-Sun. **HOURS:** 11.30-12.30am (11.30am-1.00am Fri-Sat.) **CREDIT CARDS ACCEPTED:** Visa, AmEx, Mastercard. **NUMBER OF SEATS:** 240. **SERVICE:** 12.5%. No smoking area. Wheelchair access (but not lavatory). 12 tables outside. Private room seats 90. **NEAREST TUBE STATION:** Hyde Park Corner/Green Park.

MAP REF: 12/A4

Harvey's Cafe

358 Fulham Road, SW10

071-352 0625 £16

'Ideal for a casual, non-ethnic night out'

Harvey Sambrook is not an upstart in catering. I reviewed a restaurant he owned in Battersea Park Road called Harvey's twenty years ago. Before that he was running a place in Sardinia. His latest enterprise joins the category of Good Use Made of Pubs. In fact so successful is his reasonably priced first floor restaurant at The Black Bull on Fulham Road that he now runs the whole pub and masterminds the better-than-average bar snacks. The food in the restaurant is modish, appetizing and the right price. Typical dishes are aubergine bruschetta, roasted peppers with feta cheese, fish soup, salmon fishcakes with anchovy sauce, spiced chicken with raita and cassoulet. You get the drift. Wine prices are fair which makes for a night out that does not require a lot of financial forethought. The dining rooms are large and seemingly furnished on a shoe-string but with a gallery of paintings displayed. Service under pressure can be slow and/or muddled.

OPEN: **LUNCH:** Tues-Sun. **DINNER:** Tues-Sat. **HOURS:** 12.30-3.00pm (12.30-5.00pm Sun) and 7.00pm-12.00am. **CREDIT CARDS ACCEPTED:** None. **NUMBER OF SEATS:** 65. **SERVICE:** 12%. **SET PRICE LUNCH:** £5 (Tues-Fri). Private room seats 35. **NEAREST TUBE STATION:** Fulham Broadway. MAP REF: 14/A4

Hilaire

68 Old Brompton Road, SW7

071-584 8993 £35

'Not far from, and for when you can't afford, Bibendum'

Chef Bryan Webb had a hard act to follow when he took over Hilaire after Simon Hopkinson had gone to Bibendum. It was made the more so by the fact that their cooking style is similar – although Hopkinson has developed more finesse – and owes much to the influence of Franco Taruschio of The Walnut Tree Inn in Abergavenny. Webb actually comes from a village near Llandewi Skirrid where The Walnut Tree is located. Currently he seems to have lost some of his enthusiasm for Thai spicing and the ever-changing menu concentrates on the sort of dishes that have come to be classified as modern English food. This definition happily allows Mediterranean incursions as Webb shows with, for instance, tagliatelle with chorizo, peppers and parsley or English asparagus with balsamic vinegar, olive oil and Parmesan or fillet of lamb with tapenade, couscous and broad beans or Bresse pigeon with pancetta, peas and baby onions. He is loyal to his homeland in the use of laverbread – a kind of seaweed – both deep-fried as an amuse-gueule or as a component in a butter sauce for sea bass served with samphire. A popular dish of his which does not beguile me is oysters au gratin with laverbread and Stilton. The regime at Hilaire aims valiantly to please with various set price menus including a very reasonable lunch and a two-course supper and an unusually long list of half bottles of wine plus a range of wines by the glass. A similar over-eager approach is sometimes evident in the cooking which can clutter a plate with too many ingredients and flavours or occasionally miss the point with what seems like slapdash enthusiasm. I have had very fine cooking at Hilaire and also perfectly ordinary. It could be that a shorter menu would produce more consistent results.

The look of the place dices with dullness and it seems high time a new coat of a different colour paint was brushed over the sludge green tongue and groove panelled room. Upstairs is preferable to down. Lunchtime attracts a well-dressed clientele, some of whom drift over from Christie's opposite. The wine list is commendable.

HILAIRE'S WINE LIST IS well-organized, with useful annotation; has an excellent selection of halves (thirty-seven in all); and gives plenty of provoking choice for less than £20 (as, for example, between the softness of the 1985 Viña Ardanza Rioja at £19.45 or the peppery vigour of Cape Mentelle's 1989 Shiraz at £19.85).

OPEN: LUNCH: Mon-Fri. DINNER: Mon-Sat. HOURS: 12.15-2.30pm and 7.00-11.30pm. CLOSED: Bank Holidays. CREDIT CARDS ACCEPTED: Access, AmEx, Diner's Club, Visa. NUMBER OF SEATS: 40. SERVICE: Optional. SET PRICE LUNCH: £10.95 (2 courses). SET PRICE DINNER: £25 (4 courses). Wheelchair access (but not lavatory). Downstairs can be privately booked and seats 24. NEAREST TUBE STATION: South Kensington. MAP REF: 14/A3

Ho Ho

29 Maddox Street, W1

071-493 1228 **£20**

'A smart Chinese restaurant where you might least expect it'

The most original thing about Ho Ho – and perhaps an explanation of its name – is its Mayfair address. Ho ho, you cry, fancy being able to have won-ton soup and moo shu pork so close to Bond Street. Behind the black venetian blind at the Maddox Street premises lies a trim, modern dining room with well-spaced pink-clothed tables. Service is from friendly Chinese girls. There is a wide range of set price menus including a good value (for the area) set price lunch. As well as a trawl through the familiar territories of Peking, Szechuan and Canton there is the more surprising inclusion of Singapore/Malaysian specialities, e.g. a first course of crispy fried lamb in a chilli sauce and main courses of chicken nuggets in spicy soy sauce and prawns served with a sambal, a combination of chillis and spices. Should you for any reason be seeking anonymity, Ho Ho in the evening would be a good choice.

OPEN: Mon-Sat. HOURS: 12.00-3.00pm and 6.00-11.00pm. CLOSED: Bank Holidays. CREDIT CARDS ACCEPTED: All major cards. NUMBER OF SEATS: 80. SERVICE: 12.5%. SET PRICE LUNCH: £12. Wheelchair access (but not lavatory). Private room seats 30. NEAREST TUBE STATION: Oxford Circus. MAP REF: 12/B3

Imperial City

Royal Exchange, Cornhill, EC3

071-626 3437   **£28**

'An Oriental asset to the Square Mile'

Imperial City, a new Chinese restaurant with English ownership, is doing
brisk business. In the City word of mouth is replaced by messages flicking
between the computer screens of money men. The method has been
successful; the brick barrel-vaulted basement bar and red, blue and gilt
detailed dining rooms tucked discreetly below the Royal Exchange are
thronged with a mixture of Orientals and Westerners and, blow me, even
some women. The consultant to the venture is cookery book writer and TV
chef Ken Hom. This much-travelled Chinese/American is well qualified to
understand what is wanted from a Chinese restaurant by a fairly
sophisticated clientele. Hom made the important and unusual decision of
hiring neophyte cooks and instructing them in his own ways rather than
employing kitchen-weary cynics well-schooled in slip-shod practices and
clichéd dishes. The wisdom of this is immediately apparent in the first
choice on the relatively short à la carte menu. Imperial cold platter served for
two is an assortment of items to which considerations of balance, colour,
texture and originality have been applied. It is a far cry from the usual
round-up supplied for mindless ordering. The plate displays chilli prawns,
crunchy sesame jelly fish, duck in mustard sauce (excellent), half of a
marbled tea egg, Szechuan cold peppers (a version of marinated but
unskinned peppers) and caramel walnuts (syrup overboiled). It makes an
ideal, diverting start to a meal, better, I suspect, than the Imperial hot platter
for two in which one constituent is spring rolls. The kitchen prepares an
authentic Peking duck as well as the deep-fried crispy aromatic kind.
Szechuan braised fish features pieces of quick-fried sole in an intense
translucent sauce. Crackling Northern style chicken with garlic is made with
fresh not frozen chicken, dry roasted to give the skin the correct salty
brittleness. Braised red pork casserole features belly pork more carefully
trimmed of fat than you would find elsewhere, steeped in and imbued with a
deeply savoury soy-based sauce. As far as I am concerned, that and the
savoury home style steamed egg custard are reasons enough to go to the City
and even to eat an early evening meal (last orders are at 8.30pm). The
vigorously-seasoned custard, balancing in a rim of fine chicken stock, is the
sort of 'home cooking' difficult to find in the user-jaded lists of the average
Chinese restaurant. It marries well with a green vegetable such as ginger
broccoli or seasonal greens (bok choy). Imperial City hearty Northern style
bean sauce noodles with a minced meat and cucumber julienne topping is a
self-contained entity rather than an accompaniment; a perfect one-dish
snack. Desserts are unusually enticing, e.g. steamed Northern style pears,
firecracker sweet wontons and orange cream pudding. Espresso coffee is
available. It has a likeable mocha flavour. Service is slender, demure and tries
hard to please.

OPEN: Mon-Fri. **HOURS:** 11.30am-8.30pm. **CLOSED:** Bank Holidays and 23rd-25th
December. **CREDIT CARDS ACCEPTED:** All major cards. **NUMBER OF SEATS:** 180. **SERVICE:**
12.5%. **SET PRICE LUNCH:** £13.50 or £18.50. Wheelchair access. Private room
seats 12. **NEAREST TUBE STATION:** Bank.   MAP REF: 8/C2

Inaho

4 Hereford Road, W2

071-221 8495 **£20**

'Gives a new meaning to lunch box'

The friend who came with me accused me of luring him into a sauna cabinet, a reference not to temperature but to the tiny wood panelled dining room. Despite the size, it is calm and orderly inside. The menu is also scaled down compared to more spacious Japanese places, with sashimi (not sushi), tempura, grilled meat and very good noodle dishes. At lunch time there are six simple and inexpensive set menus.

OPEN: LUNCH: Mon-Fri. DINNER: Mon-Sat. **HOURS:** 12.30-2.30pm and 7.00-11.00pm. **CLOSED:** 4 days at Easter and 10 days at Christmas. **CREDIT CARDS ACCEPTED:** Visa, Access, Mastercard. **NUMBER OF SEATS:** 20. **SERVICE:** 10%. **SET PRICE LUNCH:** £7-£9. **SET PRICE DINNER:** £18- £20. **NEAREST TUBE STATION:** Notting Hill Gate.

MAP REF: 11/E

L'Incontro

87 Pimlico Road, SW1

071-730 6327 **£50**

'Incontestably expensive and smart Italian'

The proprietor of L'Incontro is Gino Santin, who also owns the restaurant Santini in Ebury Street, a restaurant in Milan and is author of *La Cucina Veneziana* (Ebury Press £14.95). L'Incontro, opened in the autumn of 1987, is incontestably chic and incontestably expensive. It is not worth visiting unless you are prepared to spend money carelessly and you enjoy the sight of the gilded middle-aged at play. That said, some parts of the menu, notably the home made pastas, risottos, frittata made with imported saffron-yellow yolked eggs, and Venetian specialities such as creamed salt cod (baccala mantecato) and scallops baked in their shells (cappe sante) are usually extremely well-prepared. To enjoy scottatine biriicchine, beef escalopes with a hint of truffle, you must be able to take a hint. There is scant truffle presence. Despite a bold statement of intent in the foreword of his recipe book to the effect that good food is beautiful in itself, S. Santin's kitchen seem unable to resist flourishes of unnecessary garnish. Wines are expensive. Furthermore be sure to check the price of any bottle you are offered as a replacement for one out of stock. It has been known for a waiter to produce a much more expensive wine than the one originally requested. When you book (as you must) stipulate a table on the ground floor.

OPEN: LUNCH: Mon-Fri. DINNER: Mon-Sun. **HOURS:** 12.30-2.30pm and 7.00-11.30pm (7.00-10.30pm Sun). **CLOSED:** Bank Holidays and Christmas Day. **CREDIT CARDS ACCEPTED:** AmEx, Diner's Club, Access, Visa. **NUMBER OF SEATS:** 55. **SERVICE:** 12%. **SET PRICE LUNCH:** £13.50. Wheelchair access (but not lavatory). Private room seats 25-30. **NEAREST TUBE STATION:** Sloane Square. MAP REF: 14/D3

Indian Connoisseurs

8 Norfolk Place, W2

071-402 3299 £20

'Game, lobster and luxury fish Indian style'

My search for the perfect Indian restaurant, much more problematic than the search for the perfect bra, came a little closer to success with the discovery of Indian Connoisseurs in Paddington. The restaurant's name had somehow not held out much promise but certain sections of the menu entitled seafood dishes, game dishes and regional cuisine showed that something was going on in the kitchen more interesting than the usual knee-jerk response to the provision of Indian food. Ingredients such as sea bass, parrot fish, pheasant, venison, grouse (in season), goat and duck reveal a wider vision. Using more commonplace ingredients in daring pairings as in awshi king prawns – large prawns cooked with pumpkin – also pays off. The pieces of pumpkin imbued with spices are an ideal foil in flavour and colour for the shellfish. Tandoori lobster can be ordered as a first course but is more interesting in the main course cooked jalfarezi, with chillis and onions. Among the first courses aloo chops, patties of remarkably light potato mash coated in ground lentils and deep-fried, stand out. They partner well the starter-size tandoori lamb chops. Console yourself during any long waits for food with the fact that there is obviously more last-minute preparation involved in this enterprising approach. The premises are simply decorated. The service can be attentive to the point of intrusive.

OPEN: Mon-Sun. **HOURS:** 12.00-3.00pm and 6.00pm-12.00am. **CREDIT CARDS ACCEPTED:** All major cards. **NUMBER OF SEATS:** 48. **SERVICE:** Optional. **SET PRICE LUNCH:** £9. **SET PRICE DINNER:** £12. No smoking area. Private room seats 20. **NEAREST TUBE STATION:** Paddington. MAP REF: 11/D

Istanbul Iskembecisi

9 Stoke Newington Road, N16

071-254 7291 £15

'The place to start getting to know the Turkish restaurants of North-East London'

There are many Turkish restaurants in the Stoke Newington/Islington area and each has its following. Istanbul Iskembecisi, now located in larger, plusher premises than its original site on the opposite side of the road, has the virtue, as far as I am concerned, of serving among its several offal specialities (iskembecisi means tripe restaurant) kokarec. Having discovered this dish in Athens – where it is known as kokoretsi – and having long ago enjoyed it in a Greek restaurant in Percy Street now closed, I was delighted to find it here. The most alluring way to describe it is as similar to the principle of andouillette but with the pieces of intestine wound round a skewer and charcoal-grilled. Were you not to know the origin it just comes across as delicious crisp little bits which you eat with finely chopped salads, crushed wheat salad and little heaps of cayenne and oregano. For those who like their food more recognizable there is a strong selection of kebabs and grills. There is a dish of the day – layered minced meat baked dishes and the Turkish version of ravioli, manti. Tripe soup which you flavour to your liking with salt, pepper, lemon juice and vinegar would be the appropriate start but if that is not to your liking roam among the meze which includes cips (chips). Everything is eminently reasonably priced.

OPEN: Mon-Sun. **HOURS:** 12.00pm-5.00am. **CLOSED:** Christmas Day and New Year's Day. **CREDIT CARDS ACCEPTED:** Access, AmEx, Switch, Visa. **NUMBER OF SEATS:** 78. **SERVICE:** Optional. Wheelchair access (but not lavatory). **NEAREST TUBE STATION:** Highbury & Islington. MAP REF: 8/C2

The Ivy

1 West Street, WC2

071-836 4751 £34

'Beautifully managed theatrical restaurant'

At last 'the industry' has formally recognized what has been clear to everyone for a long time. This year (1993) in their version of the Oscars – The Catey Awards – Christopher Corbin and Jeremy King, proprietors of Le Caprice and The Ivy, were voted Restaurateurs of the Year, an award which you may or may not be interested to know is sponsored by Foster Refrigerator (UK). Corbin and King took over The Ivy in 1990 and devised a contemporary version of the theatricality and glamour the restaurant enjoyed in the 1920s and 30s. The decor is not shiny, as at Le Caprice, in fact it is almost dangerously low-key, but little pleasures unfold as you study your surroundings, particularly in the works by artists such as Howard Hodgkin and Eduardo Paolozzi. The clientele are also relied upon to add their tuppence ha'penny worth of decoration and distraction. The graphics of the large menu card bring to mind the classic long lists of old-fashioned stately restaurants but the content is, for the most part, thoroughly modern. Chef Des McDonald has a deft touch and the kitchen seems as competent with the mildly exotic as with the earthy. It is also possible to structure a deeply conservative meal, starting with, for example, potted shrimps, moving on to deep-fried plaice with chips and minted pea purée and finishing with port and damson trifle. All in all it is a clever menu, devised to avoid boredom or complacency among regulars of which there are many. Service copes well, especially considering that many of the customers view themselves as deserving of special treatment. Last orders at midnight is an additional lure to the stars of the stage and screen. The good value of the weekend set price lunch menu is somewhat dented by the cover charge of £1.50 (also imposed on à la carte meals), an anachronistic and annoying practice which I think Restaurateurs of the Year should consider dropping.

OPEN: Mon-Sun. **HOURS:** 12.00-3.00pm and 5.30pm-12.00am. **CLOSED:** Bank Holidays and Christmas. **CREDIT CARDS ACCEPTED:** Access, AmEx, Diner's Club, Visa. **NUMBER OF SEATS:** 90. **SERVICE:** Optional, £1.50 cover charge. **SET PRICE LUNCH:** £12.50 (weekends only). Wheelchair access (but not lavatory). Private room seats 60. **NEAREST TUBE STATION:** Leicester Square. MAP REF: 12/C2

Jashan

19a Turnpike Lane, N8

081-340 9880 or 081-347 8770   **£15-£20**

'Impressive Indian cooking by chefs flown in from Bombay'

Jashan claims to have chefs chosen in Bombay by catering consultants who are obliged by their contract to visit regularly to check that standards are maintained. I find this a much more impressive claim than the ones you come across that promise to reveal the secrets of a maharajah's kitchen or explore the cuisine of a little-known backwater of the subcontinent. The cooking is impressive here with some of the items seemingly cooked to order. From the section coyly entitled From the Deep Sea, try machhi kithmiri, whole pomfret marinated with herbs and spices and grilled. Among the chicken specialities there are some unfamiliar titles such as murg zaibunissa, pieces of charcoal-grilled chicken cooked in a rich white gravy – presumably one based on ground nuts and seeds.

One of the strengths of Jashan – the word means celebration – is the attention to the important details of an Indian meal such as breads, rice and raitas. Paratha lachedar, not offered everywhere, is available as is masala kulcha, the Indian equivalent of a sourdough bread. As well as cucumber, raitas feature carrot and gram flour pearls in their yogurt bases. Desserts are there for those who spent their formative years with a finger in the condensed milk tin. The salted lassi, dehati chaas, is good. Showing interest in what you order will be rewarded by the helpful staff.

OPEN: Mon-Sun. **HOURS:** 12.00-2.30pm and 6.00pm-12.00am. **CLOSED:** Christmas Day and Boxing Day. **CREDIT CARDS ACCEPTED:** All major cards. **NUMBER OF SEATS:** 50. **SERVICE:** 10%. Wheelchair access. **NEAREST TUBE STATION:** Turnpike Lane.

MAP REF: 8/C2

Jin

16 Bateman Street, W1

071-734 0908   **£25**

'The place to discover Korean food'

Korean food has not been embraced by the English as fondly as has Thai. There is an austerity to it but this will unbend on prolonged acquaintance and subtleties can be uncovered. I like the clean flavours and strident spicing and find it actually more appealing than much Japanese food. Indeed Korean restaurants tend to have a significant Japanese clientele as the dishes, similar in some ways, are invariably less expensive. Jin means authentic and this friendly, civilized restaurant is a good place to start an exploration of the cuisine or confirm a liking. The centrepiece of a meal – and the table – is the Korean barbecue where, with some instruction from the friendly staff, you cook certain dishes for yourself. Bulgogi is strips of sweet/sharp marinated beef, a meat held in high esteem by the Koreans, which is grilled. There is also pork, chicken marinated in sake and chilli and seafood to play with.

Around this you choose dishes which double as starters and/or condiments; cold, tender bracken stalks, cucumber in sesame oil, and the sine qua non of Korean food, kim chee. This pickled vegetable, usually Chinese cabbage, brined, spiced and fermented, is thrillingly hot. No Korean would eat a meal without it. (There is a kim chee museum in Seoul). Soups are not intended as first courses. They are part of a meal. A good one, yuk ke jang, is made with beef and vegetables and a confident amount of chilli. There are main courses not dependent on the barbecue. Bee bim neg myun features pears – a rather startling but good notion – mixed with beef, noodles and cucumber in a hot sauce. The owner, Tony Wee, is usually on hand to advise. Barley tea is a traditional accompaniment or finish to a meal. Wines are only adequate, making sake probably the answer.

OPEN: LUNCH: Mon-Sat. DINNER: Mon-Sun. **HOURS:** 12.00-3.00pm and 6.00-11.00pm. **CLOSED:** Easter, Bank Holidays, Christmas and New Year's Day. **CREDIT CARDS ACCEPTED:** All major cards. **NUMBER OF SEATS:** 65. **SERVICE:** 12.5%. **SET PRICE LUNCH:** £5.50 or £7.90. **SET PRICE DINNER:** £15.50 or £19.50. Wheelchair access (but not lavatory). Private room seats 14. **NEAREST TUBE STATION:** Tottenham Court Road/Leicester Square. MAP REF: 12/C2

Joe Allen

13 Exeter Street, WC2

071-836 0651 £20-£25

'A genuine American urban experience'

Joe Allen, the restaurant, came to London from New York City about the same time as the Broadway musical *A Chorus Line*. It seemed that those who did not make the cast of the show waited on tables. From the start, with no overt publicity and little signage to the side street basement premises other than a discreet brass plaque, Joe Allen was a hit. Sixteen years later, the advent of many new boys on the block seems scarcely to have dented its popularity. It retains its theatrical clientele, due to some extent to last orders being at the accommodating hour of 12.45am. The menu has developed over the years, moving away from Norman Rockwell Americana to a more Californian approach with some south-western touches. The once famous salads served in large bowls now being lacklustre (and smaller) affairs, it makes more sense if you are being calorie-conscious to go for items like panfried calamari with balsamic vinegar and rocket. What you might classify as brunch dishes – eggs Benedict, omelettes, crab cakes – are well-prepared and grills competently done. There is no burger shown on the menu but if you ask for one it will be done and, who knows, someone might gaze at you admiringly for your insider knowledge. Famous faces may get friendlier treatment and the two-sitting evening booking system annoys some but one answer would be to go for a late lunch and while away the afternoon. Joe Allen is open all day every day and was one of the first to wish you a nice one.

OPEN: Mon-Sun. **HOURS:** 12.00pm-1.00am (12.00pm-12.00am Sun). **CLOSED:** Christmas Eve and Christmas Day. **CREDIT CARDS ACCEPTED:** None. **NUMBER OF SEATS:** 170. **SERVICE:** Optional. No smoking area. **NEAREST TUBE STATION:** Covent Garden/Embankment. MAP REF: 12/D3

Joe's Cafe

126 Draycott Avenue, SW3

071-225 2217   **£30**

'For stylish folk who like things in black and white'

The wavy, navy line look of Joe's Cafe with its black and grey surfaces and black and white photographs is sometimes complained of as forbiddingly fashionable. The mood changes depending on the crowd. Sometimes the bar right by the door is busy with raffish drinkers, at other times uncannily well-groomed folk in Japanese couture take over and you can hear a pin tuck drop. Staff operate with the polite competence of those used to being at some fashion editor's beck and call. The menu begins just as expected, with trendy but trouble- (in the form of calories) free food that can be picked over with a fork. Fancy seeing you here Caesar salad; mozzarella with tomatoes (sun-dried, of course); gazpacho and carpaccio. This last is sliced too thin to leave much taste and served with a huge mound of Grana cheese. The starters as a whole seem anodyne, and pasta dishes and the plate of sashimi can apparently not be scaled down to make a first course. Second courses are more lively: enormous tortelloni filled with crab meat and served with a warm, bisque-like Americaine sauce and a flagrant amount of basil; particularly good chopped steak; veal fillet with mushrooms, artichokes and meat juices. But with puddings the kitchen is back on automatic pilot producing dull tarte Tatin and gratin of oranges. The wine list is annoyingly minimalist about vintages and includes Roederer Cristal at £119. The advent of Charles Fontaine as consultant chef should produce changes.

OPEN: BREAKFAST: Sat-Sun. LUNCH: Mon-Sun. DINNER: Mon-Sat. **HOURS:** MON-FRI: 12.00-4.00pm, 6.00-11.30pm. SAT: 9.30am-4.30pm, 7.30-11.30pm. SUN: 9.30am-3.30pm. **CLOSED:** Christmas Day and Boxing Day. **CREDIT CARDS ACCEPTED:** Access, AmEx, Diner's Club, Visa. **NUMBER OF SEATS:** 90. **SERVICE:** 15%. Wheelchair access (but not lavatory). **NEAREST TUBE STATION:** South Kensington.

MAP REF: 14/C3

Kalamaras

76 Inverness Mews, W2

071-727 9122   **£22**

'A popular restaurant serving specialities from mainland Greece'

The menu at Kalamaras evokes something more than nostalgia for sunny Aegean holidays. This Bayswater kitchen often shows up that taverna of fond memory in its range and quality. A long list of mezedes (small dishes for sharing as starters) includes light little pastries of feta and oregano or spinach and spring onion; artichoke hearts casseroled with broad beans and dill; grilled mussels; wild greens and lemon juice; fried salt cod with garlic dip: twenty-eight interesting choices in all, not counting the familiar dips and salad. Main courses read equally well but don't necessarily match the mezedes in finesse. A rich Athenian moussaka is dependably good for those not set on avoiding every stereotype. It is all Greek on the wine list, with some good enough examples. Wine buffs have the alternative of taking their own bottle to the smaller, unlicensed Microkalamaras a few doors away which has essentially the same menu. Of course the setting of both, in a bottle-necked mews near Queensway, does not compete with the homeland, though owner Stelios Platonos has worked wonders in turning a low oblong full of ducting into a likeable, lived-in room. Whether the live entertainment he is sometimes inspired to provide has a similar charm must be left to personal judgement.

OPEN: Mon-Sat. **HOURS:** 6.30pm-12.00am. **CLOSED:** Bank Holidays. **CREDIT CARDS ACCEPTED:** Access, Visa, Diner's Club, AmEx. **NUMBER OF SEATS:** 86. **SERVICE:** 10%. **SET PRICE DINNER:** £15.50. Wheelchair access (but not lavatory). 5 tables outside. Private room seats 28. **NEAREST TUBE STATION:** Queensway.   MAP REF: 11/E

Kenny's Cajun Creole Bar & Restaurant

70 Heath Street, NW3

071-435 6972   **£19**

"Jambalaya, crawfish pie, filé gumbo ... "

Kenny Miller, owner of the eponymous restaurants, has spent time in Louisiana researching the subject of Creole and Cajun food. Indeed he has been made both an Honorary Senator of Louisiana and an Honorary Citizen of New Orleans. He has installed American chefs in the kitchens of both his restaurants and imported some ingredients, such as andouille, crawfish and catfish, that are the sine qua non of this cuisine. Despite the sincere effort and staff trained to be so friendly you fear you are being indoctrinated into a cult, some dishes can be imprecise and thus disappointing.

As anyone who has been to Paul Prud'homme's New Orleans restaurant or read his book will know, Cajun-Creole food is rich and many-layered and can easily slip over the edge from gastronomic to gross. For that reason choose buttermilk fried softshell crab coated in a light batter in preference to blue crab and crawfish enchilada smothered with cream and cheese. Have griddle corn flapjacks, crisp and distinct, with tomato salsa and soured cream rather than the gloopy andouille 'gnocchi' served in a murky 'tomato-corn tarter (sic) sauce'. Blackened steak and barbecued chicken are other sane choices or you could just prop up the bar and punctuate your Dixie beers with cajun angels in devil's blankets – shrimp wrapped in bacon and blackened served with rémoulade sauce. Poor quality ice cream lets down the baked goods for desserts. Music, not exclusively Cajun, plays ceaselessly. But when all is said and done, if it's Cajun food you're after, Kenny's is probably the best place.

ALSO AT: 2a Pond Place SW3 (071-225 2916).

OPEN: Mon-Sun. **HOURS:** 11.45am-11.45pm (12.00-10.30pm Sun). **CLOSED:** Christmas Day and Boxing Day. **CREDIT CARDS ACCEPTED:** AmEx, Mastercard, Visa. **NUMBER OF SEATS:** 70. **SERVICE:** Optional. Wheelchair access (but not lavatory). **NEAREST TUBE STATION:** Hampstead.   MAP REF: 10/A

Kensington Place

201-205 Kensington Church Street, W8

071-727 3184 £25-£30

'Eat up and speak up'

Kensington Place is one of London's restaurant success stories and perhaps because of that tends to polarize opinion. There are those who love it (plenty of them) and those who talk crossly of the noise, crowd and clatter. I admire it. I think it is an incredible feat of chef Rowley Leigh and his brigade to feed so many so well for such a fair price. I salute Nick Smallwood and Simon Slater for their management of the usually efficient and friendly service. But when I go to Kensington Place I try to plan it for either very early or late in a mealtime in order to be able to chat to my companion with ease. In 1992 the floor to ceiling glazed premises (designed by Julyan Wickham) were seamlessly extended, moving the far wall with its mural about forty covers north. Kensington Place now qualifies as one of London's large restaurants with the concomitant dynamism and sense of egalitarianism that allows.

The menu, which, in this world of word processors, is typed in a beguilingly amateurish style, always features daily specials and in the appropriate season concentrates creatively on reasonably priced game. There are certain dishes that have become a fixture due to their popularity; foie gras with sweetcorn pancakes, chicken and goat's cheese mousse, scallops with lentil purée (a brilliant dish). Soups, risottos and pasta dishes are well executed. In the saucing and garnishing of main courses traces of Leigh's training with the Roux brothers can make a positive impact. I remember with pleasure some brilliant fondant potatoes. Some desserts have a slight boarding school quality – steamed pudding with custard, caramelized rice pudding with pineapple – but there are also confections with vulgar appeal. The interesting, rolling wine list complements perfectly the food.

My criticism of the uncomfortable chairs at KP resulted in the architect having a monogrammed cushion made for me. If your initials also happen to be FM, ask to borrow it.

AS WITH SISTER Launceston Place, it's price which ranks the wines; there is some overlap, but the lists are different, this one nosing further off the beaten paths than its sibling. Around half is under £20, and half over. Chardonnay seems to be the white grape of preference, from four continents, including two of Australia's best: the Leeuwin '86 (£29.75) and the Mountadam '90 (£25.25). Zinfandel (Ravenswood '91 £15.50), Merlot (Weinert 1989 £16), Mourvèdre (Jade Mountain 1990 £23.25) and Grenache (Charlie Melton's Nine Popes 1991 £21) are some of the red interlopers in the Cabernet and Pinot show. Fair halves; and a very creditable fifteen wines by the glass. The house white is awfully dull, though.

OPEN: Mon-Sun. **HOURS:** 12.00-3.00pm (12.00-3.30pm Sat-Sun) and 6.30-11.45pm (6.30-10.15pm Sun). **CLOSED:** 3/4 days at Christmas. **CREDIT CARDS ACCEPTED:** Visa, Mastercard, Access. **NUMBER OF SEATS:** 90. **SERVICE:** Optional. **SET PRICE LUNCH:** £13.50 (3 courses). Wheelchair access. **NEAREST TUBE STATION:** Notting Hill Gate. MAP REF: 11/F

Kettners

29 Romilly Street, W1

071-437 6437 £14

'Less august than Auguste might have liked'

I think Kettners could and should be turned into a stylish and particular hotel but until that day arrives we must be grateful that this historic Victorian address has not been rendered a poncy, pricey Frenchified restaurant but a place for the people (seating 300). Unfortunately the standard of cooking even at the level of burgers, pizzas and chilli con and senza carne could be upped considerably and the decor given a good clean and mend. Maybe now that owner Peter Boizot has sold the Pizza Express chain he will have the funds to lavish some of the attention he is bringing to bear on the hotel he has bought in Peterborough to this Soho landmark. Kettner's is well-placed for a meal after the movies. The champagne bar provides a handy meeting place.

OPEN: Mon-Sun. **HOURS:** 12.00pm-12.00am. **CLOSED:** Christmas Day and Boxing Day. **CREDIT CARDS ACCEPTED:** All major cards. **NUMBER OF SEATS:** 300. Wheelchair access (but not lavatory). Private room seats 80. **NEAREST TUBE STATION:** Leicester Square/Tottenham Court Road. MAP REF: 12/C2

Khan's Restaurant

13-15 Westbourne Grove, W2

071-727 5420 £12

'A spicy relic of seventies fashionability'

This is the sort of restaurant that flouts the rules most guide books impose. The quality of food can be erratic, the service is perfunctory and the system of no bookings which means that once in a while you should get lucky and be given a table in the infinitely prettier front part of the large lofty premises never seems to work out. However, Khan's has a period charm in terms of London life and also resembles somewhat the sort of eating house you might find in an Indian city should you tire of hotel food. Chicken dishes are the best bet and Khan's do a creditable butter chicken and chicken jalfarezi. Dishes are very reasonably priced and the trade-off is that you, the customer, understand that Khan's is not a place where you linger over coffee.

OPEN: Mon-Sun. **HOURS:** 12.00-3.00pm and 6.00pm-12.00am. **CLOSED:** Christmas Day. **CREDIT CARDS ACCEPTED:** Access, AmEx, Barclaycard, Diner's Club. **NUMBER OF SEATS:** 300. **SERVICE:** 10%. Wheelchair access (but not lavatory). **NEAREST TUBE STATION:** Bayswater/Paddington/Royal Oak/Queensway.

MAP REF: 11/E

Lahore Kebab House

2 Umberston Street, E1

071-481 9737   **£9 (Bring your own wine)**

'Where those in the know go for Indian food'

Lahore Kebab House is a name that comes up when I ask Indian friends where they go out for Indian food. Apparently Imran Khan is also a fan. It is a small, unprepossessing place with the vinyl, veneer and formica look of a greasy spoon but the food, prepared in an open kitchen, has thrilling immediacy and surprising subtlety in the spicing. The short meat-based menu is centred on kebabs, karahi dishes and wonderful breads, all of which are cooked to order over leaping flames. Quail is sometimes offered as is offal. There is always at least one vegetable assembly, such as potatoes with spinach, and a salad of cucumber, onion and coriander. The dessert of kheer (cardamon flavoured creamed rice pudding) is notable. It is tempting to order one of everything but difficult to spend much money even doing that. The only standing on ceremony at Lahore Kebab House takes the form of queuing when it is busy. At such times service can be curt, but it is an acceptable part of the package and I have known it to be charming. On the price/deliciousness index Lahore Kebab House scores highly. As the Michelin guide might put it, it is vaut le detour. Drinking alcohol is not frowned upon and there is an off-licence about three minutes' walk away.

OPEN: Mon-Sun. **HOURS:** 12.00pm-12.00am. **CREDIT CARDS ACCEPTED:** None. **NUMBER OF SEATS:** 70. **SERVICE:** Optional. 2 tables outside. **NEAREST TUBE STATION:** Whitechapel/Aldgate East.   MAP REF: 8/C2

Langan's Brasserie

Because of some critical reviews of the restaurants in which Richard Shepherd is partner, Mr Shepherd has banned me from visiting them. I am therefore unable to provide topical reviews.

The Lansdowne Public House

90 Gloucester Avenue, NW1

071-483 0409   **£17**

'The Stringalongs of NW1 can now get
good Mediterranean food in a pub'

The Lansdowne joins the still too short list of reconstructed pubs, a list headed by The Eagle (q.v.) in Farringdon Road. The chef at The Lansdowne, Amanda Pritchett, has cooked at The Eagle and also at Sutherlands. A blackboard in the large space decorated with bed-sit style tables, chairs and sofas displays her dishes of the day. There is a soup or two e.g. roast tomato with pesto, a terrine, a pasta, an interesting sandwich or bruschetta, something grilled, something stewed, something borrowed, something new. Recently I liked fresh tuna with borlotti beans and a frisée salad that incorporated chorizo as well as bacon, croûtons and poached egg. I also looked covetously at two gents tucking into Italian sausages with mash and tinned peas. The staff are young and helpful up to a point but ordering is something you do yourself at the bar, paying before the food is brought.

OPEN: LUNCH: Tues-Sun. DINNER: Mon-Sun. **HOURS:** 11.00am-11.00pm. (6.00-11.00pm Mon; 12.00-3.00pm and 7.00-11.00pm Sun). **CREDIT CARDS ACCEPTED:** None. **NUMBER OF SEATS:** 60. **SERVICE:** Optional. Wheelchair access (but not lavatory). 8 tables outside. Private room available. **NEAREST TUBE STATION:** Chalk Farm.   MAP REF: 10/C

Launceston Place

1a Launceston Place, W8

071-937 6912   **£29**

'Civilized atmosphere, civilized food'

Perhaps now that a prying paparazzo has identified Launceston Place as an occasional choice of the Princess of Wales Kensington Place will cease to steal all the thunder. Both are owned by the partnership of Simon Slater and Nick Smallwood, but their place at Launceston on a quiet Kensington street is the more pukka restaurant. Here you may sit comfortably and hear what your companion is saying (see Kensington Place entry for comparison). The curving layout of the rooms means that some tables are tucked out of sight and the look is reminiscent of a tasteful country house hotel. Cookery is the point of least contrast; similar in confidence to KP but quieter in style. Simple English treatments and modern eclectic recipes are mixed together on both daily and à la carte menus, making it a good place to entertain someone whose tastes are unsure of. Chaps of either sex can stick to smoked salmon and a good roast while the more adventurous try squid stir-fried with oriental flavourings, deep-fried oysters with chilli and chicken spiked with garlicky gremolada. In winter the various braised or boiled dishes are dependably good, and it is a joy to be able to eat them somewhere where the atmosphere is not stiffly English and the wine list not stiffly priced. Cheeses are well-kept, puddings good and some regulars would not think of leaving without downing a glass of Somerset cider brandy.

THOSE USED TO STRICT wine-list apartheid may be taken aback to see South Africans, Australians, Californians and Spaniards muddled together – until it's realized that the wines are arranged in price order. An admirable idea; would that the prices were a little lower. The selection shows occasional flashes of originality – the 1991 Le Volte from Ornellaia (£17.50), for example; or curranty depths from Langlois-Château's 1981 Saumur Vieilles Vignes (£14.75) – but it's mainly solid stuff from solid names. Skip the dull house wines at £8.50; you'd be better off with the halves at the same price or less.

OPEN: LUNCH: Sun-Fri. DINNER: Mon-Sat. **HOURS:** 12.30-2.30pm (12.30-3.00pm Sun) and 7.00-11.30pm. **CLOSED:** Easter and Christmas. **CREDIT CARDS ACCEPTED:** Access, AmEx, Visa. **NUMBER OF SEATS:** 75. **SERVICE:** Optional. **SET PRICE LUNCH:** £12.50-£15.50 **SET PRICE DINNER:** £12.50-£15.50 (7.00-8.00pm). Wheelchair access (but not lavatory). Private rooms seat 16 and 30. **NEAREST TUBE STATION:** High Street Kensington/Gloucester Road.   MAP REF: 14/A1

Laurent Restaurant

428 Finchley Road, NW2

071-794 3603 £16

'The place to go for couscous'

Laurent, a family-run restaurant in Child's Hill, originally offered a basic bistro menu that had as its speciality couscous. It has now sensibly abandoned offering dishes other than couscous and provides as a first course only brik a l'oeuf, a paper-thin sheet of pastry folded diagonally across an egg and deep-fried. Eating it must have provided the inspiration for the image of ending up with egg on your face. The couscous come vegetarian, complet with lamb and merguez sausages and royal which adds a mixed grill of brochette of lamb, lamb chop and merguez. For dessert there is sorbet, ice cream, crème caramel or crêpe Suzette. It is a good formula, well-executed, and there are few other places in London where you can get that particular pleasure of mixing a mound of steaming grains with the soupy sauce and enlivening each mouthful with the sting of harissa. Algerian or Moroccan wine and mint tea are the appropriate drinks. Service is charming.

OPEN: Mon-Sat. **HOURS:** 12.00-2.00pm and 6.00-11.00pm. **CLOSED:** First 3 weeks in August. **CREDIT CARDS ACCEPTED:** Access, AmEx, Visa. **NUMBER OF SEATS:** 36. **SERVICE:** Optional. Wheelchair access (but not lavatory). **NEAREST TUBE STATION:** Golders Green. MAP REF: 8/B1

Lemonia

89 Regents Park Road, NW1

071-586 7454 £16

'One of the most successful restaurants in London'

Lemonia recently moved across the road to premises that were formerly a spacious pub in order to deal with a greater volume of business than the original cosy, crooked three-storey building could handle. There are still queues for the reasonably priced, carefully cooked Greek/Cypriot food. The secret of success lies in both those factors but also in the warm welcome, agile service and the palpable feel of a family-run business with local employees. In addition to the more or less standard Greek/Cypriot list – notably vivaciously prepared (don't miss the tabbouleh) – there are dishes of the day featuring casseroles (try kleftiko) and fresh fish. The good value is enhanced by the spirit of generosity implicit in olives on the table to start and Turkish (Greek?) Delight with coffee. The wine list has been expanded to include a wider selection of half bottles.

OPEN: LUNCH: Sun-Fri. DINNER: Mon-Sat. **HOURS:** 12.00-3.00pm and 6.00-11.30pm. **CREDIT CARDS ACCEPTED:** Access, Visa. **NUMBER OF SEATS:** 155. **SET PRICE DINNER:** £9.25. Wheelchair access. Private room seats 40. **NEAREST TUBE STATION:** Chalk Farm. MAP REF: 10/C

The Lexington

45 Lexington Street, W1

071-434 3401 £25

'Hip West Soho hang-out'

If you eat out in London with any regularity you have probably been waited on or managed by Martin Saxon. He has done the rounds of fashionable places but now has a financial interest in this restrained looking Soho restaurant no longer recognizable as having previously been the yuppy haven Sutherlands. Saxon came to The Lexington having helped open The Square (q.v.) and with the sous-chef of The Square in tow. That chap has apparently got his green card and the chef at time of writing is Mark Holmes who has also worked at The Square. A few Square features remain such as the paysanne, an intricate composed salad with everything chopped small, a favourite at lunch with the diet-conscious sector of the clientele. The menu changes daily but roughly follows an outline of two soups, a salad, a fish and vegetable terrine, pasta and the paysanne then fish, meat and a vegetarian main course and desserts of which the Full Monte gives you a taste of most. It is a list sometimes more hip than highly-tuned and dishes can underwhelm e.g. a thin tomato and spring onion soup, a bland fricassée of rabbit and chicken with pastry. However, it is all reasonably priced, especially the theatregoers' menu available all evening at £10 for three courses, and the place is smart in a New York kinda way. Banquettes are dark green leather-look, tables bare, napkins white linen and on the walls are Bruce MacLean enamel prints on loan from the artist. The wine list roams the world with most bottles priced under £20.

SHORT BUT SHARP, terse but intelligent, this minima-list is good for whites but better for reds (don't despise the Argentinians). The ten choices by the glass (£2.25-£4.50) plunder the range at the right spots, too – like Pellé's leafy Menetou-Salon Morogues, the creamy Hess Select Chardonnay, and the wide-awake Barbera Ceppi Storici.

OPEN: Mon-Sat. **HOURS:** 12.00-3.00pm and 6.00-11.30pm. **CLOSED:** Christmas and Easter. **CREDIT CARDS ACCEPTED:** Access, AmEx, Diner's Club, Visa. **NUMBER OF SEATS:** 50. **SERVICE:** Optional. **SET PRICE DINNER:** £10. No smoking area by request. Wheelchair access (but not lavatory). 2 private rooms each seat 20. **NEAREST TUBE STATION:** Oxford Circus/Piccadilly Circus/Tottenham Court Road. MAP REF: 12/B3

Ley-On's

56-58 Wardour Street, W1

071-437 6465 £15

'Part of old Soho rather than contemporary Chinatown'

Nostalgia plays a part in Ley-On's, a Chinese restaurant that existed when Chinatown was equated with Limehouse and before we all started to distinguish between Peking and Canton, Hunan and Shanghai. The spacious

L-shaped interior retains some of the marbled grandeur of the old days, but only some. Dim sum is wide-ranging and notably good. Colour photographs in the windows will help the uninitiated. Ley-On's offers shark's fin dumplings which not everyone else does. There is also a long list of rice and noodle assemblies and one plate meals suited to lunching. From what we now recognize as a Cantonese menu, try salt roast chicken and some of the more unusual dishes such as crispy fried duck with prawn pâté and casserole of eel with roasted pork. Ley-On's tends to be less frantic than those places in the Gerrard Street/Lisle Street axis, but not worth a very long march.

OPEN: Mon-Sun. **HOURS:** 12.00-11.30pm (11.30am-10.30pm Sun). **CLOSED:** Christmas Eve and Christmas Day. **CREDIT CARDS ACCEPTED:** All major cards. **NUMBER OF SEATS:** 250. **SERVICE:** Optional. **SET PRICE DINNERS:** From £7-£30. **NEAREST TUBE STATION:** Leicester Square/Piccadilly Circus.   MAP REF: 12/C3

The Lobster Pot

3 Kennington Lane, SE11

071-582 5556   **£25-£30**

'In that slim volume of Good Fish Restaurants
South of the River, The Lobster Pot can be included'

Restaurant as stage set does not fill one with confidence about the quality of the food. A fish restaurant fitted out like a ship's cabin with portholes through to the kitchen, coiled ropes and nets hanging off the pine-panelled walls, a portrait of a pipe-smoking old tar, staff in Breton fisherfolk outfits and recordings of the whoosh of waves would give you every reason to suspect the calibre of the cooking. However, chef/proprietor Hervé Régent is a regular at Billingsgate market and his ambitiously long (overlong) menu is on the whole very well prepared. Fish soup, mussels, a plateau de fruits de mer or of smoked fish is a sound way to start. Lobsters priced at £25-£30 per person according to the market are cooked any way you want them. Otherwise prawns, brill, sole, sea bass and brochettes of fish are all grilled and served with various sauces. The couscous de poisson would be a dish hard to find elsewhere. In addition there are various meat dishes including tongue with a gherkin and red wine sauce should you want to stick it out at the idea of making a meal of fish. The wine list could use more choice in the whites. Service is sweet but sometimes slightly uncomprehending.

OPEN: Tues-Sun. **HOURS:** 12.00-3.00pm (12.30-4.00pm Sat) and 7.00-11.30pm. **CREDIT CARDS ACCEPTED:** All major cards. **NUMBER OF SEATS:** 24. **SERVICE:** 12.5%. **SET PRICE LUNCH:** £12.50. **SET PRICE DINNER:** £18.50. Wheelchair access (but not lavatory). **NEAREST TUBE STATION:** Kennington.   MAP REF: 8/C2

Lou Pescadou

241 Old Brompton Road, SW5

071-370 1057 **£23**

'Fish, simple dishes and famous badinage'

You cannot reserve tables at Lou Pescadou and there are those who ask why should anyone want to? They are timid types with insufficient respect for their stomachs. Lou Pescadou serves oysters and shellfish and other dishes that are an authentic taste of Southern France; wonderful fish soup or soupe au pistou, pissaladière and thin, cheese-free pizzas, several sorts of salad, sea bass and John Dory lightly cooked, and even a decent steak/frites. Its look is plain and slightly nautical, and there is a pocket handkerchief-sized patio at the back. The hazard is the brusque, bantering behaviour of the staff who make comments in French which the paranoid might take as criticism of their choice of main course, or of tie, or, indeed, of partner. Writers reporting this are likely to be greeted by 'How dare you say the service is rude.' It is never that. It is more like a running joke which many of the customers love. The brave banter back. Faint hearts miss some of the most honest, fairly-priced food to be found the length of both Brompton Roads.

OPEN: Mon-Sun. **HOURS:** 12.00-3.00pm and 7.00pm-12.00am. **CREDIT CARDS ACCEPTED:** All major cards. **NUMBER OF SEATS:** 60. **SERVICE:** 15% optional. Wheelchair access (but not lavatory). 8 tables outside. Private room seats 50. **NEAREST TUBE STATION:** Earls Court. MAP REF: 14/A3

Ma Goa

244 Upper Richmond Road,
Putney, SW15

081-780 1767 **£12**

'Goan recipes handed down from an "aunty"'

The former manager of Shezan in Knightsbridge, Mr R Kapoor, his wife and their son run this small neighbourhood restaurant with its Goan specialities that were taught to Mrs Kapoor when growing up in Goa. 'The legend' (their phrase) of Ma Goa concerns a 'kind lady' and her lost recipe book. In fact the women cooks in Goa are usually referred to as aunties and it is highly unlikely that any one of them would bother putting down measurements and methods in a book but that is neither here nor there since the food is unusual and good. The first courses are small in price and in quantity. Two hungry people could probably easily manage all five. Stuffed papodoms (sic) are an interesting concept with a reference to Mexican cooking; the soft dough discs being used as a wrap for lightly spiced minced meat and potatoes and then fried. Nareal and curd soup, based on corn and coconut flavoured with turmeric, is for those who like subtle, delicate broths.

The predisposition to lyrical copywriting, quite sweet in the 'legend', may raise expectations too high in the main course menu descriptions. However, the food is clearly freshly made and individually herbed and spiced. The cooking method using a sealed terracotta pot – as featured in the hundee dishes – produces particularly delicious casseroles. Potato curries are notable as is the pullao rice cooked in a rich stock. Putney has embraced Ma Goa enthusiastically; to be expected when something different is done in the preparation of Indian food.

OPEN: Tue-Sun. **HOURS:** 12.00-3.30pm (11.30am-3.30pm Sun) and 6.30-11.00pm (7.00-11.00pm Sun). **CREDIT CARDS ACCEPTED:** Access, Visa. **NUMBER OF SEATS:** 30. **SERVICE:** Optional. Wheelchair access (but not lavatory). **NEAREST TUBE STATION:** East Putney. MAP REF: 8/B3

Mamta

692 Fulham Road, SW6

071-736 5914 **£15**

'High quality Indian vegetarian food in Fulham'

Rather more chic surroundings than are usually associated with Indian vegetarian food are matched by greater than average care and attention paid to its preparation. It is the sort of attention to culinary detail that you might find in a domestic setting. Should you need to be converted to this style of eating – and, indeed, if you are a follower – start with sev puri, crisp spheres of pastry filled with boiled potatoes and topped with yogurt, tamarind sauce and fine crisp noodles (sev). Sweet and sour, soft and crackly, the puris are a great mouthful – the only way to eat them. Uttapam, a rice-flour based pancake topped with onions, potatoes and chillies, served with coconut chutney and masala dosa, dramatically large pancakes made from naturally fermented batter filled with spiced potatoes, served with a dal and vegetable gravy (sambhar) and more coconut chutney are the most delicious and meticulously prepared I have encountered outside India. Try patra for its singular flavour of aravi leaves which are spread with chick-pea paste, rolled into a pinwheel, steamed and fried. Vegetable dishes are served in three categories, without spices, dry and curried. From the last, try miser and panir matter, the first based on yellow peas, the second on green. Both are cooked to preserve the identity of the legumes rather than letting them mush. Chef's specialities, more complex assemblies, have been given daft names such as Panjab or Bust and Aubergine Sparkel (sic). But try the latter where slender slices of aubergine in sauce manage to retain crispness. For the initiate or hesitant, there are thalis, complete meals on a tray, including ones suitable for vegans and Jains, the last containing no proscribed onion or garlic. Mamta is licensed. Service is gentle and helpful.

OPEN: Mon-Sun. **HOURS:** 12.30-3.00pm and 6.00-11.30pm (6.00pm-12.00am Sat-Sun). **CLOSED:** Christmas Day, Boxing Day and New Year's Day. **CREDIT CARDS ACCEPTED:** All major cards. **NUMBER OF SEATS:** 45. **SERVICE:** Optional. **SET PRICE LUNCH:** £4.95. No smoking area. Wheelchair access (but not lavatory). **NEAREST TUBE STATION:** Parsons Green. MAP REF: 8/B3

Mandarin Kitchen

14-16 Queensway, W2

071-727 9012/9468   **£25**

'Included for shellfish reasons'

Something about the curved ceiling of this cavernous restaurant is reminiscent of a Spanish disco. Curt greetings from female staff who seem to have been carefully coached by the Soho school soon knock such nonsense out of the head. They may as well say 'Sit over there and behave yourself.' Possibly they do, in Cantonese. Fish and shellfish are the specialities here, well-chosen and fairly priced. Two people would be wise to share either a crab or a lobster dish to begin with. Baked lobster with spring onion sauce and fine noodles is especially good but messy, very messy. A pot of crab with bean noodle, dried shrimp and chilli is more pungent. Flavour is conserved by deft cooking and the staff thaw enough to wonder at the quantities consumed. Although the menu then goes into familiar territory (pancake rolls, Peking duck), there are more adventurous items translated into English: cucumber and preserved hot cabbage head; abalone and sea cucumber pot; beautiful sea bass cooked with shredded pork (like lardons) and mushrooms. Prices would be fiercer in the West End.

OPEN: Mon-Sun. **HOURS:** 12.00-11.30pm. **CLOSED:** Christmas Eve and Christmas Day. **CREDIT CARDS ACCEPTED:** All major cards. **NUMBER OF SEATS:** 120. **SERVICE:** Optional. **SET PRICE LUNCH AND DINNER:** £8.90. Wheelchair access (but not lavatory). **NEAREST TUBE STATION:** Queensway/Bayswater.   MAP REF: 11/E

Mandeer

21 Hanway Place, W1

071-323 0660   **£16**

'A karma place off Tottenham Court Road'

I have never actually seen George Harrison at The Mandeer but in his hippy-dippy sitar-playing personification he would have fitted in well and appreciated the Southern Indian and Gujerati vegetarian food. An air of benevolence and idealism clings to the tinselled, tasselled basement premises and it comes as no surprise to find that the owner expresses his creativity both in cooking and in poetry. Evenings are the time to enjoy the incense and innocence. Lunchtimes are for the good-value buffet. There is organic wine for the wide-eyed drinker.

OPEN: Mon-Sat. **HOURS:** 12.00-3.00pm and 5.30-10.00pm. **CLOSED:** Christmas and Bank Holidays. **CREDIT CARDS ACCEPTED:** AmEx, Diner's Club, Mastercard, Visa. **NUMBER OF SEATS:** 150. **SERVICE:** 10%. **SET PRICE LUNCH:** £3.65-£10. **SET PRICE DINNER:** £7.25-£11.50. Private room seats 30. **NEAREST TUBE STATION:** Tottenham Court Road.   MAP REF: 12/C2

Manzi's

1-2 Leicester Street, WC2

071-734 0224   **£27**

*'A fixture in Leicester Street since the days
when Chinatown meant Limehouse'*

Sentimentality is one of my reasons for including Manzi's. I have long associated eating here with romance not least because the restaurant is (or was anyway) part of an hotel about which I have entertained fantasies of lost weekends – with much time being spent at the movies – or anyway fishy ones. Fish, simply cooked – perhaps skate or grilled plaice or sole – is what to order in the ground floor room (in my view the only one to bother with) preceded by oysters delivered from the long oyster bar that runs down one side of the room. It is foolish to expect too much of sauces or vegetables or to hope to penetrate with your charm the cynicism of the waiters. Manzi's, a family-run kind of haven in a tawdry area, is for those who think the phrase old-fashioned a compliment when applied to a restaurant and who think that the definition of restaurant tablecloths is red and white check gingham.

Open: Lunch: Mon-Sat. Dinner: Mon-Sun. **Hours:** 12.00-2.45pm and 5.30-11.30pm (6.00-10.30pm Sun). **Closed:** Christmas Day. **Credit cards accepted:** All major credit cards. **Number of seats:** 80. **Service:** Optional, £1.50 cover charge. Wheelchair access. **Nearest tube station:** Leicester Square.   MAP REF: 12/C3

Marché Mövenpick

Swiss Centre,
1 Swiss Court, W1

071-494 0498   **£15**

'Bargain basement food freshly served Swiss style'

Cafeterias, such as those you find on motorways and in department stores, have improved almost immeasurably in the last decade but the Swiss-owned Marché Mövenpick nevertheless provides an object lesson in how it can be done. Stacks, sacks and piles of fresh produce is the immediate impression on entering the basement premises (formerly the restaurants of the Swiss Centre). Much of it is cooked to order. Mussels are steamed open to order, meat grilled and basted while you wait, pasta fresh from the pasta-making machine simmered and then stirred with your choice of garnish, vegetables are finely sliced and quickly sauteed rendering them unusually healthy and fresh-tasting for an operation of this size and scope. The selection of cold cuts and salads is imaginative and the range of freshly-baked breads temptingly displayed. A set-up of this kind depends heavily not only on the wit and skills of staff but also on the good sense and patience of customers. As you might imagine there can be hiccups caused by both sides of the counters and tedious waits. The surroundings are Heidi-hokey and muzak a mistake. But for office-workers, tourists, movie-goers and groups who have disparate ideas about what they fancy eating, Marché Mövenpick is a godsend. Drink the (expensive) Swiss wine rather than the characterless stuff served in carafes. From 6.00pm and all day Sunday, fondue and raclette are served.

OPEN: Mon-Sun. **HOURS:** 8.00am-12.00am (9.00am-12.00am Sun). **CLOSED:** Christmas. **CREDIT CARDS ACCEPTED:** All except AmEx. **NUMBER OF SEATS:** 400. **SERVICE:** Optional. No smoking area. 35 tables outside. Private rooms seat 15 and 40. **NEAREST TUBE STATION:** Piccadilly Circus/Leicester Square.   MAP REF: 12/C3

Mélange

59 Endell Street, WC2

071-240 8077   **£20-£25**

'For the eternal student in you'

You get the feeling that if the bass player of Grateful Dead had met a young Dutch art student and they'd opened a restaurant in Covent Garden, Mélange would be it. The exterior is understated to the point of being distressed. Inside chaos seems to be the guiding spirit of the decor. The food is a casual, culinary trawl through the eclectic cookbook and comes described in a babel of menuspeak with often two languages in the same title – e.g. saumon cru en mille pezzo (salmon tartar with onion, lime and coriander). Even matzo balls make an appearance as a garnish of chicken and watercress soup. There are attempts at a joke; M. Maigret et les cerises is pan-roast duck breast with dark cherries on spiced lentils. The Mezze Bar provides small dishes resembling tapas priced from £1.50-£3. One assumes this is mainly to facilitate drinking. The cooking is not skilled but adequate. Staff laugh and chat and somehow in the process deliver the goods. Patronizing Mélange can feel like doing someone a good deed. It is a visit to a curious but not unlikeable timewarp.

OPEN: Mon-Sat. **HOURS:** 11.30am-11.30pm (3.00-11.30pm Mon, Sat). **CLOSED:** 1½ weeks over Christmas. **CREDIT CARDS ACCEPTED:** All except AmEx and Diner's Club. **NUMBER OF SEATS:** 65. **SERVICE:** 12.5% for 5 or more. Private rooms seat 20 and 40. **NEAREST TUBE STATION:** Covent Garden.   MAP REF: 12/D2

Melati

21 Great Windmill Street, W1

071-734 6964   **£20**

'Skilful sambals and satays in Soho'

Despite the colonial connections, Malaysian food is not represented here in anything like its true brilliance and variety. The influence of different peoples (Malay, Southern Indian, Nonya) makes the food unique, but Cantonese cooking is so popular that in British Malaysian restaurants it seems to edge out the others. Also the city hawker stalls are specialists who are bound to do a better job than a London restaurant serving more than a hundred different dishes, and some of the ingredients that give savour are unimportable (tiny oysters and local shellfish), or unacceptable (fresh blood). The two Melati restaurants persevere, and succeed in producing bright, authentic dishes and attracting a young crowd to eat them. Unsurprisingly, though, a decision has been taken not to serve raw squid with the fruit and vegetable salad called rujak. Portions are not vast but prices are low; it seems unlikely that anyone thrilled by fiery flavours and aromatics will be dissatisfied. The staff in both restaurants are helpful.

ALSO AT: 31 Peter Street, W1 (071-437 2011).

OPEN: Mon-Sun. **HOURS:** 12.00-11.30pm (12.00-2.30am Fri-Sat). **CLOSED:** Christmas Day. **CREDIT CARDS ACCEPTED:** All major cards. **NUMBER OF SEATS:** 120. **SERVICE:** 10%. **SET PRICE LUNCH AND DINNER:** £19.75. Wheelchair access (but not lavatory). **NEAREST TUBE STATION:** Piccadilly Circus.   MAP REF: 12/C3

Meshwar

128 Edgware Road, W2

071-262 8304   **£15-£17**

'Unprepossessing place but excellent Lebanese food'

Amongst the parade of Arab restaurants on Edgware Road, you might easily miss Meshwar or think it only a take-away. Go in past the cold cabinet to the small, innocently-decorated dining room at the back. Here a long Lebanese menu is served, much of it prepared with extra care. From the list of forty-eight cold and hot d'oeuvres do not omit their particularly fine versions of tabbouleh, cracked wheat salad, muhamara, spicy hot mixed chopped nuts, makdous batinjan, stuffed baby aubergines, and arayes, minced meat grilled on Lebanese bread. In addition to the usual main course grills there are specialities of the days of the week. Notable is Saturday's molukhieh (spinach-like leafy vegetable) cooked with lamb, coriander and garlic, served with rice. Drink Lebanese wine.

OPEN: Mon-Sun. **HOURS:** 10.00am-12.00am (10.00am-1.30am take-away). **CREDIT CARDS ACCEPTED:** All major cards. **NUMBER OF SEATS:** 28. **SERVICE:** Optional, £1 cover charge. Wheelchair access (but not lavatory). **NEAREST TUBE STATION:** Marble Arch/Edgware Road.   MAP REF: 11/D

Le Metro

28 Basil Street, SW3

071-589 6286   **£19**

'Appealingly priced food and good wines by the glass'

Hidden away in a basement in Basil Street is a pretty little wine bar owned by the Capital Hotel a couple of doors down. When grand luxe operations set out to do simple things they often end up tricksy, but Le Metro has a life and a clientele of its own: Harrods' buyers having a tea break, back packers proclaiming the food to be 'brilliant', local women out for a chat and those who work in the area. The look is Gallic and the wine list, a lure. There is a strong French bias but many unusual and fairly priced bottles. A Cruover allows a dozen fine wines to be dispensed by the glass in perfect condition. The left hand side of the menu provides a distillation of the Capital kitchens with dishes such as warm fish terrine with crayfish butter, roasted best end of lamb on a light mustard sauce and caramelized apple tart. There are slightly cheaper plats du jour and snacks such as croque monsieur and bacon sandwich, both served with salad. It is a neat operation, skilfully managed.

OPEN: Mon-Sat. **HOURS:** 7.30am-10.30pm (8.30-10.30pm Sat). **CREDIT CARDS ACCEPTED:** Visa, AmEx. **NUMBER OF SEATS:** 55. **SERVICE:** Optional. **NEAREST TUBE STATION:** Knightsbridge.   MAP REF:14/C1

Mezzaluna

22 Shorts Gardens, WC2

071-379 3336   **LUNCH £13; DINNER £20**

'A bright spot in Covent Garden'

There is a Mezzaluna in New York, Beverley Hills, Aspen and now Covent Garden. This London branch, run by Neal Grossman, brother of the more famous Loyd, is in colourfully decorated premises on the lower ground floor of the Thomas Neal development, a shopping mall plus flats that can serve to remind us of the heady optimism of the eighties. The menu strives to convince that new and unusual Italian assemblies are being offered, a fantasy easily shattered by buying the 'unusual' ingredients in Carluccio's delicatessen on the other side of the street. However, the pizzas cooked in the wood-fired oven on view in the restaurant are the U.S.P. of Mezzaluna. The dough is thin and light, but a pizza not a poppadum, and the toppings are, on the whole, well-judged. There is an above-average selection of Italian wines. Service is bouncy and enthusiastic, sometimes cloyingly so.

OPEN: Mon-Sun. **HOURS:** 12.00pm-1.00am (12.00-11.00pm Sun). **CLOSED:** Christmas Day and Boxing Day. **NUMBER OF SEATS:** 120. **SERVICE:** Optional. No smoking area. Wheelchair access. 10 tables outside. **NEAREST TUBE STATION:** Covent Garden.   MAP REF: 12/D2

Le Midi

488 Fulham Road, SW6

071-386 0657   LUNCH £16; DINNER £19

'Inexpensive, unpretentious Southern French cooking'

Le Midi is the sort of small French restaurant that all over London has been displaced in the dash for fashionability. A menu featuring baked field mushrooms with garlic, a version of bouillabaisse, daube of beef, rognons à l'ancienne and navarin of lamb – in style circa Elizabeth David *French Country Cooking* 1951 – has become almost a rarity. Juliet Graham cooks and she and her husband run this aiming-to-please neighbourhood Fulham restaurant. The pricing allows unpremeditated eating out and as such the standard of cooking is fine. Charcoal-grilled mixed fish is a nice hors d'oeuvres and the two fish casseroles, Marseillaise (similar to bouillabaisse) and Dieppoise (the broth thickened with cream and saffron) are popular main courses. Wines are regional French. Lunch is a bargain.

OPEN: LUNCH: Sun-Fri. DINNER: Mon-Sat. **HOURS:** 12.00-2.30pm and 7.00-10.30pm. **CLOSED:** Christmas Eve, Christmas Day, Boxing Day and Bank Holiday lunches. **CREDIT CARDS ACCEPTED:** AmEx, Visa, Access. **NUMBER OF SEATS:** 30. **SERVICE:** Optional. **SET PRICE LUNCH:** £6.95. **SET PRICE DINNER:** £8.95. Private room seats 14. **NEAREST TUBE STATION:** Fulham Broadway.   MAP REF: 8/B3

Mijanou

143 Ebury Street, SW1

071-730 4099   **£36**

' "Bingo", says Neville Blech, if you can match the food and wine: it is probably worth the gamble'

Neville and Sonia Blech are husband and wife, wine merchant and chef, and proprietors of this singular restaurant named after the pet name of one of their daughters. Mrs Blech states her own approach to cooking; to read Escoffier in order to understand the techniques. And then, she has said, 'When I had that I could force the ingredients to become what I wanted them to be.' This strong-arm technique has occasionally bizarre results and criticisms of Mijanou tend to focus on the complexity of dishes which quite often – like a woman with too many jewels and accessories – would be better minus a few ingredients. One wonders, if in some version of marital sparring she is challenging her husband's expertise with wines. Mr Blech's response is to devise a scheme called winematch, described by Andrew Jefford below.

Air-dried venison, which you can inspect hanging in the shed in the small back garden, is one of the simpler first courses and Mrs Blech's mastery of technique is apparent in the jellied foie gras. A passion for nuts seems to have calmed down but fruit still plays a part in main courses, for example medallion of venison saddle, Tatin of apples and shallots, served with a blackcurrant and juniper sauce. Game is an obvious enthusiasm and meat generally seemingly the preferred area of attack. Indeed, a vegetarian dish I tried of ravioli stuffed with pine kernels, tomatoes and herbs had such an alarming garnish of rearing, bucking, shying vegetables that the most ardent veggie would have sought refuge with the horseradish, shallots and marrow tucked inside a fillet of beef. However, Mijanou is a very personal and particular place, one of the few serious mom and pop operations, and it does have a stunning wine list. It can perhaps be best appreciated on a sunny day from a table in the back garden, reached through the small, efficient kitchen.

THE WINEMATCH SCHEME (dishes keyed in to wine list sections for compatibility, like a kind of mealtime Dateline) is a good idea, though unless you're eating on your own it quickly gets fiendishly complicated, and is best handled by the systems analyst in the party. If you don't have one, never mind: the twenty sections, and the intermittent annotation, gives this big list plenty of shape to grab hold of. Many of the wines are sourced by Neville Blech himself, and those which aren't are chosen with an enthusiast's care; the strengths are California and Burgundy; the prices, for Belgravia, fair.

OPEN: Mon-Fri. HOURS: 12.00-2.00pm and 7.00-11.00pm. CLOSED: 1 week at Easter, 2 weeks at Christmas and 3 weeks in August. CREDIT CARDS ACCEPTED: Access, Visa, AmEx. NUMBER OF SEATS: 30 SERVICE: Optional. SET PRICE LUNCH: £12 (2 courses) or £15 (3 courses). SET PRICE DINNER: £36. No smoking area. Wheelchair access (but not lavatory). 6 tables outside. Private room seats 20. NEAREST TUBE STATION: Victoria/Sloane Square.   MAP REF: 14/D2

Ming

35-36 Greek Street, W1

071-734 2721   **£17**

'Unusual for London; a female Chinese restaurateur'

A Chinese restaurant close to Chinatown that deliberately courts Westerners (they advertise in the *Spectator*), Ming aims to cover all bases. Perhaps having noted the success of Wagamama (q.v.) there is a menu of one-dish noodle-based meals but considerably more varied than the Japanese approach. These make an ideal, inexpensive lunch. There is also a selection of Mantou dishes based on a type of grilled or steamed bread. More Peking style food is offered than is customary in the Cantonese restaurants on the other side of Shaftesbury Avenue. Some approved dishes are mushu pork with onion pancakes, shredded duck imbued with ginger, small tender salt and pepper squid, and slow-cooked Emperor's beef flavoured with star anise. In the effort to be original and different the flights of fancy can disappear over the horizon of good taste; pomegranate prawns in the shape of a pomegranate looks to be avoided. The owner Christine, is usually on hand to advise and make customers feel at home but I sometimes finish a meal feeling that the promise in Ming has not quite been fulfilled. The blue of the paintwork, inside and out, is not a cosy colour.

OPEN: Mon-Sat. HOURS: 12.00pm-12.00am. CLOSED: Christmas Day and Boxing Day. CREDIT CARDS ACCEPTED: All major cards. NUMBER OF SEATS: 70. SERVICE: Optional. SET PRICE LUNCH: From £7.50. SET PRICE DINNER: From £12. No smoking area. NEAREST TUBE STATION: Leicester Square/Piccadilly Circus. MAP REF: 12/C2

Mirabelle

56 Curzon Street, W1

071-499 4636   **£40-£45**

'A grand old name of quondam glamour'

Should there be funds enough, and time, a comparative study of how to re-create once great restaurants might be made by dining at the Mirabelle and Quaglino's (q.v.). Sadly the Mirabelle, which used to be a byword for sophistication, has been redone by its Japanese ownership in a stiff, unimaginative style. Money and manpower have been lavished upon it, but not enough thought. The decorative scheme is neither a re-creation of the past nor an update; it gives an impression of having descended into hotel lounge limbo. Michael Croft's food is some consolation; either plain fish and roast meat from the traditional menu or modern, multi-faceted creations in the style supported by the men from Michelin. Faint spirits are warned to shut the wine list after the 'Sommelier's recommendations' for the prices rise rapidly.

YOU CAN DRINK INEXPENSIVELY here – Antinori's pleasant though unexceptional Orvieto is £10, and there's a Minervois and a Bourgogne Rouge at £13 – yet the really hot action starts at £500, when it's time to pit Margaux '61 against Romanée-Conti '75. Burgundy in general has the edge on Bordeaux; the Latours and Jadots are much in evidence, but so are the various Gagnards, Armand Rousseau, Gros Fräre et Soeur, Grivot and Dujac. There are fifteen 1982 clarets, from Potensac (£37) to Lafite, Mouton and Pétrus (£600). A place to call in favours.

OPEN: LUNCH: Mon-Fri. DINNER: Mon-Sat. **HOURS:** 12.00-2.00pm and 6.30-10.30pm. **CLOSED:** Bank Holidays. **CREDIT CARDS ACCEPTED:** Diner's Club, AmEx, Visa, Access, JCB. **NUMBER OF SEATS:** 74. **SERVICE:** Optional. **SET PRICE LUNCH:** £19 (2 courses) or £25 (3 courses). **SET PRICE DINNER:** £28. No smoking area. Private rooms seat 10 and 34. **NEAREST TUBE STATION:** Green Park.   MAP REF: 12/A4

Monkeys

1 Cale Street, SW3

071-352 4711   **£35-£45**

'Hoorays (and others) hooray for the serious cooking here'

Proprietors Tom and Brigitte Binham are chef and front of house at this Anglo-French neighbourhood restaurant, a neighbourhood distinguished by the confident and carrying voices of its inhabitants. The fact that it is open only Monday to Friday doubtless reflects the fact that on Saturday nights the clientele (and perhaps the chef too) would have to be bussed in from their second homes in the shires. So good and serious is the food at Monkeys – the derivation of the name is apparent only in the primatial pictures – you might think it better than that lot deserve. Game is particularly well-handled and the accompaniments such as game chips, clear gravy and bread sauce are given meticulous attention. The quality of ingredients is generally high as can be ascertained from the chunks of lobster inside ravioli, the scallops that are caramelized in quick-cooking and perched on alternate heaps of Puy lentils and finely diced sauteed peppers and the foie gras served as part of a salad. Desserts are country house rich. Hot treacle tart comes with cream, ice cream or custard. Millefeuille of pancakes and Cointreau is teeth-on-edge sweet. The premises divide into two rooms, the front room preferable, I think, in terms of its decor. Service is efficient and agreeable. The wine list offers occasional bin ends of interest.

OPEN: Mon-Fri. **HOURS:** 12.30-2.30pm and 7.30-11.00pm. **CLOSED:** 2 weeks at Easter, 3 weeks in August and 3 weeks at Christmas. **CREDIT CARDS ACCEPTED:** Access, Mastercard, Visa. **SERVICE:** Optional. **SET PRICE LUNCH:** £12.50, £17.50 and £35. **SET PRICE DINNER:** £22.50 and £35. Wheelchair access with assistance (but not lavatory). Private room seats 12. **NEAREST TUBE STATION:** South Kensington/Sloane Square.   MAP REF: 14/B3

Mon Petit Plaisir

33c Holland Street, W8

071-937 3224   **£25-£28**

'A sentimental Kensington bistro'

A branch of the original Mon Plaisir (q.v.), this small, cramped bistro tucked away on picturesque Holland Street fulfils unevolved definitions about a romantic place to eat. The French menu has a satisfactory bourgeois structure in terms of its dishes; salade tiède de lentilles au petit salé, soupe de poissons avec croûtons et rouille, tarte aux escargots et Stilton, escalope de veau aux champignons, coq au vin et pâtes fraîches, coquilles St Jacques persillées, tarte Tatin are just some of the bones of it. In addition there is a set lunch menu which changes daily. The wines are all French domaine bottled. My very first job in the restaurant business – working as a waitress in the school holidays – was at this address when, if I remember correctly, the restaurant was called The Londoner. Consequently, I have fond feelings for the place.

OPEN: Mon-Fri. **HOURS:** 12.00-2.30pm and 6.30-10.30pm. **CLOSED:** Bank Holidays and 10 days at Christmas. **CREDIT CARDS ACCEPTED:** All major cards. **NUMBER OF SEATS:** 30. **SERVICE:** 12.5%. **SET PRICE LUNCH:** £13.50. **SET PRICE DINNER:** £13.70 (from 6.30-7.30pm). 6 tables outside. **NEAREST TUBE STATION:** High Street Kensington.
                                                        MAP REF: 11/E

Mon Plaisir

21 Monmouth Street, WC2

071-836 7243   **£27**

'London's quintessential French bistro for nigh on fifty years'

There are many Londoners for whom the phrases Mon Plaisir and French bistro are synonymous. Despite the restaurant's longevity (close on fifty years) it has only had two owners, first the Viala family and now Alain Lhermitte. M. Lhermitte has had the sense to let the place evolve but not, in essence, to change except for the fact that there are now several rooms at different levels seating nearly 100, whereas originally only thirty covers could be accommodated at any one time in the agreeably dog-eared front room. The current chef, Daniel Gobet – who came to London to work at La Tante Claire but got sidetracked – has added a gloss to the cooking but not betrayed its fundamental bourgeois quality. You can still start a meal with a gratinée à l'oignon or escargots à l'ail and move on to an entrecôte with Béarnaise and unputdownable pommes allumettes or a canonical gratin dauphinois (both priced separately). You might, however, prefer farcon au Reblochon (Gobet comes from the Savoie) followed by a panaché de poissons, sauce Vierge (very Michel Guerard). Filet d'agneau en croûte, a tricky dish to get right, is got right. Chapon grand'mère is a disappointment. The plateau de fromage was always a feature of Mon Plaisir and it remains well-stocked and well-kept. If you see the climax of a meal as an either/or situation, go for the cheeseboard rather than dessert. Producers and vintages of the French wines are carefully chosen. It will be a sad day – and I hope it never dawns – when Mon Plaisir no longer underpins the restaurant culture of the West End.

OPEN: LUNCH: Mon-Fri. DINNER: Mon-Sat. **HOURS:** 12.00-2.15pm and 6.00-11.15pm. **CLOSED:** Bank Holidays. **CREDIT CARDS ACCEPTED:** Access, Visa, AmEx, Diner's Club. **NUMBER OF SEATS:** 90. **SERVICE:** 12.5%. **SET PRICE LUNCH AND DINNER:** £13.95. Wheelchair access (but not lavatory). Private room seats 30. **NEAREST TUBE STATION:** Covent Garden.   MAP REF: 12/C2

Motcombs

26 Motcomb Street, SW1

071-235 6382   **£30**

'A Belgravia hang-out'

On the ground floor the wine bar open all day provides a useful meeting place as an alternative to the bars of the nearby luxury hotels. Downstairs is a minor period piece clustered with oil paintings and with old-style waiters who should be, and probably are, called Luigi and Alfonso and who have known some of the customers since they were knee-high to a trust fund. The menu provides for those whose nursery tastes have moved on to their understanding of exotic; Caesar salad, Peking duck, spare ribs, steamed sea bass with mint and coriander and steak tartar. There are also the reass

uring and hang-over absorbing stalwarts such as fishcakes, smoked haddock
with poached egg and grills. The wine list is not bad value and strong on
white burgundies.

OPEN: LUNCH: Mon-Fri. DINNER: Mon-Sat. **HOURS:** 12.00-2.30pm and 7.00-
11.00pm (7.30-11.30pm Sat). **CLOSED:** Bank Holidays. **CREDIT CARDS ACCEPTED:** All
major cards. **NUMBER OF SEATS:** 70. **SERVICE:** 12.5%. **SET PRICE LUNCH:** £15. No
smoking area. 4 tables outside. Private room seats 25. **NEAREST TUBE STATION:**
Sloane Square/Knightsbridge. MAP REF: 14/D1

Mr Kong

21 Lisle Street, WC2

071-437 7341 **£20**

'One of Chinatown's reliable fixtures'

Along with nearby Fung Shing (q.v.) the restaurant Mr Kong (also the name
of the chef) has offered consistently high standards in Peking and Cantonese
(but mainly Cantonese) food over a relatively long period. One way of
dealing with the daunting length of the menu – and a much better one than
settling for the set meals – is to concentrate on the specialities. From this list
I have enjoyed satay eels cooked over charcoal, sauteed venison with ginger
wine, stuffed bean curd, casserole of stewed duck with yam and the rather
spectacular sauteed scallop and king prawns Szechuan style in 'bird's nest'.
Baked spare ribs with chillis in a paper bag sounds a good bet but I am
doubtful about the restaurant's enthusiasm for meat and fruit as in sauteed
chicken with mango. It is a moving gesture of moving with the times but
probably little more than that. The ground floor dining room is the one
to aim for. There are wines but I don't think Hugh Johnson has advised on
the list.

OPEN: Mon-Sun. **HOURS:** 12.00pm-1.45am. **CLOSED:** 4 days at Christmas. **CREDIT
CARDS ACCEPTED:** AmEx, Diner's Club, Visa, Access, JCB. **NUMBER OF SEATS:** 115.
SERVICE: 10%. **SET PRICE LUNCH:** £8.60. **SET PRICE DINNER:** £8.60-£18. Private room
seats 30. **NEAREST TUBE STATION:** Leicester Square. MAP REF: 12/C3

Le Muscadet

25 Paddington Street, W1

071-935 2883 **£30-£34**

'An authentic, steady French bistro'

François Bessonard, owner of Le Muscadet, once owned Le Bressan in
Kensington, a restaurant which in its heyday – over twenty years ago – was
one of the serious French restaurant contenders in London. His Marylebone
establishment has relatively modest aspirations but, importantly, fulfils
them. The dishes on the blackboard – painstakingly recited to each table –
exemplify French provincial cooking and come close to a flip through

Elizabeth David's book of that name. Details change but the list of first courses revolves around two soups, oysters and perhaps mussels, a terrine, a croustade or feuilleté, a version of asparagus and usually an escalope of foie gras. Regulars in the main course are salmon with sauce Hollandaise, Dover sole done this way and that, duck breast with blueberries, stuffed quail and a treatment of rabbit. Authentically dull vegetables are included in the prices. There seems to be a faithful clientele, middle-aged in demeanour if not actuality. Service can be rather arch but is nice when you are known to them. The French wine list is short with not a great deal of choice under £20, but embellished with moderately priced wines of the day.

OPEN: LUNCH: Mon-Fri. DINNER: Mon-Sat. **HOURS:** 12.30-2.30pm and 7.30-11.45pm (7.30-11.00pm Sat). **CLOSED:** Last 3 weeks of August and Bank Holidays. **CREDIT CARDS ACCEPTED:** Visa, Access. **NUMBER OF SEATS:** 40. **SERVICE:** 12.5%. Wheelchair access (but not lavatory). **NEAREST TUBE STATION:** Baker Street.

MAP REF: 12/A1

Museum Street Cafe

47 Museum Street, WC1

071-405 3211   LUNCH £16; DINNER £21 (Bring your own wine)

'You are under strict orders to have a good meal'

The popularity of the Museum Street Cafe seems to me to say a lot about the mentality of the English diner. It is a place of prohibitions; no smoking, no alcohol (save that you have brought yourself), no privacy if you are obliged, as often you are, to share a table, no eating at weekends (when it is closed), no credit cards accepted and from the demeanour of the owners you might think no laughing or joking. If Sally Clarke – with whom Gail Koerber has worked – is head nanny, Koerber would seem to be the rather nervous and even stricter under-nanny. However, she has honed well her baking skills in breads, tarts and desserts at Clarke's. Her partner and grill chef Mark Nathan, who has worked at The River Cafe, is similarly skilled in his area of providing. I am willing to believe they would like to relax the rules if space and licensing laws would allow but the Museum Street Cafe requires a certain reined-in approach to the ideas of enjoyment or hanging out. When first I reviewed the Cafe, I used the phrase 'Californian style' with regard to the cooking. The owners wrote to say they hadn't even heard of such a thing. Well, perhaps they also deny themselves reading or travelling. The fact is that the well-handled grills of fish, meat and vegetables, the use of roasted peppers and sun-dried tomatoes, the trading of sauces for vinaigrettes, pestos or the mixtures that have come to be defined by the word salsas, the emphasis on delicious desserts all justify the description. Go, but take plenty of wine. And your tickling stick.

OPEN: Mon-Fri. **HOURS:** 12.30-2.15pm and 7.15-11.00pm. **CLOSED:** 1 week at Easter, 1 week at Christmas and 2 weeks in August. **CREDIT CARDS ACCEPTED:** None. **NUMBER OF SEATS:** 24. **SERVICE:** Optional. **SET PRICE LUNCH:** £11 (2 courses) or £14 (3 courses). **SET PRICE DINNER:** £19.50. No smoking in restaurant. Wheelchair access (but not lavatory). **NEAREST TUBE STATION:** Tottenham Court Road/Holborn.

MAP REF: 12/C2

Nautilus

27-29 Fortune Green Road, NW6

071-435 2532   **£16**

'Outstandingly good fish and chips'

There is nothing simple about fish as fried in the Nautilus. You may order it on the bone, filleted or – obviously only in the case of large fish – in satisfying cutlets sliced through the spine. It may be lightly coated in matzo meal flour (a Jewish tradition and probably as close as possible to healthy fish and chips) or coated in a richer egg and matzo mix for an extra charge. Real sissies can have their fish grilled. The variety offered is huge too, all impeccably fresh and fried to order. There is only one sort of chip – huge ones cooked in clean groundnut oil and included in the price of the fish which ranges from £6.50-£10. There are starters and puddings but bear in mind that the main attraction is served in immense portions. The dining room next to the take-away counter is a standard caff interior made exuberant by flowers, statues classical and Chinese, glass fish and other carefully dusted treasures. Stately women serve here and offer to wrap up any remnant of the vast pieces of fish so that it may be taken home to the cat.

OPEN: Mon-Sat. **HOURS:** 11.30-2.30pm and 5.00-10.30pm. **CLOSED:** Christmas Day, Boxing Day and New Year's Day. **CREDIT CARDS ACCEPTED:** None. **NUMBER OF SEATS:** 50. **SERVICE:** Optional. **NEAREST TUBE STATION:** West Hampstead.

MAP REF: 10/A

N.B.

17 Princess Road, NW1

071-722 9665   **£21**

'Note well this pleasant restaurant near Primrose Hill'

There is a genial tweeness to this restaurant which sports a pretty garden. Owned and run by two friends Paul Nielsen and chef Paul Brans, who have previously worked together at L'Opera and Bates in Covent Garden, N.B. provides reasonably priced and inventive enough food often distinguished by an interesting accompaniment to a main ingredient. For example, pumpkin polenta is the inspired accompaniment to fried chicken livers, an apple and fig chutney sets off the richness of crispy duck. In the first course seafood sausage with saffron sauce and red pepper and Parmesan flan have been a success. For dessert, dark chocolate torte and sticky toffee pudding satisfy. The locale is well served by N.B. but it could also be a destination for eating after a walk through Regent's Park and over Primrose Hill.

OPEN: LUNCH: Sun-Fri. DINNER: Mon-Sat. **HOURS:** 12.00-2.30pm (12.00-3.00pm Sun) and 7.00-10.30pm. **CLOSED:** Christmas Day, Boxing Day and New Year's Day. **CREDIT CARDS ACCEPTED:** Access, Visa, AmEx. **NUMBER OF SEATS:** 70. **SERVICE:** Optional. **SET PRICE LUNCH:** £10.50. **SET PRICE DINNER:** £14.50. Wheelchair access (but not lavatory). 10 tables outside. Private room seats 48. **NEAREST TUBE STATION:** Chalk Farm/Camden.   MAP REF: 10/C

The Neal Street Restaurant

26 Neal Street, WC2

071-836 8368   **£45-£50**

'Owned by Antonio Carluccio, the wild mushroom man'

There is something incongruous about the cultivated image of the canny
wild mushroom hunter plucking his booty for free from under the noses of
the uninitiated and the almost carelessly high prices at this style-conscious
mushroom-fixated Covent Garden restaurant. Of course some of the fungi
served here have to be bought, and at considerable cost, but the residual
feeling for the customer is of having been gulled. The outrage is not so much
at £12 (+ 15% service) for tagliolini with truffle sauce – although that is
pretty outrageous – but more at a salad containing the dismal leaves of lollo
rosso being priced at £4 (+ 15% service) or some spinach at £3 (+ 15%
service). However, the cheekiness does not seem to deter for The Neal Street
Restaurant is consistently busy with evening bookings often needing to be
made a day or two ahead. At the moment of writing chef Santiago Gonzalez
who has been at The Neal Street since its inception twenty years ago is about
to retire but it is Antonio Carluccio, famous for his TV appearances and his
excellent books, who guides the kitchen. Very particular ingredients – some
of which are for sale in Carluccio's shop next door – are the pegs on which
the dishes are hung. Thus bottarga (dried mullet roe) lifts up a mass of black
angel hair pasta garnished with a few, more or less dispensable, clams. Slices
of soft classy beef, flashed for moments into a hot oven, are made infinitely
more luxurious by shavings of truffle cheese. Densely flavoured mushrooms
in a sauce are played off against mostarda di Cremona as garnishes for
medallions of rosy venison. Some dishes are to English eyes perhaps
insolently plain, e.g. a first course of a plate of Italian salami or hand-cut raw
ham, main courses of noisettes of veal cooked with butter and sage, or a
skewer of prawns and bacon, but it actually makes Neal Street one of the
more Italian Italian restaurants in London. The look, originally conceived by
Terence Conran, the pictures originally assembled by Kasmin, still please
and the Stephen Buckley at the end of the long room commissioned,
according to Carluccio, to absorb noise does a great deal more than that.
Pricing of wines, more of which should be Italian, sustains the ongoing
impertinence.

ABOUT HALF THE LIST IS Italian, and strays creditably from beaten paths;
some annotation, however, is needed to help us differentiate Baldi from
Peppoli, Rocco Rubia from Turriga. The four house wines (at £12.50) are
well-chosen; it's best to leave Italy for aromatically emphatic whites like the
1991 Sauvignon from Morton Estate (£14.50).

OPEN: Mon-Sat. **HOURS:** 12.30-2.30pm and 7.30-11.00pm. **CLOSED:** Bank
Holidays and 1 week at Christmas. **CREDIT CARDS ACCEPTED:** Access, AmEx, Diner's
Club, Switch, Visa. **NUMBER OF SEATS:** 60. **SERVICE:** 15%. Wheelchair access (but not
lavatory). Private room seats 26. **NEAREST TUBE STATION:** Covent Garden.

MAP REF: 12/C2

Neshiko

265 Upper Street, N1

071-359 9977   LUNCH £15; DINNER £30-£45

'East meets N1 for accomplished Japanese food'

The occidental problem with Japanese restaurants is that Japanese customers (on whom most establishments depend) are early eaters. Some of the best are solitary places after 9.30pm. One attraction of Neshiko is that enough Islington types patronize it to keep it buzzing later on. It is a pretty place lined with light wood and fringed with blue curtains. There is seating at a counter too which looks into the kitchen. If the food is a bit slow, it is evidently not from idleness on the chef's part – the waiter and waitress were in there helping out on a busy Friday. Standard items are done well: light tempura, beautiful teriyaki, delicate sushi and sashimi. Servings are commendable too and set dinners are filling. There is evidence of extra care, and of creativity, for example in exquisite dobinmushi soup in a tiny teapot, or yams with a hint of vanilla served with salty fish roe as a daily special. Those not trying to achieve Zen purity with vegetables, fish and green tea will find many alcoholic temptations – martinis, champagne cocktails, New World wines and old malt whiskies.

OPEN: LUNCH: Mon-Fri. DINNER: Mon-Sat. **HOURS:** 12.00-3.00pm and 6.00pm-12.00am. **CLOSED:** Bank Holidays. **NUMBER OF SEATS:** 40-50. **SERVICE:** 10%. **SET PRICE LUNCH:** From £13. **SET PRICE DINNER:** From £35. **CREDIT CARDS ACCEPTED:** All major cards. **NEAREST TUBE STATION:** Angel/Highbury & Islington.

MAP REF: 8/C2

Newton's Restaurant

33-35 Abbeville Road, SW4

081-673 0977   £23

'Eclecticism writ large in South London'

Abbeville Road and its many restaurants serves to illustrate my theory that people who live south of the river eat out with greater ferocity than do their northern counterparts. The eclectic menu at Newton's seems particularly to appeal as if there is something inherently racy and sophisticated about starting a meal with, say, chicken bang-bang salad with spicy peanut sauce and moving on to fillet of lamb wrapped in aubergine with pesto. Eating out as much as I do brings out the purist in me and such opportunities do not appeal. I like the simpler dishes here such as a first course of dark, meaty field mushrooms grilled with garlic butter followed by bangers and mash with flageolet beans or, alternatively sticking to an Oriental slant throughout the meal. The well-chosen, well-annotated wine list strives to mix with and match the babble of flavours. Different wines each month offered by the glass promote a learning curve. A large terrace facilitates eating outside. At weekends easygoing hours and a children's menu encourage families to eat out and Sunday brunch is popular.

JAMES ROGERS IS ONE of the great tasters of his age; combine his selections with Zue Newton's emphasis on value and you have the best inexpensive wine drinking in London. Fifteen wines at under £10 is a remarkable feat; the flavours (light and easy whites to rich and meaty reds) are there, too. The rest of the list falls into price bands; and of fifty-two largely memorable wines, only two (the delinquent Champagnes) are over £20. The annotations are simple and accurate, so choosing wine here is as near painless as it ever gets.

OPEN: Mon-Sun. **HOURS:** 12.30-2.30pm (12.30-4.00pm Sat) and 7.00-11.30pm (12.30-11.30pm Sun). **CLOSED:** 23rd-26th December and Easter. **CREDIT CARDS ACCEPTED:** Access, Visa. **NUMBER OF SEATS:** 80. **SERVICE:** Optional. **SET PRICE LUNCH:** £6.95. **SET PRICE DINNER:** £11.95. No smoking area. Wheelchair access (but not lavatory). 8 tables outside. Private room seats 35. **NEAREST TUBE STATION:** Clapham South. MAP REF: 8/B3

Nico at Ninety

It is to be hoped that in next year's edition our relationship with Nico Ladenis will permit reviews of his restaurants which rightfully belong in a London guide.

The Nosh Brothers

773 Fulham Road, SW6

071-736 7311   **£20**

'Mick and Nick make you an offer you shouldn't refuse'

Without fanfare – although presumably with some pretty ferocious word of mouth – the Nosh Brothers, Mick and Nick, opened a small establishment far down the Fulham Road and at time of writing are talking of expanding to larger premises near Brompton Cross. Their image is of catering thugs, a sort of Cook-with-the-Krays double act. Mercifully the look is not translated into the biff-bang chuck it in, it'll be fine, sometime English approach to grub and plonk, still nurtured in certain areas of the cookery press and TV. In fact in that way that big men often move daintily, there is surprising delicacy in much of the cooking. From a menu that changes constantly, slices of notably good bresaola are served with shavings of Parmesan, truffle oil and a salad dressed with a honey-sweetened vinaigrette. Spinaci con salcicce comprises the wilted vegetable strewn with the result of frying sausage meat until reduced to crumbs. Panfried scallops come with lime pesto that has a nice zest and sting to it. Desserts of chocolate rum mousse and apple tart al'coloche deliver all that a body could want from a dessert. The wine list is short and savvy in choice. Service in the minimally decorated ground floor room, where you will avoid the large groups that tend to gather in the basement, is reasonably efficient.

OPEN: Tues-Sat. **HOURS:** 6.00-11.00pm. **CLOSED:** Bank Holidays. **CREDIT CARDS ACCEPTED:** Visa, Access. **NUMBER OF SEATS:** 60. **SERVICE:** 12.5%. Wheelchair access (but not lavatory). Private room seats 45. **NEAREST TUBE STATION:** Parsons Green.
MAP REF: 8/B2

Now & Zen

4a Upper Saint Martin's Lane, WC2

071-497 0376   **£15-£25**

'Glamorous surroundings for as much Chinese food as you can eat'

This was the third and last of the Lawrence Leung/Rick Mather London Zen enterprises combining evolved Chinese food with purist design. Mather has made spectacular use of a theoretically dull space but sadly efforts by the owner to attract more custom have resulted in design compromises and fudging of decor. However, Now & Zen remains an exciting place in the West End and the introduction of an eat-as-much-as-you-like set price menu means that the hungry and greedy get good value. For after-theatre it is ideal, but best of all I like Now & Zen for dim sum at weekends (served until about 4.30pm). Notably skilled dim sum chefs from Hong Kong are employed and customers can enjoy the steamer baskets full of intricate treasures in spacious comfort. Staff are usually smiling and on the ball.

OPEN: Mon-Sun. **HOURS:** 12.00-3.00pm and 6.00-11.30pm. **CLOSED:** Christmas Day. **CREDIT CARDS ACCEPTED:** All major cards. **NUMBER OF SEATS:** 140. **SERVICE:** 12.5%. **SET PRICE LUNCH:** £10.50. **SET PRICE DINNER:** £16.80. Private room seats 40. **NEAREST TUBE STATION:** Leicester Square/Covent Garden.   MAP REF: 12/C3

Nusa Dua

11 Dean Street, W1

071-437 3559   **£8**

'Explore Indonesian cooking in Soho'

The Soeharjono family run this Soho Indonesian restaurant with mum and her son-in-law in the kitchen. A long menu may drive you towards the set meals but don't be so spineless; there is much delectable to discover. In the first course try martabak udang, prawns, egg and spring onions fried in squares of rice paper and served with a pickle based on cucumbers and shallots. Tahu telur, a bean curd omelette with its crisp crust smothered in a piquant gravy is a main course to order even if your brushes with bean curd in the past have not been successful. From the list of vegetable dishes do not omit to order terong belado, aubergine and anchovies fried in hot chilli oil. The above is only a fraction of what is available and whatever you do choose should be bedded down on either a rice or noodle assembly. The staff are helpful if you are flummoxed. The corner aspect of the premises in my view makes the ground floor preferable as a place to sit. The management say the downstairs is more intimate but I say it is a basement.

OPEN: LUNCH: Mon-Fri. DINNER: Mon-Sat. **HOURS:** 12.00-2.30pm and 6.00-11.30pm (6.00pm-12.00am Sat). **CREDIT CARDS ACCEPTED:** Visa, Access, AmEx. **NUMBER OF SEATS:** 60. **SERVICE:** Optional. **SET PRICE LUNCH:** £2.95 (three courses). Private room seats 12. **NEAREST TUBE STATION:** Tottenham Court Road.
MAP REF: 12/C2

Oak Room

Le Meridien, 21 Piccadilly, W1

071-734 8000   LUNCH £40; DINNER £65

'Quiet luxury and top calibre cooking'

One hotel dining room that manages to be grand without intimidating: the delicate coffee colour of the oak panelling is like a giant gâteau – not a frightening image. Sofas and little table lights domesticate the lofty space. A piano plays somewhere behind banks of flowers. Tables are far enough apart to encourage soppy or scandalous conversations, and the staff seem particularly in tune with customers' moods. Notably, it is also the only hotel where the idea of employing a chef from France as a consultant and visiting genius has been sustained. The reason seems to be that the arrangement has become a genuine joint effort between David Chambers, the man on the spot, and Michel Lorain of La Côte Saint-Jacques at Joigny. In a business where egos inflate like unruly dough, such co-operation is rare. Their menu used to be divided between 'tradition' and 'creative' recipes but has now reverted entirely to modern French food listed with the prices in words, as if to soften the blow. Though lovely, the Oak Room is an expensive place to dine. Raw materials are first class and what might sound fancy on the menu (shellfish with scrambled eggs and a sweet garlic and sherry sauce, duck with braised endive with a sauce infused with Arabica coffee beans) often turns out to be bold and intelligently structured. Fish and game cooking is accomplished and foie gras terrines, formidable. There is rarely a fault in food or service from the first bread roll to the final cup of coffee.

SOLID, SOBER AND STRAIGHT-LACED, this longish, grandish wine list is everything it should be (save properly proof-read), but as yet little that it might be. The Californian irruption looks promising (Ridge's Geyserville – here spelt Gerserville – Zinfandel 1989 at £27 is a good way to gauge the break-in); but it finds only the slightest of echoes in Australia, New Zealand and Italy. Burgundy, by contrast, flows in torrents, and the good (Lafarge, de Montille) mingle with the ordinary (Mommesin, Latour). Allow £35 for choice.

OPEN: LUNCH: Mon-Fri. DINNER: Mon-Sat. **HOURS:** 12.00-2.00pm and 7.00-10.30pm. **CLOSED:** Bank Holidays. **CREDIT CARDS ACCEPTED:** All major cards. **NUMBER OF SEATS:** 45. **SERVICE:** Optional. **SET PRICE LUNCH:** £24.50. **SET PRICE DINNER:** £46. Wheelchair access. **NEAREST TUBE STATION:** Piccadilly Circus.   MAP REF: 12/B4

Odette's

130 Regents Park Road, NW1

071-586 5486/8766   £35

'Ambitious neighbourhood restaurant in a well-heeled neighbourhood'

Simone Green has always run this densely mirrored, fairly romantic restaurant as a tight ship. She minds very much indeed about the quality of the food and I would imagine that her chefs have to welcome proprietorial input. Paul Holmes who worked his passage as sous-chef is currently in charge of the thoroughly modern menu which might on any one day admit influences from British, Creole, Italian, Chinese and French cooking. Thus you could choose in the first and main courses of a daily changing list from cream of Jerusalem artichoke soup, spicy fish gumbo, pappardelle of creamed wild mushrooms, pork and coriander faggots with Chinese-style noodles or roasted venison with haricot beans, bacon and prunes. You might infer that a jack-of-all-trades is needed in the kitchen and it is true that not every dish is a hit but the standard is reasonably good and the energy sustained. Interestingly lunch often has a more diverting choice than dinner. For example, consider hot gravad lax with salt cod mash, cucumber, mustard and dill, or sauteed foie gras with pigeon breast and parsnip soufflé pancake with prune and cinnamon sauce. Actually, I can imagine that last going distressingly wrong. There are always more straightforward dishes for those who like them and for Kingsley Amis who lives nearby and wanders in from time to time. Dessert is a course taken seriously with rich and complex creations on offer; chocolate mousse pavlova with fudge sauce and praline, hot toffee apple cake, saffron bread and butter pudding. You could have as well, or instead, a selection of Spanish cheeses served with quince jelly. The wine list is compiled with the help of the wine merchants Bibendum located at the far end of Regent's Park Road. On sunny days the doors that give on to the attractive shopping street are folded aside, but you might prefer the conservatory which is at the back of the premises. The basement houses a popular wine bar.

THIS WINE LIST is intelligently organized, and every wine is given a descriptive note – though some of these are so far over the top in terms of superlatives and absolutes that they might have been written in a hot-air balloon. No matter: there's lots that's good here anyway (Basedows, Rolly Gassmann, Saintsbury, Ghislaine Barthod, Paul Avril). Most are fairly priced, and there's still a choice for under a tenner.

OPEN: LUNCH: Sun-Fri. DINNER: Mon-Sat. **HOURS:** 12.30-2.30pm (12.30-3.00pm Sun) and 7.00-11.00pm. **CLOSED:** 1 week at Christmas. **CREDIT CARDS ACCEPTED:** AmEx, Visa, Diner's Club, Barclaycard, Access. **NUMBER OF SEATS:** 60. **SERVICE:** Optional. **SET PRICE LUNCH:** £10. 3 tables outside. Private rooms seat 8 or 30. **NEAREST TUBE STATION:** Chalk Farm. MAP REF: 10/C

O Fado

50 Beauchamp Place, SW3

071-589 3002   **£17**

'They put their bacalhao into it'

There used to be a concentration of Portuguese restaurants in Beauchamp Place, of which Ports (now closed) was the least tourist office in appearance. O Fado may lose the prize for the best eponymous singing to Caravela down the road but their seafood and bacalhao (salt cod) is excellent. The catch, or more accurately, the delivery, is displayed in a cold cabinet at the entrance of the basement premises. Start with lobster or fish salad and then have a thick slice of centre-cut bacalhao simply grilled and served with a heap of lightly fried sliced onions and some boiled potatoes. The salt cod comes in various other ways but in my view this serves it best. Finish the meal with Portuguese pastries. If live music in a confined space is not your sort of thing, go to O Fado at lunchtime when the clientele seems almost completely Portuguese and there is the quite nice, desultory air of a place out of season.

OPEN: LUNCH: Mon-Sat. DINNER: Mon-Sun. **HOURS:** 12.00-3.00pm and 7.00pm-1.00am. **CLOSED:** Christmas Eve and Christmas Day. **CREDIT CARDS ACCEPTED:** All major cards except Diner's Club. **NUMBER OF SEATS:** 80. **SERVICE:** 10%. No smoking area on request. Private room seats 40. **NEAREST TUBE STATION:** Knightsbridge.   MAP REF: 14/C2

Ognisko Polskie
55 Exhibition Road, SW7

071-589 4635   £25

'A refuge from rocket and bruschetta'

The splendid, if slightly faded, yellow dining room of the Polish Hearth Club is called Ognisko Polskie and it is patrolled by particularly pretty girls. Customers are a mixture of London Poles and other Londoners. The beer, on the last visit at least, was Norwegian. Old-fashioned and often overwhelming Polish cooking (fondly remembered but also an excuse for not visiting very often) has been transformed by a lighter touch. Quantities are more manageable and traditional recipes show refinements of technique, flavouring and presentation; pierogi dumplings are on the point of turning into filled pasta and there is a vegetarian version of the salmon pie kulibijaka which uses sauerkraut and mushrooms to good effect. There is a wine list but there is also a big range of vodkas. After a few of the latter an evening spent eating to the tunes from *Twin Peaks* under the gaze of portraits of Rula Lenska and Robert Carrier seems perfectly normal. Take a taxi home.

OPEN: Mon-Sun. **HOURS:** 12.30-3.00pm and 6.30-11.00pm. **CLOSED:** Easter Sunday and Monday, Christmas Day and Boxing Day. **CREDIT CARDS ACCEPTED:** AmEx, Visa, Mastercard. **NUMBER OF SEATS:** 90. **SERVICE:** Optional. **SET PRICE LUNCH AND DINNER:** £7.50. Wheelchair access. 6 tables outside. Private room seats 100. **NEAREST TUBE STATION:** South Kensington.   MAP REF: 14/B1

O'Keefe's
19 Dering Street, W1

071-495 0878   £20

'The way forward for sandwich bars'

O'Keefe's is the dream cafe to have near your place of work. Started in the autumn of 1992 by the art dealer Thomas Dane when he converted a run-of-the-mill sandwich bar in a street off Hanover Square, the first chef was Alaphia Bidwell, now running a floating barge restaurant moored at Little

Venice (081-964 5033 for details). Having set a style for great soups, imaginative sandwiches, assiettes of cheeses and charcuterie, simple roasts and delectable baked goods, Bidwell's approach is now well-served by Caroline Brett and Sam Russell. Brett has worked at 192 and at All Saints, where she met Russell. The daily-changing menu follows more or less the above formula offering on one day two soups; rocket and rice or red pepper and chilli with basil oil; a sandwich of smoked salmon, watercress and horseradish on pumpernickel; a meat dish of cotechino with lentils and salsa verde and two vegetarian main dishes, saffron focaccia with buffalo mozzarella roasted vegetables, rocket and olives and radicchio risotto with balsamic vinegar; four desserts including a maple pecan tart. How very different from spag. bol. or ham and cheese on white. O'Keefe's also serves breakfasts, dinner on Thursday evenings (ring to check) and sells a small range of produce, much of it seemingly chosen for the beauty of the packaging. There is a short wine list with all of the wines available by the glass.

OPEN: LUNCH: Mon-Sat, DINNER: Only on Thur. **HOURS:** 8.00am-5.00pm (7.30-10.30pm Thur; 10.00am-5.00pm Sat). **CLOSED:** Easter, Christmas Day, Boxing Day, New Year's Day and last 2 weeks in August. **CREDIT CARDS ACCEPTED:** None. **NUMBER OF SEATS:** 38. **SERVICE:** Optional. Wheelchair access. **SET PRICE DINNER:** £13.50. 6 tables outside. **NEAREST TUBE STATION:** Oxford Circus. MAP REF: 12/A2

Old Delhi Restaurant

48 Kendal Street, W2

071-724 9580   **£20-£25**

'An Indian restaurant with a Middle Eastern accent'

This small, brightly decorated corner restaurant, in the ownership of an Iranian family, offers a hybrid of Northern Indian and Middle Eastern cooking. The straightforward Indian dishes and mildly spiced curries are authentically prepared using better raw ingredients than is the norm. Specialities have reference to the nationality of the ownership. Koubideh kebab has sumac in its spicing. Lamb, chicken and seafood dishes include fruit in the flavourings, Persian style. Rice is treated with the reverence typical of that cuisine. Jeera aloo – potatoes with cumin – and channa masala – chick-peas cooked with tomatoes and spices – are a good choice of side dishes and, as you might expect, breads are excellent. Those who find chillis a stimulant should ask for the lethal home made sauce. Service is keen and interest in the menu will be rewarded by a visit from the owner who is proud of his food and keen to proselytize. Old Delhi is worth seeking out as a reminder that good ingredients are the basis of good cooking and that Indian food can develop without missing the point. Count on paying more than you would usually budget for 'an Indian'.

OPEN: Mon-Sun. **HOURS:** 12.00-3.30pm and 6.00-11.30pm. **CLOSED:** Christmas Eve and Christmas Day. **CREDIT CARDS ACCEPTED:** Visa, Access, AmEx, Diner's Club. **NUMBER OF SEATS:** 56. **SERVICE:** 15%. Wheelchair access (but not lavatory). 5 tables outside. Private room seats 20. **NEAREST TUBE STATION:** Marble Arch.

MAP REF: 11/D

Olivo

21 Eccleston Street, SW1

071-730 2505   **£25**

'Jolly Italian has replaced demure French at this address'

Changes at this address – some would say for the better – encapsulate the way eating out has been evolving in London. In what seemed like a lightning transformation scene, a rather prim and precious French restaurant called Ciboure turned into a fairly groovy, boldly decorated Sardinian/Italian restaurant called Olivo and the ownership remained snugly the same. The decoration of the walls in swimming pool blue and Dijon mustard yellow is striking. The menu features ingredients that often get slighted elsewhere; chick-peas (as a basis for soup), pumpkin (as a filling for ravioli), grilled cuttlefish, wings of skate. However, the transition between one style and another has meant that the rustic and robust is sometimes inappropriately buttered up in the cooking process. The good value of the lunchtime menu can easily be undone – as can your virtue – by lapsing into grappa.

OPEN: LUNCH: Mon-Fri. DINNER: Mon-Sat. **HOURS:** 12.00-2.30pm and 7.00-11.00pm. **CLOSED:** Bank Holidays and first 3 weeks of August. **CREDIT CARDS ACCEPTED:** Access, Visa, Mastercard, AmEx. **NUMBER OF SEATS:** 45. **SERVICE:** Optional. **SET PRICE LUNCH:** £13-£15. Wheelchair access. **NEAREST TUBE STATION:** Victoria.

MAP REF: 14/D2

192

192 Kensington Park Road, W11

071-229 0482   **£25**

'Will expansion mean growing up or selling out?'

This recently enlarged and revamped establishment has been a forcing ground for the style of food now referred to as modern English and the style of person known as a Notting Hillbilly. A roll call of some of the chefs who have been associated with the place – Alastair Little, Rowley Leigh, Adam Robinson, Rose Gray, Sebastian Snow, Maddalena Bonino, Margot Clayton – reverberates through the pages of this guide. Josh Hampton, previously cooking at Canal Brasserie (q.v.), is currently chef and the changeover from what was happening before if not seamless is also not shocking. The light, bright Italianate and Orientally-inspired dishes suit the clientele whose concerns may often be more social and sartorial than centred on the texture of a sauce. The menu changes regularly with the dinner list extending and embellishing what is on offer during the day. Vegetables are the basis for many of the dishes; a subtle distinction this from 'catering for vegetarians'. They come grilled (of course) and also roasted but in among the modish assemblies such as grilled vegetable tortilla with guacamole and nutty couscous with lime and ginger there are stalwarts such as celeriac rémoulade (rarely found these days even in London's French bistros). Fish and meat tend to be simply, quickly cooked – often grilled – with the creativity more evident in the garnishes and mostly olive oil-based sauces. There are a few cloth-cap dishes such as deep-fried cod and chips with tartare sauce. Desserts are effortful. Lime meringue pie looked pretty as a picture – a Swiss scene of snow-dusted peaks – but the lime filling was stiff with cornflour. 192 has always been noted for its wine list and for the very civil habit of offering many bottles by the glass, standard or large. It remains an attraction.

Service at time of writing is a desultory affair. The waiter showed most animation when discussing with some other customers his real role in life as a film director/super model/Formula One driver/something like that. The new spaciousness and playschool colours remove the clubby feel from the place. This may have distressed the regulars but I suspect it suits the fact that, a decade on, talk amongst them has moved from scandal to school fees.

OPEN: Mon-Sun. **HOURS:** 12.30-3.00pm (1.00-3.00pm Sun) and 7.30pm-12.00am (7.30-11.30pm Sun). **CLOSED:** Bank Holidays. **CREDIT CARDS ACCEPTED:** Visa, Access, AmEx. **NUMBER OF SEATS:** 110. **SERVICE:** Optional. **SET PRICE LUNCH:** £7.50. Private room seats 28. **NEAREST TUBE STATION:** Ladbroke Grove.

MAP REF: 11/E

The Oriental

Dorchester Hotel,
53 Park Lane W1

071-629 8888   **LUNCH £28; DINNER £38**

'High class, high price Cantonese cooking'

There are Chinese restaurants in Hong Kong – Fook Lam Moon is one – where part of the point of going there is for hosts of a meal to spend outrageous and theoretically impressive amounts of money on their guests. Were you anxious to do that sort of thing in London, The Oriental is your place. Prices (inclusive of tax and service) are startlingly high especially when, as with shark's fin and abalone, ingredients are specially imported directly from Hong Kong. The cost will strike some as additionally cheeky given the subtlety and restraint – that you could confuse with lack of taste – in the cooking. This is sophisticated Cantonese food, not the stridently sauced assemblies with which Chinatown makes us familiar. The method of service – formally and in well-defined courses – adds to a sense of prissiness. Dishes can be impressive or they can be dull; it pays to go to The Oriental as – or with – an aficionado of Cantonese cooking. A way of trying the place on a 'budget' is via the set price lunch which features dim sum made by Ngan Tung Cheung, a dim sum chef of twenty-three years' experience. Making a meal of dim sum, the price per portion (£3) is twice that of Chinatown but it is a temptation given the banality of the rest of the set price lunch menu. The spacious, sparsely decorated dining room is a pleasure.

OPEN: LUNCH: Mon-Fri. DINNER: Mon-Sat. **HOURS:** 12.00-2.30pm and 7.00-11.00pm. **CREDIT CARDS ACCEPTED:** AmEx, Visa, Diner's Club, Access, JCB. **NUMBER OF SEATS:** 60. **SERVICE:** Included. **SET PRICE LUNCH:** £20. **SET PRICE DINNER:** £28. Wheelchair access. Private rooms seat 6,10 and 14. **NEAREST TUBE STATION:** Hyde Park Corner.

MAP REF: 12/A4

Orso

27 Wellington Street, WC2

071-240 5269 £30

'Joe Allen's Italian brother'

Orso uses the same discretion in announcing itself as does Joe Allen, sited in what is in fact an adjacent basement. When booking a table you are frequently obliged to fit in with the management's ideas of when you should arrive and when you should leave rather than impose your own. This sort of spirit of service continues upon arrival when it becomes apparent that the famous and the frequent customers get a noticeably better reception and tend not to be seated at the back near the wall of lavatorial tiles. However, Orso has an infectious buzz and sometimes excellent, cleanly cooked Italian food. An ideal pairing of first courses to share would be one of the poppadum-thin pizzas topped with, say, spinach, pancetta, black olives, mozzarella and Parmesan, and a composed salad, say, tuna, new potato, red onion and tomato or perhaps roast duck and pickled radicchio. Main courses are stronger on meat than fish. I have had memorable calf's liver flash-fried with thyme and balsamic vinegar and also wonderful roast suckling pig with garlic potatoes. Green vegetables such as beans or broccoli are served tiède dressed with olive oil and lemon. Pecorino cheese and pear is a nice finish to a meal. The wine list shows the same careful choosing of elements as does the menu. Note the easygoing hours – daily from noon to midnight – and the bore of Orso taking no credit cards.

ALSO AT: 119 Portland Road, W11 (071-221 3299). Scheduled for 7.9.93.

OPEN: Mon-Sun. **HOURS:** 12.00pm-12.00am. **CLOSED:** Christmas Eve and Christmas Day. **CREDIT CARDS ACCEPTED:** None. **NUMBER OF SEATS:** 110. **SERVICE:** Optional. No smoking area. Wheelchair access (with assistance). **NEAREST TUBE STATION:** Covent Garden/Charing Cross. MAP REF: 12/D3

Osteria Antica Bologna

23 Northcote Road, SW11

071-978 4771 £17

'The Lavender Hill mob is alerted to life after lasagne'

Almost all of the many Italian restaurants to have opened in the last five years proclaim their colours by ordering decorative schemes that immediately distinguish them from the Trattoria Era, which you will recall was slightly shorter than the Jurassic period. The Osteria is, in looks, more like a half-way house; still rustic and reassuring with warm wood, bits of clutter and the totem of the Ancien Regime, a big pepper grinder. Some continuity with the past, perhaps, as well as reasonable prices, has enabled this restaurant to attract a much wider audience. All credit to the owner and chef Aurelio Spagnuolo for doing so. But huge demand and the opening of a second restaurant in Putney (q.v. del Buongustaio) seem to be responsible for inconsistent standards. On the last visit crostini was strafed with raw garlic and the fennel risotto featured that vegetable woefully undercooked – not mistakes that would be tolerated back in Bologna. A meatloaf fulfilled all the worst fears of dull density and, to add a real sour note, the waitress recommended an awful bottle of wine from an otherwise interesting and fairly priced list.

OPEN: LUNCH: Tues-Sun. DINNER: Mon-Sun. **HOURS:** 12.00-11.00pm (6.00-11.00pm Mon, 12.30-10.30pm Sun). **CLOSED:** Easter, Bank Holidays and 2 weeks at Christmas. **CREDIT CARDS ACCEPTED:** Access, AmEx, Switch, Visa. **NUMBER OF SEATS:** 70. **SERVICE:** Optional. **SET PRICE LUNCH:** £6.50. Wheelchair access (but not lavatory). 5 tables outside. **NEAREST TUBE STATION:** Clapham Common.

MAP REF: 8/B3

Le Palais Du Jardin

136 Long Acre, WC2

071-379 5353   **£23**

'A fair deal for a meal in Covent Garden'

The fatuous name of this relatively new establishment is particularly irritating in light of the fact that it is one of the few places in London that could correctly claim the definition brasserie i.e. open all day for food and drink. The oyster and seafood bar and cafe at the front of the premises provide justification for invoking the word Parisien. The high quality of the shop-fitting throughout the extensive premises suggests investment of a more exotic kind, which is apparently the case. The menu is fundamentally French bistro with some quasi-fashionable additions such as fishcakes and the need to title one section 'Cuisine Grand'mère'. Notably reasonable pricing has the useful effect of keeping culinary expectations in check but for the most part one is agreeably surprised by the competence of the cooking and the authenticity of the food. What I like about Le Palais du Jardin is the apparent assumption that customers eat out in order to satisfy hunger and sociability not to buy into some theme or fantasy. The square footage and the style of service confer an anonymity that some, including myself, find relaxing. The wine list is French to a bottle and, in keeping with the general policy, reasonably priced.

OPEN: Mon-Sun. **HOURS:** 10.00am-1.00am. **CREDIT CARDS ACCEPTED:** Visa, Mastercard, AmEx, Diner's Club. **NUMBER OF SEATS:** 175. **SERVICE:** 12.5%. Wheelchair access. 10 tables outside. Private room seats 20. **NEAREST TUBE STATION:** Covent Garden.   MAP REF: 12/C3

Il Passetto

230 Shaftesbury Avenue, WC2

071-836 9391   **£25-£27**

'For when too much bruschetta induces nostalgia
for the trat. values'

A certain sort of middle-brow Italian menu popularized in the swingin'
sixties, peculiar to Britain rather than any province of Italy, still finds favour
– as do waiters proficient in pepper-mill semaphore and the understanding
that women, like babies, are fragile creatures who must be flattered into
eating. Il Passetto has been packing the customers in for years. They enjoy
selections from the well-stocked hors d'oeuvres trolley, main courses
dominated by veal and chicken and the specials that always include fresh fish
dishes. There are few surprises, mercifully the bill is not one of them.

OPEN: LUNCH: Mon-Fri. DINNER: Mon-Sat. **HOURS:** 12.00-3.00pm and 6.00-
11.30pm. **CREDIT CARDS ACCEPTED:** All major cards. **NUMBER OF SEATS:** 39. **SERVICE:**
Optional. Wheelchair access (but not lavatory). **NEAREST TUBE STATION:** Tottenham
Court Road/Holborn/Covent Garden.   MAP REF: 12/C3

Pavilion Restaurant

Grosvenor House Hotel,
Park Lane, W1

071-499 6363   **£20**

'One of the better attempts at a hotel to emulate
the standards of independent casual dining'

Hotel restaurants, by the very nature of the thing, are lumbered with one sort
of clientele – the hotel's transient guests – who are unlikely to attract the
sector of the indigenous dining-out population able to give a restaurant a
buzz. These folk show reluctance to run the gauntlet of hotel lobby staff and
go along with the (sometimes presumed) formality of hotel eating. Even a
separate entrance can fail to overcome the problem. A valiant attempt has
been made at the Pavilion Restaurant of Grosvenor House Hotel where
theming by way of the design has been kept to a tolerable minimum and chef
Sean Davies, previously chef of Ninety Park Lane, seconded to provide a
modern menu. First courses are light and salady, main courses enterprisingly
garnished, a fact belittled and mocked by an off-the-peg veg selection being
brought unbidden and charged for separately. Desserts exemplify the
fashion for back to the nursery. Service is vivacious, even touching, as in a
manager's confidence that they were hoping to rival Kensington Place.

OPEN: Mon-Sun. **HOURS:** 7.00-11.00am, 12.30-2.30pm and 6.00-10.00pm
(6.00-10.30pm Sat-Sun). **CREDIT CARDS ACCEPTED:** All major cards. **NUMBER OF
SEATS:** 130. **SERVICE:** Optional. **SET PRICE LUNCH:** £13.50 (3 courses). **SET PRICE
DINNER:** £19.93 (2 courses). No smoking area. Wheelchair access (2 steps).
NEAREST TUBE STATION: Hyde Park Corner/ Marble Arch.   MAP REF: 12/A4

Le Petit Max

97a High Street, Vicarage Road,
Hampton Wick

081-977 0236   **£21 (Corkage £1.50)**

---

*'Twins from Essex cook fine French food in
Hampton Wick'*

Before Marc and Max Renzland begin their mise-en-place for dinner at Le
Petit Max in Hampton Wick they heave a tea urn off the restaurant counter.
During the day Le Petit Max is a cafe called Bonzo's run by two women. In
the evenings it becomes a restaurant run by the twin brothers with the help
of Matthew Jones who has worked in the kitchens of Gidleigh Park and
Bibendum. The system of relatively cheap, unlicensed premises operated for
one meal only, but seven days a week, suits the Renzlands who at their
previous restaurant, Chez Max in Richmond, fell victim to the demands of
the bank and VAT department and were forced into voluntary liquidation.
Le Petit Max is very much a restaurant of the recession but none the worse
for that. Max and Marc themselves launder the red and white check
tablecloths and napkins. The only concession to decor and clue to their lofty
culinary aspirations within the simple surroundings are framed menus of
French Michelin-starred restaurants on bare brick walls. Customers good-
naturedly put up with cramped seating and elbows-in eating. There is a
feeling of everyone pulling together, the sort of camaraderie that you are led
to believe distinguished wartime Britain.

The menu at Le Petit Max is £18 for three courses. Corkage for wine the
customers supply is £1.50 a bottle. The handily situated Wine Warehouse
next door to the cafe is being encouraged to upgrade the stock and discover
areas such as dessert wines. The list of dishes changes daily, in part in
response to marketing. It encompasses French bourgeois cooking kicking off
with a soup, a terrine maison and a staple such as harengs pommes à l'huile
tiède but takes off in flights of fancier food such as a delectable parfait of foie
gras and chicken livers and exquisite scallops scorched to a sweet crust and
served with a sauce velouté. Max seems to find more reward in cooking meat
rather than fish. His daube, fillet steak and magret de canard are superb. The
Renzlands' stated aim to offer good, simple, well-prepared food is exceeded
through cooking of immense attention to detail and sheer deliciousness. It is
the ideal synthesis of the care you might take at home lavished onto the
ingredients by professionals. The tempo is sustained in the desserts.
Throwing all calorific caution to the winds, take Matthew's crème brulée
(supplement of £1.50). A more sober choice would be tarte à la crème, a
dessert seldom offered elsewhere, perfectly simple confection of pastry and
custard. Such effort is put in by the twins who do their own marketing in
order to trim costs that they take off a few days at the beginning of each
month. Be prepared either to eat late – there is a post-theatre (in Hampton
Wick?) two course dinner served from 10.30pm – or to book ahead.

OPEN: LUNCH: Sun. **DINNER:** Mon-Sun. **HOURS:** 12.30-3.45pm and 7.00-11.30pm.
CLOSED: 3-4 days a month. **CREDIT CARDS ACCEPTED:** None. **NUMBER OF SEATS:** 35.
SERVICE: 10%. **SET PRICE LUNCH AND DINNER:** £18. Wheelchair access (but not
lavatory). **NEAREST BR STATION:** Hampton Wick.   MAP REF: 8/B3

Le P'tit Normand

185 Merton Road, SW18

081-871 0233   **£23**

'A travel poster for Normandy comes alive'

'Allo 'Allo, here's a little bit of Northern France in Southfields. Le P'tit Normand does more than fulfil comedy series expectations of a French bistro although the set dressing is all there; gingham tablecloths, dripping candles and chansons. The printed menu is supplemented by a blackboard list of daily dishes. Duck in various manifestations waddles to the centre of the menu. I have enjoyed a beautifully roasted poulet de grain with great sauté potatoes and coveted a formidable choucroute. A mode of ingesting a trou Normand is via a sorbet packing a good slug of Calvados. The cheeseboard is kept in good condition and provides a rationale for ordering another bottle. It was a French restaurateur who works in London who tipped me off about Le P'tit Normand. He went there when homesick.

OPEN: LUNCH: Sun-Fri. DINNER: Mon-Sun. **HOURS:** 12.00-2.00pm and 7.00-10.00pm (7.00-11.00pm Fri-Sat). **CREDIT CARDS ACCEPTED:** All major cards. **NUMBER OF SEATS:** 35. **SERVICE:** Optional. **SET PRICE LUNCH:** £9.75-£11.95. Wheelchair access (but not lavatory). **NEAREST TUBE STATION:** Southfields.

MAP REF: 8/B3

Phoenicia Restaurant

11-13 Abingdon Road, W8

071-937 0120   **£24**

*'A Lebanese restaurant that offers unbeatable
value at lunchtime'*

The Lebanese in London resemble the Japanese to the extent that both rarely produce a bum restaurant. They have in common their respect for food, innate courtesy and the support of their countrymen in London who keep restaurateurs up to the mark. Phoenicia is true to form in its welcome and the variety of vividly flavoured meze it provides. And, unlike others, the stocking of Chateau Musar wine from the homeland has not been abandoned. There is even a rare white. Eating here is marginally cheaper and – how to say this without offending the charming staff? – the room seems a little more lived in than other restaurants. But the greatest difference is at lunchtimes (Sunday excepted) when a long table is covered with meze, main courses and supremely sweet cakes and puddings to which customers help themselves for a very reasonable set price (£9.95 at the time of writing). Waiters help with explanations and clean plates for second helpings.

OPEN: Mon-Sun. **HOURS:** 12.00pm-12.00am. **CLOSED:** Christmas Eve and Christmas Day. **CREDIT CARDS ACCEPTED:** Access, AmEx, Diner's Club, Visa. **NUMBER OF SEATS:** 80. **SERVICE:** 15%. **SET PRICE LUNCH:** £8.95 (Buffet). **SET PRICE DINNER:** From £14.30. Wheelchair access (but not lavatory). **NEAREST TUBE STATION:** High Street Kensington.   MAP REF: 11/F

Pied-à-Terre

34 Charlotte Street, W1

071-636 1178   **LUNCH £30; DINNER £50**

'A young contender for the haute cuisine stakes'

What goes down must come up is perhaps an optimistic way of viewing these straitened times but the restaurant Pied-à-Terre in Charlotte Street provides some ammunition for the claim. Only weeks after Jamdami, an ambitious Indian restaurant of high design, folded in late 1991, the premises were bought from the receivers, a lick of white paint, a few decorative plates, some borrowed Richard Hamilton prints applied (but much else sensibly kept) and chef Richard Neat installed in the kitchen. Neat has worked with Joel Robuchon in Paris, with Raymond Blanc of the Manoir aux Quat' Saisons in Oxfordshire and with Marco Pierre White at Harvey's in Wandsworth; good credentials. Partner and manager is David Moore who has also worked at the Michelin two-star Manoir. Apart from a less expensive set price lunch at £17.50 offered in addition to the main menu, Pied-à-Terre boldly commands an inclusive price of £36 for three courses, tax and service charge. Picky eaters are not their target audience. Indeed, with the little bites offered before the meal and the 'taster' dessert of crème brulée served before your particular choice, the invitation is to the serious and dedicated consumer. Such a person will happily while away time in contemplation of Neat's treats for the chef does not make life easy for himself. There can be long waits while you imagine Neat – or someone – plaiting chives or some other similarly daft intricacy of garnish considered essential to Michelin star-studded food (Pied-à-Terre has one star). It is the same school of catering that could not envisage a menu that omitted foie gras. In fact Neat's heart seems to be in meat and offal, a claim supported by his dishes of lamb served with its kidneys, sweetbread and tongue and braised pig's head served with a purée of swede. This is not to say he cannot handle fish as a tranche of turbot sensitively cooked and surrounded by neatly turned batons of cucumber, courgettes and celery proved. Sometimes the finicky approach to garnish pays off as in the skinning of the tiniest, sweetest, most emerald-green broad beans you can imagine surrounding best end of lamb. Desserts after the heart-stopper of crystalized custard seem otiose but you have paid so try a fruit tart, some sorbets or the intense chocolate soufflé. The wine list is adequate and larded with fashionable names but reflects a restaurant recently assembled.

EXPENSE IS WHAT first strikes you about this wine list – the cheapest bottles, two plain Australians, are £12 apiece; you'll need £25 for a bottle of claret and £30 for burgundy. Fortunately eight wines by the glass (£3.25 to £5) come to the rescue, among them Trimbach's dry, silvery 1989 Muscat (£4) and St Hallett's well-rounded 1989 Cabernet-Merlot (£3.50). A decent selection of halves is further mitigation.

OPEN: LUNCH: Mon-Fri. DINNER: Mon-Sat. **HOURS:** 12.15-2.00pm and 7.00-9.30pm (7.00-10.15pm Sat.). **CLOSED:** Last week of December, first week of January and last 2 weeks of August. **CREDIT CARDS ACCEPTED:** Visa, AmEx, Diner's Club, Mastercard. **NUMBER OF SEATS:** 40 **SERVICE:** inclusive. **SET PRICE LUNCH:** £19.50. **SET PRICE DINNER:** £36. Wheelchair access (but not lavatory). Private room seats 10. **NEAREST TUBE STATION:** Goodge Street.   MAP REF: 12/B1

Pizza Express

30 Coptic Street, WC1

071-636 3232 **£9**

'They've got the dough down pat'

The first Pizza Express opened in Wardour Street in 1965. It was owned by pizza-devotee Peter Boizot, a chap who is still involved with the company nearly thirty years and seventy branches later. In my view Pizza Express is the best of the pizza chains, not just because they have got the properly kneaded, yeast-raised dough just right, but also because elements like cleanliness, efficiency, good design (thanks to Enzo Apicella) and good music (jazz or classical) are standard for every outlet and can be relied upon. The most popular pizza is apparently Marguerita (mozzarella and tomato) but I invariably go for American Hot (pepperoni sausage, hot green peppers, mozzarella, tomato). My two favourite outlets are Dean Street for the jazz in the basement and Coptic Street for the surroundings and the clientele.

Branches too numerous to list. Please check the telephone directory for details.

OPEN: Mon-Sun. **HOURS:** 12.00pm-12.00am. **CLOSED:** Christmas Day. **CREDIT CARDS ACCEPTED:** All major cards. **NUMBER OF SEATS:** 100. **SERVICE:** Optional. No smoking area. 4 tables outside. **NEAREST TUBE STATION:** Tottenham Court Road/Holborn.

Pizza on the Park

11-13 Knightsbridge, SW1

071-235 5550 **£9**

'Pizzas and all that jazz'

As pizza premises grow and mutate to produce doughy discs smothered in pretension, Peter Boizot's enterprises become more and more attractive. What bliss not to be offered pizza in several thicknesses topped with tuna, pineapple, minced beef, sweetcorn and satay sauce. The founder stays true to his own foundation, which is fresh dough made into thin, crisp pizzas that are topped with tasteful combinations of ingredients of good quality. However, he has varied the formula somewhat and given the Pizza on the Park a bigger menu and dressed its staff in formal uniform. The burgundy tiles outside date back to the days when this building was part of another popular chain: the Lyons Tea Houses. Inside is a high room completely revamped by Enzo Apicella with white tiles, geometrical wood panelling and a semicircular work surface as the focal point behind which chefs make pizza. Downstairs another room serves pizza with live music, often very good jazz. There are starters of smoked salmon and soup, vegetarian 'Chilli senze Carne', ham and eggs, generous main course salads (the dressing could be improved) and big sandwiches. Tea is served in the afternoon. This restaurant is deservedly popular with families and parties but manages, even with the jukebox, to be lively rather than raucous. Staff are so well-trained that they even close credit card slips although no service charge is included.

Open: Mon-Sun. **Hours:** 8.15am-12.00am. (9.30am-12.00am Sat-Sun). **Closed:** Christmas Day. **Credit cards accepted:** All major cards (payments in Ecus also). **Number of seats:** 220. **Service:** Optional. No smoking area. Wheelchair access. 12 tables outside. Private room seats 100. **Nearest tube station:** Hyde Park Corner (exit 4). MAP REF: 14/D1

Pizzeria Castello

20 Walworth Road, SE1

071-703 2556 £14

'The castle is the one with the elephant'

It seems tough on Pizzeria Castello always to be praised for being useful in the area. It is true that there is not a great deal of competition around Elephant & Castle but the formula executed here with much brio would flourish anywhere. Huge pizza ovens confront you when you arrive and you may well find yourself studying them at length as you queue for a table – either further back or downstairs. The dough that emerges is dramatically puffy and described by another restaurant reviewer as the best in London. If you like the kick of chilli, choose the topping called Sicilian. If you are a ditherer, Four Seasons or Castellana incorporate most of the garnishing ingredients. If you are perverse and don't want to eat pizza at all, there are some pasta dishes. It is worth having antipasto to start in order to accompany it with garlic pizza-dough bread. The Montepulciano d'Abruzzo '87/88 is an ideal accompaniment and cheap at £9. There is live music most evenings, serving to raise the decibel level ever higher.

Open: Lunch: Mon-Fri. Dinner: Mon-Sat. **Hours:** 12.00-11.00pm (5.00-11.00pm Sat). **Closed:** Bank Holidays. **Credit cards accepted:** Mastercard, AmEx, Visa. **Number of seats:** 150. **Service:** Optional. Wheelchair access. **Nearest tube station:** Elephant & Castle. MAP REF: 8/C2

PJ's Bar & Grill

52 Fulham Road, SW3

071-581 0025 £20

'The nearest London has to a New York Bar and Grill'

More or less immune to the supposed charms of pubs, I can nevertheless see the point of bars where drinks are properly made, where glasses of wine are not served from screwtop litre bottles and where reasonable food is served all day with something close to a smile; bars such as most American cities possess in quantity. The Fulham Road branch of PJ's – in look and feel infinitely preferable to the larger establishment in Covent Garden – features a basically American menu with soft-shell spicy crabs, Caesar salad, Creole crab cakes, ribs, steaks, and such like. Service is slick in response to the pressure that builds up as locals crowd in. There is no obligation to eat more than a snack or anything at all. Many just hang out at the large bar which dominates the room. P. J. McMahon was a polo player hence the polo memorabilia that serves as decoration.

ALSO AT: 30 Wellington Street, WC2 (071-240 7529).

OPEN: Mon-Sun. **HOURS:** 12.00pm-12.00am. **CLOSED:** Christmas Day and Boxing Day. **CREDIT CARDS ACCEPTED:** All major cards. **NUMBER OF SEATS:** 130. **SERVICE:** 15%. No smoking area. Wheelchair access (but not lavatory). 4 tables outside. Private room seats 32. **NEAREST TUBE STATION:** South Kensington.   MAP REF: 14/B3

Le Pont de la Tour

36 Shad Thames, SE1

071-403 8403   £45-£55; BAR & GRILL £22

'Gastronomy meets the Thames, almost for the first time'

A Gastrodrome is how Sir Terence Conran describes the restaurant/ bar/ grill/ oystery/ bakery/ smoked fish shop/ wine shop/ delicatessen/ salon privé built alongside the river Thames by Tower Bridge, named, aptly enough, Le Pont de la Tour. Conran, now most famous for Quaglino's (q.v.) turned part of what seemed a development casualty of the recession into a humming hotspot. People, it seems, will beat a path to the better mousetrap or perhaps, in this case, cheeseboard. The City, of course, is not far away. Conran comments with glee on a certain bimbo element among the punters. Making clever use of the river frontage – nevertheless most easily appreciated by sitting outside – the premises stretch from the oyster bar close to the entrance through a bar where simple meals and grills are served all day (no bookings taken) to the dining room furnished in pale, subtle colours, a flourish of Sem prints, and cream linen-cushioned chairs based on the original design for the second class dining room of the transatlantic liner *La Normandie*. As you might expect much thought has been applied to details such as glassware, table lights and the unusually deep large plates that signal serious eating. The kitchen, visible both back and front, throbs like an engine room at the heart of the premises. In charge is chef David Burke who has worked with Simon Hopkinson at Bibendum. The guiding principle of the food is ingredients luxuriating in their own identity, the sort of dishes the patron likes to eat quand il mange ici. Start simply with fruits de mer or more richly with prawn bisque, crêpes à la Bordelaise or foies de volaille sur croûton, sauce vin rouge. Main courses tend to be straightforward. In season, game is capitalized on. What can be done with potatoes is not ignored. Colcannon, an Irish notion of mixing pureed potatoes with sauteed cabbage, is well worth ordering. Among desserts are items as English as apple crumble or as universally pleasing as chocolate and brandy terrine. Complaints, and there are complaints, sometimes concern the economy of portions, sometimes just slips in kitchen performance. Lunchtimes, when there is a set price menu, minimize any risks financially. The wine list, the work of Joel Kissin, is astutely assembled and wide-ranging.

THE FACT THAT this wine list feeds on a wine shop gives it both magnitude and variety, though its core remains firmly French. Within France, the disposition of forces is a traditional one, with stimulating representations from the Loire, the Rhône and Alsace; Italian wines (from Mascarello, Quintarelli, Isole e Olena and Villa Ligi among others) offer the most fun. Prices, after the addition of 15% service, are discouraging; though the list does begin with an annotated selection of wines below £20 (before service) which includes Basedow's quilted 1990 Semillon at £13.50 and the savorous 1991 Quinta de la Rosa red at £11.50.

OPEN: Mon-Sun. **HOURS:** 12.00-3.30pm and 6.00pm-12.30am (6.00-11.00pm Sun.) Bar and Grill open all day. **CLOSED:** Telephone for advice. **CREDIT CARDS ACCEPTED:** AmEx, Visa, Diner's Club, Access. **NUMBER OF SEATS:** 105 in Restaurant, 70 in Bar and Grill. **SERVICE:** 15%. **SET PRICE LUNCH:** £25. Wheelchair access. Restaurant seats 65 outside; Grill seats 35 outside. Private room seats 20. **NEAREST TUBE STATION:** London Bridge/Tower Hill.   MAP REF: 8/C2

Poons

4 Leicester Street, WC2

071-437 1528   £17

'No pretensions but some of the better cooking in Chinatown'

Consistency is sometimes the only ingredient missing from those long Cantonese menus in Chinatown, where the restless cooks seem only too happy to fit into Saki's aphorism. This particular branch of Poons, though, is able to maintain its standards. Favourite dishes are good year in and year out – senior chefs of the fashionable, occidental set meet here to eat the hot pot of stewed eels with crispy pork with garlic. Original hot pots, rice hot pots and wind-dried food are house specialities. Hot pots are individual crocks of rich stew; rice hot pots are one dish meals that, with two exceptions, are served dry – sauce cravers won't like them; the wind-dried food is a form of charcuterie: duck and dark, intensely flavoured sausages that have been air cured. The list of specialities runs on and on – the duck ham quickly fried with celery, whole chickens baked in salt, vegetables and nuts fried with kidney and squid – but commoner things are also carefully prepared. Nothing disappoints. The service is, of necessity, brisk but not unfriendly. Leicester Street Poon's plain room is spotless and it is often possible for solo lunchers to find a companionable place at one of the large round tables, where the topic of conversation is what a reliably good restaurant this is.

BONIFACE'S 1991 APREMONT (£11), Von Bassermann Jordan's 1985 Forster Jesuitengarden Spätlese (£19), Bruno Clair's 1988 Marsannay Rosé (£14), and a terrific range of beers (including Fuller's ESB, Courage's Russian Imperial stout, German and Belgian wheat beers, two Swiss lagers, Anchor Steam and Coopers) suggest a thoughtful approach.

OPEN: Mon-Sun. **HOURS:** 12.00-11.30pm. **CLOSED:** 3/4 days at Christmas. **CREDIT CARDS ACCEPTED:** None. **NUMBER OF SEATS:** 100. **SERVICE:** Optional. **SET PRICE LUNCH AND DINNER:** £13. Wheelchair access (but not lavatory). Private room seats 30. **NEAREST TUBE STATION:** Leicester Square/Piccadilly.   MAP REF: 12/C3

Prost

35 Pembridge Road, W11

071-727 9620 **£15**

*'One of the few places to offer German and
Eastern European food'*

I was sad when the cafe called The Galleon in Pembridge Road W11 closed
down. A prim, spinsterly place serving cheap, solid English food it held out
for a long time against the relentless trendification of Notting Hill Gate. The
Galleon became something else which was short-lived. Now it is Prost, a cafe
and restaurant serving German and Eastern European food. The owners
apparently – correctly – feel that in London there is a lack. They are well-
served in their ambition to right this situation by their chef John-Paul
Habermann who has previously worked at the Sheraton Park Tower and the
Capital Hotel among other places. The surroundings remain those of a tea
shop with the first floor room designated as restaurant, managing a little
more formality. Main courses such as the home made wild boar sausage and
venison ragoût tend to outshine first courses such as featureless marinated
herrings and over-fried potato pancakes served with soured cream and apple.
Vegetarians are catered for, sometimes in a novel way, as in celeriac steak
sauteed in breadcrumbs. Prices are on the low side. All day opening
encourages a drifting crowd. Sacher torte and schnapps would be one way of
using Prost.

OPEN: Tues-Sun. **HOURS:** 11.00am-11.00pm. **CREDIT CARDS ACCEPTED:** All major
cards. **NUMBER OF SEATS:** 55. **SERVICE:** Optional. **SET PRICE LUNCH:** £3. **SET PRICE
DINNER:** £7.50 (before 8.00pm). No smoking area. Private room seats 35. **NEAREST
TUBE STATION:** Notting Hill. MAP REF: 11/E

Quaglino's

16 Bury Street, SW1

071-930 6767 **£30**

'The closest in London so far to La Coupole'

Undoubtedly the talk of the town in 1993 was Quaglino's. A restaurant and
bar requiring an investment of two and a half million pounds and seating 400
might have been folly in other hands but Sir Terence Conran in his catering
ventures, from The Soup Kitchen onwards, has a knack of understanding
what suits the times. These sombre times needed gaiety, a sense of
excessiveness and the living proof that all sorts of people now derive
enjoyment from the activity of eating out, not just the chomping upper
middle classes. Whilst I anticipated, and found, all kinds of delights in the
look and feel of Quaglino's I was not expecting food much beyond
fashionable and competent. It is so easy nowadays with interesting
ingredients to do little to them and get by satisfactorily. I thought that
feeding the 400 might militate against subtlety. It does not, although the

pressure of numbers inevitably brings some culinary hiccups in its wake. And service can be all over the place. The focal point of the space, the feature that draws your eye as you stand on the mezzanine bar level looking down as if from the prow of a ship on the restaurant spread below, is the crustacea counter. Fronted by a piscatory design in green and gold mosaic it is surrounded by a frieze of scallop shells and heaped with raw shellfish on ice. Its contents count for a good many of the first courses including a plateau de fruits de mer at two prices, £14.50 and £19.50 per person, the latter enough for a whole meal. Langoustine cocktail is prawn cocktail for grown-ups. Dressed crab with mirin and soy is beautifully balanced in its zingy flavours and its aura of healthiness enhanced by a salad of Japanese seaweed and cucumber.

Grill & Rotisserie is a title on another section of the Brasserie Lipp-lifted menu and that activity can be seen through a glass panel set into the wall of the kitchen. Rabbit wrapped in prosciutto comes from it surprisingly succulent. The kick of pepper and spices informs rib of beef and lamb served with roast onions. Plaice and pommes frites are the best fish and chips in town. Oxtail in red wine, skate with mash, boudin blanc, chicken with cabbage and duck with noodles are some of the staples. Some like Sauternes custard with Armagnac prunes for dessert. I found it distressingly akin to something encountered at boarding school and parkin pudding is not my idea of parkin. Instead of a kind of flapjack, it turns out to be a gingery steamed mound surrounded with butterscotch sauce. A short wine list divided more or less by grape varieties and adequate for most outings is supplemented by a fine wine list. Because the renewed Quag's was instantaneously a huge success and because this is England, the restaurant has come in for a lot of knocking, some of it by journalists who paid half price at the running-in meals before the official opening. I'm just pleased London has got somewhere comparable to the large, egalitarian brasseries of Paris. And somewhere you can dance (at weekends) and drink and snack on antipasti. The real problem for me is the noise level. I want others to be able to hear myself speak.

REMARKABLE DEPTH of choice is compressed onto the back of the brasserie menu card and given some basic varietal organization. Jacobins will find plenty of New World and New European action (Bonny Doon's 1991 Big House Red £15.50, St Hallet's Chardonnay by the pot at £9.45); high Tories the comforts of Beaune (or, better still, Vajra's deft 1988 Barolo at £25.50). There are eight good dessert wines and ports by the glass. The fine wine list, available on request, is surprisingly short – some thirty wines at £33.50 and up. Everything that's on it merits inclusion, though some of the bins (Foreau's Vouvray Moelleux Réserve 1989 and Warre '85) also merit another decade of cellaring.

OPEN: Mon-Sun. **HOURS:** 12.00-3.00pm and 5.30pm-12.00am (5.30-11.00pm Sun.) **CLOSED:** Christmas. **CREDIT CARDS ACCEPTED:** AmEx, Visa, Diner's Club, Access. **NUMBER OF SEATS:** 400. **SERVICE:** 15%. Wheelchair access. Private room seats 40. **NEAREST TUBE STATION:** Green Park. MAP REF: 12/B4

The Quality Chop House

94 Farringdon Road, EC1

071-837 5093 **£20**

'Up the working classes'

Charles Fontaine was chef at Le Caprice before he bought this Farringdon Road Victorian caff with the legend etched into the window 'Progressive working class caterer'. He stripped out the interior and then returned it to more or less the original look with high-backed pews enclosing long narrow tables (torture, I am reliably informed, for anyone with a bad back). The surroundings are not just a gimmick, for what Fontaine has achieved is a laudable redefinition of a genre – the caff – that once was a mainstay of British catering, creating a model that could and should be emulated. This is a place not for the sentimental celebration or the meal that is going to clinch weeks of business negotiation or the chance to ogle the famous – all of those being too frequently the jumping off point for a restaurant meal; it is a place affordable on a fairly regular basis where you can enjoy good food straightforwardly prepared. The dishes are not without imagination viz. sweet potato, cabbage and coriander soup, smoked haddock and lentil salad, grilled ox tongue with caper vinaigrette, caramel cheesecake (examples taken from a daily changing menu) but you can eat totally within the vernacular with dishes like eggs, bacon and chips, sausages, mash and onion gravy (although they will be Toulouse sausages), bread and butter pudding. The necessity to share a table unless you go out in a party of six can add to the conviviality but it is quite possible as a couple to keep yourselves to yourselves. The drinks list suits the food. Most wines are modestly priced but there are a couple of good bottles and champagne for celebration and to toast the legend of the Chop House, 'quality and civility'.

OPEN: BRUNCH: Sun. LUNCH: Mon-Fri. DINNER: Mon-Sun. **HOURS:** 12.00-3.30pm (12.00-4.00pm Sun) and 6.30pm-12.00am (7.00pm-12.00am Sun). **CLOSED:** Christmas Day, New Year's Eve and New Year's Day. **CREDIT CARDS ACCEPTED:** None. **NUMBER OF SEATS:** 48. **SERVICE:** Optional. Wheelchair access (but not lavatory). **NEAREST TUBE STATION:** Farringdon. MAP REF: 8/C2

Ragam

57 Cleveland Street, W1

071-636 9098 **£13**

'Notable Southern Indian dive with specialities from Kerala'

In the shadow of the Post Office Tower, Ragam is a small, untidy room where atmosphere is mainly provided by an enthusiastic clientele (keen on the value offered) and smiling staff. It would be foolish to use Ragam for meat dishes only (there is no tandoori cooking) as the U. S. P. of the place is the Southern Indian vegetarian cooking featuring particularly well-made versions of masala dosai, uthappam and iddli – a steamed patty that serves well as a foil to sambar and avial – and the Keralan staple, the buttermilk and coconut-based kalan. An omnivorous approach pays off the best as all the cooking, including that of meat and fish, is done with care, retaining an unusual-for-an-Indian-restaurant air of freshness. The wine list is dull. This is a moment to whistle for lassi.

OPEN: Mon-Sun. **HOURS:** 12.00-3.00pm and 6.00-11.30pm (6.00-11.00pm Sun.) **CLOSED:** Christmas Day and Boxing Day. **CREDIT CARDS ACCEPTED:** Visa, Access, Mastercard, Diner's Club, AmEx, LVs. **NUMBER OF SEATS:** 36. **SERVICE:** 10%. Wheelchair access. **NEAREST TUBE STATION:** Warren Street/Goodge Street/Tottenham Court Road/Great Portland Street. MAP REF: 12/B1

Rani

7 Long Lane, N3

081-349 4386/2636 £22

"Who can set a price on paradise?"
(Paul Levy, Observer April '92)

The above might be just slightly overstating the case, but the fact is that Rani is an exceptionally fine Indian vegetarian restaurant (tendency Gujerati). The Pattni family are dedicated to and determined that you should appreciate and enjoy the food, to which end they offer set meals, various deals, and even a sort of credit card which they call an exchequer card that entitles you to discounts depending on the day, the time and even the weather – 'additional discount of further 5% if it snows'. There is also – commendably – a menu in braille. Such lures are well-intentioned and perhaps build up a core clientele but the food alone is attraction enough. What can be done in the name of deliciousness and gratification without recourse to eggs, fish, meat or animal fats is a revelation, enough to make you send off your sub. to the Vegetarian Society, or at least its Indian branch. For those on wheat-free or dairy products-free diets there are useful markers.

Start with bhel poori, bean papri chat, the well-made bhajias or the daily choice, for example Friday's kachori, spicy peas and moong dal rolled in pastry and deep-fried. Follow with vegetable curries, some also served according to the day of the week, for example Saturday's undhi, fried gram flour and fenugreek balls cooked with exotic vegetables, and accompany them with the outstanding breads. Mithi roti is roasted bread stuffed with a sweetish lentil mix flavoured with cardamom and saffron. Methi bhatoora is puffed deep-fried bread flavoured with fenugreek. If you developed a liking for Indian desserts, they are nearly all here; kulfi, ras malai, shrikand, bundi, falooda and more. The decoration at Rani is clean and clear-cut. The service is friendly and there is a noble note on the menu saying, 'No service charge. Any money left behind as change or gratuities will be donated to charity'.

OPEN: LUNCH: Wed-Fri, Sun. DINNER: Mon-Sun. **HOURS:** 12.15-3.00pm and 6.00pm-12.00am. **CLOSED:** Christmas Day. **CREDIT CARDS ACCEPTED:** Access, Visa, Switch. **NUMBER OF SEATS:** 90. **SERVICE:** Gratuities not accepted. **SET PRICE LUNCH:** £6 and £12. **SET PRICE DINNER:** £11.50-£19. No smoking area. Wheelchair access (but not lavatory). Private room seats 23. **NEAREST TUBE STATION:** Finchley Central. MAP REF: 8/B2

Ransome's Dock Restaurant

35-37 Parkgate Road, SW11

071-223 1611 £25

'The definition of a user-friendly restaurant'

This restaurant currently flourishing in a site where other ventures have floundered is owned by Martin Lam whose previous post as chef was at L'Escargot. The move from Soho to South of the river seems to have galvanized Lam's cooking which comes across as more muscular and seductive than of old. His menu is priced with sympathy for the punters' pockets and manages in a short list to roam wide and free. To visit three countries in just three first courses from one of the monthly changing menus (June '93), you could choose between Turkish cheese and dill boreks with rocket and cos salad, Morecombe Bay potted shrimps with granary toast or terrine of aubergines, ricotta and sun-dried tomatoes with tomato vinaigrette. Some first courses have two prices and two sizes. Main courses are precise. Calves' liver served with mash (gluey on one occasion) is well-cooked and there is invariably a steak for those whose idea of a meal out is a steak. And chips. Specials of the day are fish-led. They might be grilled gambas with garlic and rocket or baked sea bream with samphire and beurre blanc. Martin Lam's wife, Vanessa, is a pâtissière. Her desserts include prune soufflé with Armagnac sauce, layered chocolate terrine with a vanilla sauce, gooseberry and muscat fool. From the interesting wine list – with better than usual house wines – different bottles are selected at different times to be offered by the glass, an admirable notion helpful to anyone keen on experimenting. More evidence that thought has gone into this business is a good value set price lunch, a note on the menu offering smaller portions for children and a Saturday and Sunday brunch which would be the time to take them. There is room for children to wander about in the blue and green painted rooms (important for their enjoyment and yours) and a window where they can peer down onto the usually muddy little inlet that gives the place its name.

OPEN: LUNCH: Mon-Sun. DINNER: Mon-Sat. **HOURS:** 11.00am-11.00pm (12.00pm-12.00am Sat; 12.30-3.30pm Sun). **CLOSED:** Easter and 1 week in August. **CREDIT CARDS ACCEPTED:** All major cards. **NUMBER OF SEATS:** 60. **SERVICE:** Optional. **SET PRICE LUNCH:** £10.50. 4 tables outside. Wheelchair access (but not lavatory). **NEAREST TUBE STATION:** Sloane Square. MAP REF: 8/B3

Rebato's

169 South Lambeth Road, SW8

071-735 6388 £20

'Good value tapas in a gimmick-free bar'

The tapas trend has been and gone, and a cairn of mediocre meatballs is its memorial. But Rebato's still thrives, pleasing its local clientele and Spanish supporters with competent tapas and friendly service. A choice which includes pickled anchovies, garlic chicken, chorizo, kidneys cooked in sherry, chicken livers, deep-fried squid, tortilla served too cold and unusually decent albondigas seems to have grown more conservative lately. But being able to order a paella in the bar is a newly added attraction. The wines are mostly supplied by the Torres company and, curiously, there is no manzanilla stocked and manzanilla sherry is one of the nicest drinks to accompany tapas. Beyond the Iberian tiles and ornateness of the bar (where tables cannot be booked) is a pretty restaurant where a mixture of unsophisticated Spanish food and such British favourites as the avocado or melon starter, the Dover sole with tartar sauce and the mixed grill can be ordered from a modestly priced set menu. The restaurant also has live music most evenings from costumed musicians whom some find too lively. This is Big Night Out territory. It seems mean to report it, but many Rebato's fans won't budge from the tapas bar.

OPEN: LUNCH: Mon-Fri. DINNER: Mon-Sat. **HOURS:** 12.00-2.30pm and 7.00-10.50pm. **CLOSED:** Bank Holidays. **CREDIT CARDS ACCEPTED:** All major cards. **NUMBER OF SEATS:** 70. **SET PRICE LUNCH AND DINNER:** £13.95. Wheelchair access (but not lavatory). **NEAREST TUBE STATION:** Stockwell. MAP REF: 8/B2

The Red Fort

77 Dean Street, W1

071-437 2525 **£25**

'Where modern day moguls eat ambitious Indian cooking'

Ten years have passed since Amin Ali opened his own, purple coloured, Soho version of Delhi's Mogul palace The Red Fort. Mr Ali is a humorous iconoclast who longed to name a restaurant 'The Empire Strikes Back'. Red Fort sounds far more romantic, and so it is when there are Indian musicians playing in the bar and women in saris bringing drinks. The temptation is to ask to be allowed to eat here watching the curious traffic of Dean Street, for the restaurant further in is not as spacious or as attractive as the bar. The menu is something to study, though, with its precise descriptions which are mostly matched on the plate by a precise use of spices and herbs: lamb chops marinaded in ginger and cooked in the tandoor oven; pomfret with chilli and coconut (roop chanda); potatoes braised with fenugreek. The chicken jalfarezi made with fresh green chilli and garlic is renowned, and there is a delicate lamb biryani cooked in the painstaking traditional way, layered with yogurt and sealed with a disposable dough crust. When ordering it is wise not to overdo the dairy richness of cream, butter, yogurt and baked cheese used in the Red Fort's mogul cuisine. By the time you read this, Manjit Gill, creator of the Bukhara restaurant at the Manrya Sheraton hotel in Delhi and reputed to be one of the best Indian chefs in the world, will have joined Red Fort as consultant chef. There is a long and fairly adventurous wine list, Cobra beer and several single malts.

OPEN: Mon-Sun. **HOURS:** 12.00-2.45pm and 6.00-11.30pm. **CREDIT CARDS ACCEPTED:** All major cards. **NUMBER OF SEATS:** 120. **SERVICE:** Optional. **SET PRICE LUNCH:** Buffet £10. Wheelchair access. Private room seats 75. **NEAREST TUBE STATION:** Tottenham Court Road/Leicester Square. MAP REF: 12/C2

The Winter Garden
at the Regent Hotel

222 Marylebone Road, NW1

071-631 8000 **£20**

'Go for the atrium – like a building turned inside out'

The Winter Garden is the name given to the interior of the Regent, the reincarnation of what was once the British Rail station hotel at Marylebone. So extraordinary is the inside of this long-neglected building with its eight-storey atrium as strange as an Escher drawing with overtones of a set for Batman's Gotham City, that a visit is a must if only for a drink or for afternoon tea. An eclectic menu of snacks and appetizers, reasonably well-prepared, is served during the day and well into the evening. Although the service tends to be incomprehending it matters little in these almost weird circumstances. The dining room adjacent is by contrast stolid and gloomy and the efforts of the Italian chef not, so far, worth the high prices.

OPEN: Mon-Sun. **HOURS:** 9.00am-12.00am (9.00-1.00am Sat-Sun). **CREDIT CARDS ACCEPTED:** All major cards. **NUMBER OF SEATS:** 60. **SERVICE:** Optional. No smoking area. Wheelchair access. **NEAREST TUBE STATION:** Marylebone.   MAP REF: 11/D

The Rib Room

Hyatt Carlton Tower
2 Cadogan Place, SW1

071-235 5411 **£55**

'If your definition of a proper meal is a steak'

Set on the ground floor of the Hyatt Carlton Tower, The Rib Room is a large, solid space where old and new money meet to eat meat. The menu revolves around staple luxury items at gold card prices. A typical meal might kick off with crab salad, then move onto the eponymous rib of beef served with some of the best chips in town. Service is formal and efficient. The quality of the ingredients could be viewed as compensation for the somewhat dull surroundings. The Rib Room bar is one of London's serious cocktail bars.

OPEN: Mon-Sun. **HOURS:** 12.30-2.45pm (12.30-2.00pm Sat-Sun) and 7.00-11.15pm (7.00-10.30pm Sat-Sun). **CLOSED:** Dinner on Christmas Day and 1st-3rd January. **CREDIT CARDS ACCEPTED:** All major cards. **NUMBER OF SEATS:** 86. **SERVICE:** Optional. **SET PRICE LUNCH:** £24.50. **SET PRICE DINNER:** £29.50. Wheelchair access. Private room seats 18. **NEAREST TUBE STATION:** Knightsbridge.   MAP REF: 14/D2

The Ritz Restaurant

Ritz Hotel,
Piccadilly, W1

071-493 8181   **LUNCH £30; DINNER £45**

'An exquisite dining room in need of better service'

The Ritz has seen several English chefs come and go since the much publicized, then singular idea of employing one was launched in the early eighties with the arrival of Michael Quinn. Patriotism was its own reward – for Quinn anyway who was awarded an OBE. Currently the chef is David Nicholls, an eminently capable chap formerly at the Royal Garden Hotel. Any chef at the Ritz has to deal with an inheritance; a dining room so wildly decorative that the food tends to take a backseat and a front of house that seems resolutely determined to remain uninterested in what they serve. Prices inclusive of tax and service do nothing to galvanize the waiters who presumably can foresee no palpable reward for nimbleness, foresight, enthusiasm, generosity, flattery or any other attribute someone might think appropriate. Lunch is the time to keep the cost of a bill in touch with reality. The set price menu for three courses and coffee is £26 inclusive, a figure that more or less covers a main course à la carte. Lunch is also the time to select traditional English dishes from the trolley, a style of food that is in complete contrast to the decorative approach apparent in dishes such as crown of asparagus with fondued (sic) crab and seasonal lettuce, fillet of sea bass with potato scales on a tomato and courgette roseace (sic) and supreme of free range guinea gowl (sic) with Alsace bacon and sweet red cabbage. Literals scattered through the menu are emblematic of the management's attitude. It is high time the Ritz – in terms of its public rooms a jewel of an hotel – threw itself behind the idea of producing classic food and did more than just make the gesture of hiring yet another English chef to pit himself against cynical service.

OPEN: Mon-Sun. **HOURS:** 7.00-10.30am (8.00-10.30am Sat-Sun), 12.30-2.30pm (12.30-3.00pm Sun) and 6.00-11.30pm (6.30-10.30pm Sun). **CREDIT CARDS ACCEPTED:** Visa, Barclaycard, AmEx. **NUMBER OF SEATS:** 100. **SERVICE:** 15%. **SET PRICE LUNCH:** £26. **SET PRICE DINNER:** £39.50. Wheelchair access. 16 seats outside. Private rooms seat up to 80. **NEAREST TUBE STATION:** Green Park.   MAP REF: 12/B4

Riva

169 Church Road, SW13

081-748 0434   **£25**

'A great Italian in Barnes'

Riva would appear on many people's list of favourite London restaurants. Opening, as it did, a couple of years after The River Cafe (q.v.) it prompted some to murmur that here was the same sort of Italian food but for less money. The food is not, in fact, necessarily comparable apart from the obvious fact that it is Italian. Francesco Zanchetta's cooking has a Venetian slant – he has worked at The Cipriani – and his larger kitchen gives greater scope in cooking methods, particularly applicable to braised and casseroled dishes, and also to the range of pasta dishes offered. In any case comparisons are invidious and there is the additional consideration of quite different architecture and atmosphere. Riva is a long narrow room painted a self-abnegating umber, decorated with a few architectural drawings. A panelled mirror down one side was probably installed in the belief it would 'widen' the space. When I first reviewed Riva soon after it had opened grilled vegetables were beautifully done, sprinkled with green chilli and mint at the moment of serive, and the baccala Mantecato, creamed salt cod served with polenta, was excellent. I was impressed by skate cooked with fava (broad) beans and slightly underwhelmed by warm goose carpaccio served with spinach and pecorino cheese. Tiramisu and a wild fruit shortbread were lovely. The restaurant's huge success means that I did not review it again, feeling that my time could be more usefully spent scouring areas like Dollis Hill for, say, an Indonesian restaurant that needed some encouragement. But subsequent meals at Riva with friends, enthusiastic reports from others and the same chef in control prove that standards remain high. From the current menu (at time of writing) I like the sound of tortino di patate, thinly sliced baked potatoes topped with mushroom caps stuffed with snails and fennel fronds (get those fronds); ravioli al ragu di pesce, pasta filled with lobster, prawns, leeks and aromatic herbs; lombatina aromatica, loin of pork filled with ham, black truffle and shallots with mashed potatoes; coniglio con spaetzli, rabbit roasted with mushrooms and carrots with spaetzli; gnocchi di latte, sweet milk gnocchi with honey-butter sauce. Andrea Riva is an able (and glamorous) restaurateur who has not let the popularity of the business go to his head in the sense of raising prices or altering the original statement. Areas where complaints have arisen are the inevitable crowding, the lighting, and the timorous, low-key service. Whilst not wishing for pepper mills to be flashed from behind pinnies, a bit of enthusiasm would not come amiss. The wine list delivers some of what is best from Italy.

OPEN: LUNCH: Sun-Fri. DINNER: Mon-Sun. **HOURS:** 12.00-2.30pm and 7.00-11.00pm (7.00-11.30pm Sat; 7.00-9.30pm Sun). **CLOSED:** Christmas, Easter and Bank Holidays. **CREDIT CARDS ACCEPTED:** Visa, Access, Mastercard. **NUMBER OF SEATS:** 50. **SERVICE:** 10%. Wheelchair access. 2 tables outside. **NEAREST BR STATION:** Barnes.   MAP REF: 8/B3

The River Cafe

Thames Wharf,
Rainville Road, W6

071-381 8824   **£35**

'Where the Italian restaurant revolution started'

When the history of Italian restaurants in London comes to be written, the opening of The River Cafe in the late eighties will be seen as a pivotal moment. That the chef/proprietors are American and English and women to boot is something that will probably ensure such a book (or pamphlet) will never exist. The story of The River Cafe is well-known but here it is: architect Richard Rogers wanted a canteen to serve the complex of architecture and design studios he had built in Hammersmith on the banks of the Thames and rather than risk a place with disappointing or unsympathetic food, his wife Ruthie decided to do it herself in partnership with Rose Gray, a friend of Richard's from art school days. It is one of the closest, best-balanced and productive partnerships that exist in catering. The commitment to making the restaurant work embraces not just the cooking but the way the staff are involved as 'family' and also the pursuit of the best ingredients. Infinite care is taken with the sourcing of ingredients, even items like polenta, Parmesan, olive oil and raw ham that most people would think adequately well-supplied here already. An allotment has been bought in order to grow cavalo nero (a variety of cabbage essential to a good ribollita) from seeds imported from Italy and other vegetables such as courgettes in order to harvest the flowers at the peak of freshness. A ludicrously small kitchen, which is part of the plainly decorated restaurant, imposes certain constraints on the cooking. Some of the dishes are simply assemblies of fine ingredients judiciously dressed, for example, fresh buffalo mozzarella with summer herbs (mint, purple and green basil) and Parmesan. There is often a wonderful bread soup (pappa al pomodoro); always a pasta dish, for example linguine con acciughe, pasta with anchovy, lemon zest, pangrattato; a long-cooked dish, for example arrosto di miale al latte, pork cooked in milk, sage and lemon with a red chard salad; and much reliance elsewhere on the charcoal grill.

The first course of chargrilled squid with chilli and rocket is usually perfectly done. The fish or meat of the main course grills are imaginatively garnished and only rarely do the combinations not add up to more than a sum of their parts. Desserts exhibit a profound understanding of the role of sweetness in a meal; lemon curd ice cream, espresso ice cream, chocolate nemesis, polenta cake with prunes and almonds in Armagnac, Pandora bread pudding with Agen prunes are just some.

The Italian wine list demonstrates equal dedication to finding the best that Italy can offer – but at a price. The price of a meal at The River Cafe is a common complaint. It is expensive but it is run in an uncost-effective way and hampered in its trading hours by local residents. There is little in the way of creature comforts – tablecloths for example – to show you value for your money and service can be too hip to be happy. But, although the restaurant has been much plagiarized and polenta now is not an oddity but a raging torrent that will probably one day have to be damned, I still think the Italian food here is the best.

AN UP-TO-THE-MINUTE Italian range of wine bringing together the talented and the trendy (Puiatti, Vajra, Aldo Conterno, Quintarelli, Isole e Olena, Ornellaia). For reds, there's a bigger range of magnums than halves, which seems strange, and prices inhibit choice a little. The range of sweet wines is magnificent: this is the place to come to assess Italy's passito traditions (wines from dried and semi-dried grapes); would that a few more were available by the glass.

OPEN: LUNCH: Mon-Sun. DINNER: Mon-Sat. **HOURS:** 12.30-2.30pm (1.00-2.30pm Sat-Sun) and 7.30-11.00pm. **CLOSED:** Christmas and Bank Holidays. **CREDIT CARDS ACCEPTED:** Access, Visa. **NUMBER OF SEATS:** 65. **SERVICE:** 12.5%. Wheelchair access. 12 tables outside. **NEAREST TUBE STATION:** Hammersmith.   MAP REF: 8/B2

River Restaurant

The Savoy,
Strand, WC2

071-836 4343   LUNCH £40; DINNER £50

*'Wear your dancing shoes and star in your own
performance of Grand Hotel'*

Anton Edelmann, maître chef of The Savoy and the chef in charge of the
River Restaurant has a hard job, I imagine, to turn round perceptions of this
longstanding venue associated with special occasion eating out – wedding
anniversaries, twenty-first birthdays, office retirements and other such
questionably enjoyable events. He has also to contend with the fact that
dancing in restaurants rarely goes hand in hand with fine food. However, his
menus these days, which include a fairly imaginative vegetarian menu, a
menu that matches dishes to specific wines and lunch and dinner table
d'hôtes as well as an à la carte, make impressive reading – and eating.
Celebrating my own wedding at The Savoy not so long ago, I was able, even
through a haze of love, to appreciate the skill in the making of boudin de
pêcheur au caviar, a delicate fish quenelle garnished with crisp vegetables.
Terrine of pheasant and foie gras was correctly unctuous and fittingly
luxurious. Part of the pleasure and romance of sharing a roast duck for two
was the knowledgeable dexterity of the waiter carving it at the table. It is just
such an element that distinguishes grand hotel dining.

Dishes from the current (at time of writing) carte that convey the chef's
style include carpaccio de langoustines au citron vert; soupière d'Atlantique
et rouille; loup de mer grillé parfumé aux lauriers; délice de canard à la
Chinois; soufflé à l'eau de vie de framboise. It remains possible to select a
more traditional meal, one of which Escoffier would approve; consommé
double Royale, tournedos de boeuf Rossini and pêche Nellie Melba en
tulipe. Because hotel kitchens are dealing with banqueting and room service
as well as the restaurant there can be slips that might not occur in a
restaurant on its own. It has been said that Edelmann's presence (a great deal
of the time it must be said) adds an edge to the cooking and presentation.
The formal service can sometimes come across as stuffy or disaffected but
not, of course, to those they know. The famous view of the Thames is
granted to relatively few diners and I can tell you it is infinitely more thrilling
from a bedroom upstairs. The comprehensive wine list is rather oddly
priced, but not over-exuberantly.

OPEN: Mon-Sun. **HOURS:** 12.30-2.30pm and 7.30-11.30pm (7.00-10.30pm
Sun). **CLOSED:** Christmas Day dinner. **CREDIT CARDS ACCEPTED:** All major cards.
NUMBER OF SEATS: 140. **SERVICE:** 15%. **SET PRICE LUNCH:** £25.20. **SET PRICE
DINNER:** £30.50-£45. Wheelchair access by prior arrangement. Private rooms
seat 6-60. **NEAREST TUBE STATION:** Covent Garden/Embankment/Charing Cross.
MAP REF: 12/D3

Rock Island Diner

London Pavilion,
Piccadilly Circus, W1

071-287 5500 £15

'If Buddy Holly were still with us . . .'

The London Pavilion is wide of the target in its desire to be the type of shopping mall that punctuates so many American cities. It does however have Rock Circus, a once is enough rock 'n' roll waxworks which pulls them in, and the logical progression is the Rock Island Diner next door. This is a pastiche fifties diner straight out of *American Graffiti* with a soundtrack to match, marshalled, in the evenings, by the resident DJ. Ebullient waiting staff break into dance routines at the drop of a baseball cap and fun is the order of the day. Food is heavily burger-led with the usual steaks, ribs, barbecue, salads and sandwiches trailing along behind. The quality is not at all bad and even those who actually had it so good in the fifties can find the enthusiasm infectious. Children adore it and weekends during the day there is a palpable effort to entertain them and feed down to them.

OPEN: Mon-Sun. **HOURS:** 12.00-11.30pm (12.00-11.00pm Sun). **CLOSED:** Christmas Day. **CREDIT CARDS ACCEPTED:** All major cards. **NUMBER OF SEATS:** 160. **SERVICE:** 10% parties of 7 or more. Wheelchair access. **NEAREST TUBE STATION:** Piccadilly Circus. · MAP REF: 12/B4

Royal China Restaurant

13 Queensway, W2

071-221 2535 £27

'An interior in which James Bond would have felt at home'

Royal China in Putney, the original, is popular with Chinese restaurateurs on their days off which says something, perhaps quite a lot. The shiny black and brassy interior may be reminiscent of Hong Kong but the menu also provides allure. There are unusual first courses such as golden scallops, the shellfish sandwiched between slices of cucumber and deep-fried in a feathery batter. If you have a yen for pork scratchings you will like the process applied to shards of duck, listed as spring onion duck. In this atmosphere of conspicuous expenditure, the appropriate behaviour is to demonstrate conspicuous consumption and order lobster or sea bass as a centrepiece to a meal or, to be more authentic, shark's fin or abalone. The management is keen to arrange lavish banquets ordered in advance. There is much else for the less financially ambitious diner including a dish I like of sizzling veal in honey and black bean sauce (good combo). At the similarly decorated Queensway branch, cooking can sometimes be over-oily, a fault that can to some extent be circumnavigated by ordering several steamed dishes from the long menu mined with typos. Two particularly good ones are the first course of chilli dumplings and the main course (listed under chef's specialities) of steamed minced pork with salted egg. Fish and shellfish are well-handled.

Crispy orange duck is tired pieces of meat seemingly bathed in lemon curd; to be avoided. Singapore noodles are notably well-assembled. Waitresses appear to have been trained at the opposite of a charm school. They are too quick to clear plates, too intrusive with wine pouring, too determined to serve you when you would rather help yourself. My tip is to let them screw up e.g. spray you with wine as they open a bottle (as happened) whereupon they feel at a moral disadvantage and become cowed but pleasanter. Dim sum is very popular here.

ALSO AT: 3 Chelverton Road, SW15 (081-780 1520).

OPEN: Mon-Sun. HOURS: 12.00-11.15pm. CLOSED: 23rd-25th December. CREDIT CARDS ACCEPTED: Visa, Access, Mastercard, AmEx, Diner's Club. NUMBER OF SEATS: 100. SERVICE: 12.5%. SET PRICE DINNER: £20-£26. Wheelchair access. Private room seats 10-14. NEAREST TUBE STATION: Queensway/Bayswater.   MAP REF: 11/E

RSJ Restaurant and Brasserie

13a Coin Street, SE1

071-928 4554/9768   **£26**

'Joist the job for lovers of Loire's wine'

The obvious clientele for Nigel Wilkinson's South Bank restaurant are those who work in the area or are going to the theatre, and indeed both groups are well-served. The ground floor dining room gives the sort of comfort those entertaining on expenses believe is their desert and theatregoers, whether sitting here or eating from the simpler menu of the hugger-mugger basement, will be served promptly. But RSJ has another sort of customer who will schlep across town just to admire and sample the wine list which reflects the owner's obsession with Loire wines. Sensibly enough the basement serves a menu of the sort of things most wine bars offer, but with superior freshness and flavour. There is gravad lax, pork and chicken liver pâté, lively soups, bowls of mussels, bangers with bubble and squeak and duck confit all attractively priced. The modern French food in the dining room is good value, and light for all its long lists of ingredients.

ANYBODY WHO WANTS to drink grand, old wine in London for less than £40 should make for RSJ. Yes, I know almost all of it comes from the Loire, but in a way that's the point: red, white, dry, sweet, the Loire has the lot, and its puzzling untrendiness means that Nigel Wilkinson has been able to source at bargain prices. Look: 1961 dry Vouvray Clos de Bourg from Huët, £35.95. Or 1976 red Bourgueil from Domaine de Chesnaies, £39.95. Sweet wines are even finer: 1970 Coteaux du Layon Faye d'Anjou, £28.95; or 1976 Vouvray Clos Naudin £28.75. If you want youth in the glass, the 1989 and 1990 vintages in the Loire were superb; almost all of them are under £20 a bottle. This list is a voyage of exploration which almost anyone can afford to make; there are treasures waiting to be discovered.

OPEN: LUNCH: Mon-Fri. DINNER: Mon-Sat. HOURS: 12.00-2.00pm and 6.00-11.00pm (5.45-11.00pm Sat). CLOSED: Bank Holidays. CREDIT CARDS ACCEPTED: Access, AmEx, Visa. NUMBER OF SEATS: 75. SERVICE: 10%. SET PRICE LUNCH AND DINNER: £13.75 (2 courses) and £15.95 (3 courses). Wheelchair access (but not lavatory). Private room seats 16. NEAREST TUBE STATION: Waterloo. MAP REF: 8/C2

Rules

35 Maiden Lane, WC2

071-836 5314 **£29**

*'Opened by Thomas Rule in the year Napoleon
opened his campaign in Egypt'*

When a place has been in business for 195 years, it can be assumed that something is being done right. In the case of Rules (est. 1798) it is not necessarily the cooking, at least not currently. The picture-hung warren of rooms is a great attraction. The roll call of famous literary and theatrical names associated with the restaurant pulls in the tourists. Businessmen like the meaty menu. Opening hours – from midday to midnight daily – are unusually accommodating. And with your nose pressed to the glass panes of the frontage, Rules can seem very alluring compared to some of the American-inspired, raucous restaurant enterprises nearby. Rules owns an estate in the High Pennines which supplies much of the game – meat, bird and fish – for which the restaurant is known. The Aberdeen Angus beef served is well hung. The roast 24oz ribs of beef with Yorkshire pudding (served for two) is an ideal Sunday lunch but why a gratin of potatoes when roasted would be so much nicer? The way to deal with Rules is to avoid ambitious or fashion-conscious preparation of dishes and go for potted shrimps or smoked salmon followed by classically cooked game or a steak and finish with English cheese. With house wine starting at £7.95 – the house red is Sandeman Claret '88/89 – you need not spend a great deal. Service is a mixture of young and old. All your efforts to bask in the romantic history of the surroundings will be wrecked when the waiter or waitress takes away your laminated menu and punches your order into an electronic pad.

OPEN: Mon-Sun. **HOURS:** 12.00pm-12.00am. **CLOSED:** 5 days at Christmas. **CREDIT CARDS ACCEPTED:** All except Diner's Club. **NUMBER OF SEATS:** 200. **SERVICE:** Optional. **SET PRICE DINNER:** £15 (weekends); £12.75 (weekdays 4.00-6.00pm only). Wheelchair access (but not lavatory). Private rooms seat 18, 30 and 60. **NEAREST TUBE STATION:** Charing Cross/Covent Garden. MAP REF: 12/D3

Sabai Sabai

270/272 King Street, W6

081-748 7363 **£20**

'Fit to be Thai'

Simon Hopkinson (chef of Bibendum), himself no slouch when it comes to turning out an ace tom yum koong, recommended this Hammersmith Thai restaurant to me. Now that Thai restaurants occupy their place in the league of nations that exists on every London high street and the thrill of lemongrass and galangal has, for most of us, worn off, it is important to pick out the places where dishes are carefully, freshly prepared. In this jolly pair of rooms decorated with what look like knick-knacks picked up on trips abroad, the food served is just that. Steamed dim sum and bean curd satay

(from the vegetarian section of the menu) are likeable first courses that have
avoided the deep fryer. Grilled pork spare ribs are unusually well flavoured
and sauced. The sweetness that creeps into some Thai food can be
capitalized upon in the omelette stuffed with minced pork and vegetables
(kahi yad sai) and contrasted with a chilli-hot salad such as pla koong,
featuring prawns. Do not omit ordering the green chicken curry (a particular
Hopkinson favourite). Oddly the dish that everyone always orders in Thai
restaurants, the noodle assembly pad thai, was here stodgy and over-
sugared. Sabai Sabai (the word means relax) as a description of a dessert
means a pancake stuffed with chocolate cream and served with ice cream.

OPEN: LUNCH: Mon-Sat. DINNER: Mon-Sun. **HOURS:** 12.00-2.30pm and 6.00-
11.30pm (6.00-10.30pm Sun). **CLOSED:** Christmas Day and Boxing Day.
CREDIT CARDS ACCEPTED: All major cards except Diner's Club. **NUMBER OF SEATS:** 70.
SERVICE: 10%. **SET PRICE LUNCH:** £6.95. **SET PRICE DINNER:** £15.00. Wheelchair
access (but not lavatory). Private room seats 14. **NEAREST TUBE STATION:**
Ravenscourt Park.   MAP REF: 8/B2

Sabras

263 Willesden High Road, NW10

081-459 0340   **LUNCH £9; DINNER £17**

'Explore the vegetarian subcontinent'

In a review I wrote of Sabras, I said, 'This is a place to take someone who
thinks they know it all where food is concerned, a French person perhaps.'
Certainly many people – and probably 99.5% of the French – are unaware of
the intricacies of Indian vegetarian food and the array of flavours and
textures that can be achieved with a relatively small palette of ingredients.
The Desai's family restaurant started as a take-away and just grew. It has
remained, however, fairly functional in appearance. It is a place to consider
when you simply want the best possible food for your money. Speaking of
which, there is a lunchtime offer at time of writing of 'Eat for £1' for which
you could get puri bhaji-shak, potatoes cooked with traditional Sindhi
spices, peas and tomatoes served with two large puris (deep-fried, puffed
bread). There are other rather more elaborate mini-thalis (set meals) for not
much more. However, it is worth exploring further than that. Bombay street
snacks, such as bhel puri and sev puri, and Gujerati savouries of mostly fried
vegetable and pulse mixtures make ideal starters. Move on to the
dramatically large, thin, crisp rice flour pancakes called dhosas stuffed or
topped with spiced vegetables and served with chutneys. There are also
interesting vegetable curries and seasonal dishes that feature the sort of
vegetables you see in ethnic greengrocers and wonder what you do with
them. The winter assembly (surati undhiu) of mini broad beans, violet yam,
sweet and new potatoes, unripe banana and baby aubergine flavoured with
fenugreek is particularly good. Breads, dals, pickles and raitas further
(deliciously) complicate the impact. For the uninitiated there are organized
meals (thalis) but the friendliness of the owners is such that you need not feel

awkward because you could not describe what is ragada patish. It is a spicy potato cake cooked on a hot plate topped with yellow peas in a mild sauce and garnished with tamarind chutney, onions and lemon juice; wonderful.

OPEN: LUNCH: Tue-Fri. DINNER: Tue-Sun. **HOURS:** 12.30-3.00pm and 6.00-10.00pm. **CREDIT CARDS ACCEPTED:** Visa, Mastercard. **NUMBER OF SEATS:** 32. **SERVICE:** Optional at lunch; 12.5% at dinner. **SET PRICE LUNCH:** £1-£2.95. **SET PRICE DINNER:** £8.50-£11. No smoking area. Wheelchair access (but not lavatory). **NEAREST TUBE STATION:** Dollis Hill/Willesden Green. MAP REF: 8/B2

Saigon

45 Frith Street, W1

071-437 7109/1672 £22

'Veterans of Saigon have tales to tell of the sometimes combative service'

Saigon is an attractive looking – in the evening oil lamps flicker – and gastronomically rewarding place to try out Vietnamese cooking and to compose, if you wish, a complete Vietnamese meal. (Most 'Vietnamese' establishments offer a few specialities plus a long list of Chinese dishes). With lettuce leaves to use as a wrap and raw grated vegetables and fresh herbs to add crunch and flavour, it is easy to convince yourself that what we have here is healthy food. It can be if you avoid too much that is deep-fried. Fried squid cakes accessorized with carrot, chilli and mint, wrapped in lettuce and brushed through a honeyed dipping sauce make a good first course. Another kind of parcel to post yourself is the one made from softened rice flour pancakes wrapped around mint and raw vegetables and strips of beef that you barbecue at the table. Vietnamese duck is bundled up in much the same way. Because it is particular to the cuisine, try minced prawn on peeled sugar cane. Steamed prawns or chilli-spiced crab and one of the cold salads predicated on bean-thread noodles follow on well. Fresh exotic fruit is probably the most appealing dessert. Complaints about Saigon centre on small portions and the female waiting staff who seem to have strayed off the set of *Tenko*.

OPEN: Mon-Sat. **HOURS:** 12.00-11.30pm. **CLOSED:** Bank Holidays. **CREDIT CARDS ACCEPTED:** All major cards. **NUMBER OF SEATS:** 80. **SERVICE:** 10%. **SET PRICE LUNCH AND DINNER:** From £14.40. Private room seats 40. **NEAREST TUBE STATION:** Piccadilly Circus/ Tottenham Court Road/Leicester Square. MAP REF: 12/C2

St Quentin

243 Brompton Road, SW3

071-589 8005   **£30**

'Leave the cares of South Kensington behind'

The restaurant St Quentin (named after Quentin Crewe, the chap who made restaurant criticism a branch of modern journalism) has kept faith with its predecessor, the Brompton Grill. It is an old-fashioned, proper place, a little piece of France transported complete with starched linen and gliding, white-aproned courteous waiters. French exiles come here for refuge from the absurdities of English eclecticism, culinary or otherwise. Specialités St Quentin, the delicatessen a few doors west, supplies the excellent bread. Chef Richard Sawyer trained with Michel Bourdin at the Connaught and vestiges of the grand hotel style sometimes surface, as in a chartreuse of game. The same thorough grounding is evident in the first course of terrine maison, the feuilleté of scallops and quenelles of pike with beurre blanc. The warm goat's cheese salad, the restaurant claims, with a peculiarly shy sort of pride, is the first instance of this dish in London. It seems to me the sort of claim no one would be bothered to challenge. The plainer main courses are consistently successful; grilled fish, roast rack of lamb, foie de veau Lyonnaise and a châteaubriand for two. It is to be hoped they bring back the roast poulet de Bresse for two, one of the nicest things to share in London. Leave space for the patisserie – particularly the tarte au citron – and the cheeses imported from Hennard in Lille. Don't visit St Quentin with secrets to impart. Tables are packed close together and, also, I get the feeling that supporters of ASH are not the backbone of the clientele.

OPEN: Mon-Sun. **HOURS:** 12.00-3.00pm (12.00-3.30pm Sun) and 7.00-11.30pm (6.30-11.00pm Sun). **CREDIT CARDS ACCEPTED:** All major cards. **NUMBER OF SEATS:** 74. **SERVICE:** 12%. **SET PRICE LUNCH:** £13.50. **SET PRICE DINNER:** £15.25. Wheelchair access (but not lavatory). Private room seats 25. **NEAREST TUBE STATION:** South Kensington.   MAP REF: 14/B2

Salloos

62-64 Kinnerton Street, SW1

071-235 4444   **£35**

'For dedicated (and rich) connoisseurs of Indian food'

Where you might least expect it – in a Knightsbridge mews house – here is a restaurant for serious lovers of Indian food or lovers of serious Indian, more precisely Pakistani, food. High prices, which are at least justified by the quality of the ingredients used and the laboriousness of preparation applied, must be swallowed as must service which can range from fawning to surly with not a great deal in between, save when the owner's sweet daughter is on hand. However, dishes such as tandoori lamb chops, chicken karahi and jheenga masala (curried prawns), cooked only after the order is taken – as is the case with many of the items – will make you forget thoughts of the bank balance and probably of ever going anywhere else for Indian food. Sadly Salloos have stopped capitalizing on offal but have retained another 'oddity', haleem akbari, a dish of the Moghul emperors where shredded lamb is cooked with whole wheat berries, lentils and spices. The side dish of chillis, fresh herbs and spices can be used here to good effect. Breads are state-of-the-art and the biryani and pulao lessons in how those rice assemblies should be prepared. Apart from some Italian bottles, the wine list compiled by Corney & Barrow – ignoring what the New World can offer in these spicy circumstances – is wholly French and marked up with the same gay abandon that can price chicken tikka at £9.50, impose a cover charge of £1.50 per person and add on 15% service charge.

OPEN: Mon-Sat. **HOURS:** 12.00-2.30pm and 7.00-11.15pm. **CLOSED:** Bank Holidays. **CREDIT CARDS ACCEPTED:** Visa, Access, AmEx, Diner's Club. **NUMBER OF SEATS:** 60. **SERVICE:** 15%, £1.50 cover charge. **SET PRICE LUNCH:** £16. **SET PRICE DINNER:** £25. **NEAREST TUBE STATION:** Knightsbridge/Hyde Park Corner.

MAP REF: 14/D1

Les Saveurs

37a Curzon Street, W1

071-491 8919   **LUNCH £31; DINNER £40**

*'Joel Antunès is a chef's name that should
be tripping off tongues'*

This Japanese-owned establishment in Curzon Street, formerly the Tandoori of Mayfair, has not had the attention and following I believe its chef Joel Antunès should command, presumably because of the prices and to some extent the bland formality of the decor in the basement dining room. Go to Les Saveurs at lunchtime when there is more of a buzz doubtless linked to the £18 three course daily-changing menu with a choice of four dishes in each course. It is one of the bargains of London, not least because it comes topped and tailed with two waves of amuse-gueules, delicious petits fours, good bread, and fine Echire butter.

Antunès, who has done his time in Michelin-starred France but also at The Oriental Hotel in Bangkok, has an idiosyncratic approach. From various dishes recently tried this is best exemplified by chestnut soup flavoured with truffle oil. As you might imagine the creamy nuttiness of chestnuts lends itself exceedingly well to soup, especially when slicked with some truffle oil which was not backward in coming forward with its singular flavour. Floating on the broth was foam looking either like the stuff you should skim off stock or the water downriver from a petrochemical plant but it tasted delicate and added a clever other texture. Terrine of duck encasing foie gras of duck was just unabashedly rich and good. One of the little bites before the meal was an over-salted tartare of smoked salmon surrounded by a thin ribbon of sauce. Much more subtle was the main course salmon smoked à la minute served on a mess of stewed leeks and some sliced fried potatoes. It was, however, a case of a dish where the absence of one of the ingredients – the potatoes – would have made it even better. Fillets of red mullet were served placed on a mixture of diced vegetables and short threads of vermicelli swimming in a spiced oil. Even more emphatic spicing would not have gone amiss with me but I can imagine others – Michelin inspectors for example – liking the reticence.

Being urged by a waiter to order dessert when you first order removes that later struggle with your diet conscience. Feeling no responsibility for, or relationship with, the calories in, say, lime soufflé with acacia honey or gratin of apples with cinnamon and calvados they can just be enjoyed. Wine prices on the studiously French list are high but the lunch menu makes some reasonable suggestions at £15 and under including a Chateau Le Raz Bergerac white or red at £13.50. In this way the lunch 'bargain' can be kept intact. Service is assiduous and not at all snooty. If money is no object, obviously dinner, or lunch à la carte, is equally desirable, if not more so.

OPEN: Mon-Fri. **HOURS:** 12.00-2.30pm and 7.00-10.30pm. **CLOSED:** 2 weeks at Christmas, New Year and 2 weeks in August. **CREDIT CARDS ACCEPTED:** Visa, Access, AmEx, Mastercard, Diner's Club. **NUMBER OF SEATS:** 55. **SET PRICE LUNCH:** £18. **SET PRICE DINNER:** £29. Private room seats 10. **NEAREST TUBE STATION:** Green Park/Hyde Park Corner. MAP REF: 12/A4

The Savoy Grill

Strand, WC2

071-836 4343   **£50**

*'Where the great, and not so great, and the good,
and not so good, chew things over'*

It is not easy for the average punter to secure a table for lunch at The Savoy Grill. Even in these recessionary times – I feel I can write that with confidence months before publication – the room is booked out by the rich and powerful. The Grill is run with an understanding of what those folk like and want. I would imagine that along with deferential, efficient service, a good deal of the time it is the plats du jour – Monday: sausage, creamed potatoes and onions, Tuesday: steak and kidney pudding, Wednesday: boiled bacon and pease pudding, Thursday: Lancashire hot pot and so on, with roast saddle of lamb on the trolley every day. The right hand side of the menu demonstrates how chef David Sharland has understood how food has moved on since the day of Escoffier. There are plenty of light dishes, some unexpectedly simple, viz. salad of tomato and feta cheese, and a few offerings for vegetarians including an enterprising chartreuse of pumpkin served on a purée of cucumber with an Amaretto butter. You can eat extremely well and comfortably here but it helps if money is no object. Adding new potatoes and beans to your choice of main course, a modest enough desire, will add £7.25 to the bill. An admirable effort is made to promote British cheeses. The wine list covers most bases with plenty of classic bottles should you want to push this particular boat – ably steered by maître d'hotel Angelo Maresca – out.

OPEN: LUNCH: Mon-Fri. DINNER: Mon-Sat. **HOURS:** 12.30-2.30pm and 6.00-11.15pm. **CLOSED:** August. **CREDIT CARDS ACCEPTED:** Access, Amex, Visa, Diner's Club. **NUMBER OF SEATS:** 100. **SERVICE:** Optional. Wheelchair access (but not lavatory). **NEAREST TUBE STATION:** Charing Cross. MAP REF: 12/D3

Scalini

1-3 Walton Street, SW3

071-225 2301/2 or 071-823 8436 £32

'What label matters quite as much as which table'

Scalini is out of Signor Sassi by, who knows?, perhaps Sandrini, Santini, Salotto or Sale e Pepe. The Italian restaurants of South Kensington and Belgravia have an interchangeable quality about their food, atmosphere and unctuous staff that I find distinctly unseductive. For reasons that may be connected with its lineage, Scalini attracts a particularly fashion-conscious crowd. Their necessary devotion to diet cola and mineral water appears to be reflected in the food prices; on the high side even within this essentially over-priced genre. The simple dishes tend to be the best and the veal chop the best of those. The point of Scalini is checking out current alliances wearing your Alaia. The statutory tile floor contributes to noise or what they might prefer to be termed buzz.

OPEN: Mon-Sun. **HOURS:** 12.00-3.00pm and 7.00-11.45pm. **CREDIT CARDS ACCEPTED:** All major cards. **NUMBER OF SEATS:** 100. **SERVICE:** Optional. **NEAREST TUBE STATION:** Knightsbridge/South Kensington. MAP REF: 14/C2

Seafresh

80-82 Wilton Road, SW11

071-828 0747 £8

'A far, far batter thing'

Authorities as reliable as London cab drivers and Mr Keith Waterhouse speak highly of the Seafresh. The grottiness of the street outside and the netted nautical decor within are further recommendations. And the fish, when it finally arrives piping hot out of the fryer, is confirmation: fresh and flaky and sealed in very good batter. Haddock and cod hang off the large, oval plates they are served on. Someone takes the trouble to buy well-flavoured potatoes that are hacked into big, uneven, appealing chips with some of those best little bits of spud shrapnel, too. Mushy peas and baked beans may go with, and there is a longer menu than can be found in most fish and chippies with main course salads, chicken, smoked salmon or Spam fritters plus a selection of puddings that are really too modern and dessert-like to be approved by the purist. Seafresh is a large place that serves the interesting, shifting crowd of the hinterland of Victoria Station which includes Pimlico locals, commuters, cabbies and a fair number of tourists. The staff are full of fun but competent, a combination almost as enjoyable as fish with chips.

OPEN: Mon-Sat. **HOURS:** 12.00pm-11.45pm. **CLOSED:** 24th December to 3rd January. **CREDIT CARDS ACCEPTED:** Visa, Mastercard. **NUMBER OF SEATS:** 100. **SERVICE:** Optional. **SET PRICE LUNCH:** £5.95 (3 courses). Private room seats 40. **NEAREST TUBE STATION:** Victoria. MAP REF: 8/B2

Seashell

49-51 Lisson Grove, NW1

071-723 8703   **£15**

*'Olde London Town's famous fish and
chip destination'*

Perhaps it is mixing metaphors too much to say that the Seashell rests on its
laurels, but this famous fish and chip restaurant does seem to have settled on
to some sandy support for self-satisfaction and is in danger of being famous
for being famous. The two-storey premises are smart and capacious and the
tourists still crowd in but the fish and chips, and sometimes even the service,
can be frazzled. Perfectly good ingredients seem over-cooked and those
arriving towards the (early) end of lunch and dinner sessions may form the
impression that they were a nuisance. The set lunch of soup, fish of the day
and chips, pudding and coffee is good value.

OPEN: Mon-Sat. **HOURS:** 12.00-2.00pm and 5.15-10.30pm (12.00-10.30pm
Sat). **CREDIT CARDS ACCEPTED:** All major cards. **NUMBER OF SEATS:** 200. **SET PRICE
LUNCH:** £8.95. No smoking area. Wheelchair access (but not lavatory). **NEAREST
TUBE STATION:** Marylebone.   MAP REF: 11/D

La Semillante

5 Mill Street, W1

071-499 2121   **£40**

*'Fashion-plate food that sometimes loses
its accessories'*

La Semillante opened in a year (1992) that also saw the start of Pied-à-Terre,
The Fifth Floor Restaurant, Ransome's Dock, The French House Dining
Room, The Canteen, The Argyll, Downstairs at One-Ninety, and The
Lexington; all showcases for young or youngish talent many of whom had
worked in the famous classic kitchens. Patrick Woodside, chef/co-
proprietor of La Semillante – the name means a libertine – has worked at
Cavaliers (now closed), La Tante Claire, Claridges, and perhaps most
formatively in the pastry section of Marco Pierre White's Harveys. The
restaurant, formerly the Indian restaurant Shikara and converted in terms of
decor only up to a point, got off to a popular and well-reviewed start in part
because of an obvious effort to contain prices while providing all the bonnes
bouches and petits fours of expensive dining. The energy seems to be
wavering as indicated by a menu offered in early summer featuring
woodcock, pheasant and hare. It was no surprise to be told they were not
available but restaurants should not attempt to be a sequel to *The Discreet
Charm of the Bourgeoisie*. Sometimes precise cooking, as of scallops, can be
muffled by their elaborate, fanciful garnishes of red and purple purées,
lavender flowers and a tangle of deep-fried vegetable raffia. Dishes can
appear without their listed accoutrements as did an assembly of quail and
spinach that arrived innocent of the advertised langoustines and noodles. It

did retain its £3 supplement. On the same evening the wine list (singular) was unavailable for the entrance floor bar – where you are encouraged to sit to order and which is the only place where smoking is allowed – as it was being used downstairs. Other dishes have been more successful, or to put it another way, complete. Fillet of beef poached in a chicken and veal consommé served with red onions and daintily turned vegetables is a case in point. Woodside's tendency to value style over content has happier results in the dessert course where this attitude can be used to positive effect as it is in soufflé of crystallized ginger with slices of caramelized William pear. There is a – presumably deliberately – louche quality about La Semillante that I like, but a definition of that word should not be chaos. Lunch, when the menu is cheaper, is perhaps the time to put your toe in the water here. The price of wines does not ruin the intent of a fairly priced meal.

OPEN: LUNCH: Mon-Fri. DINNER: Mon-Sat. **HOURS:** 12.00-3.00pm and 7.00pm-12.00am. **CREDIT CARDS ACCEPTED:** Visa, Diner's Club, AmEx. **NUMBER OF SEATS:** 38. **SERVICE:** Optional. **SET PRICE LUNCH:** £16. **SET PRICE DINNER:** £28. Wheelchair access. Private room seats 16. **NEAREST TUBE STATION:** Oxford Circus.   MAP REF: 12/B3

Simpson's-in-the-Strand

100 Strand, WC2

071-836 9112   **£29**

'The joint is passed round'

Simpson's-in-the-Strand need no longer be left to tourists and unreconstructed carnivores. The Savoy Group (the owners) have recently pulled their socks up with regards to this historic tavern, sensitively redecorated the impressive rooms, sorted out some archaic kitchen practices, and even gone so far as to provide a fish menu which also includes a list of vegetarian dishes. I can see the marketing rationale of the last but it would seem to me a great pity not to enjoy roast meat at Simpson's, consuming your share of the average daily consumption of twenty-five loins of beef, twenty-three saddles of lamb and thirty-six ducklings. It is when roasts are well-sourced and of a substantial size that they are at their best and the joints on the trolley at Simpson's far outweigh the offerings of any carvery. Vegetables are these days prepared in the modern manner. I have had some cabbage that was boiled almost treasonably briefly. Start with quails' eggs with haddock and cheese sauce and finish with Simpson's treacle roll or a savoury. You can feel proud of traditional English food.

OPEN: Mon-Sun. **HOURS:** 12.00-2.30pm and 6.00-11.00pm (6.00-9.00pm Sun). **CLOSED:** Good Friday, Christmas Day and Boxing Day. **CREDIT CARDS ACCEPTED:** All major cards. **NUMBER OF SEATS:** 450. **SERVICE:** Optional. **SET PRICE LUNCH AND DINNER:** £10 (dinner: early evening only). Wheelchair access. Private rooms seat 50 and 150. **NEAREST TUBE STATION:** Charing Cross.   MAP REF: 12/D3

Singapore Garden Restaurant

83 Fairfax Road, NW6

071-328 5314 £22-£30

*'Malay food favoured by those who recognize
the real thing'*

This family-run establishment in a rather drab little shopping parade in
Swiss Cottage has a loyal following in North London and also among those
homesick for authentically prepared, uncompromisingly spiced Singaporean
and Malyasian food. Unusually for this style of restaurant cuisine, there are
hand-written specials attached to the long printed list of over ninety items
which itself features a section of specialities that stand out from the more
generalized Chinese background. Lobster, soft-shell crab, fresh fish, braised
duck and spicy okra are specials worth pursuing but the dish not to be
missed is chilli crab, the whole creature doused in a scarlet sweet/searing
sauce. I have heard that the Singapore ambassador comes precisely for that.
Wines are mainly unexciting French choices plus four offerings from the
New World. Beers are Singapore Tiger, Becks and Sol.

OPEN: Mon-Sun. **HOURS:** 12.00-2.45pm and 6.00-10.45pm (6.00-11.15 Fri-Sat).
CLOSED: 1 week after Christmas. **CREDIT CARDS ACCEPTED:** AmEx, Diner's Club, Visa.
NUMBER OF SEATS: 100. **SERVICE:** 12.5%.**SET PRICE DINNER:** £14.85. 3 tables outside.
Private room seats 60. **NEAREST TUBE STATION:** Swiss Cottage.   MAP REF: 10/B

Smith's Restaurant

25 Neal Street, WC2

071-379 0310 £30

*'Crypt-like restaurant in the centre
of Covent Garden'*

Smith's is one of London's better-looking basement restaurants, a vaulted,
long room with whitewashed walls hung with modern paintings sent down
from the gallery above. The gallery and the restaurant, and the flowershop
over the way and the teashop around the corner, are all part of Christina
Smith's Covent Garden empire, acquired just before everyone else cottoned
on to the area's potential. The restaurant of that ilk is often labelled British,
which did not seem justified on the evidence of a last visit when the menu
was mostly Cal-Ital: a salad of ornamental cabbage with Pecorino and herbs
which was delicate and had no resemblance to the pinky-blue rose cabbage
which the description called to mind; seared tuna with a salad Niçoise;
salmon with noodles. Perhaps the avocado and prawn duo has become pretty
British, but this is a chopped-up version made from perfect ingredients and
free of the taint of sauce 'Marie Rose'. There can be no argument about the
provenance of a good summer pudding. This has proved an inconsistent
kitchen in the past, but now there is evidence of good taste and proficiency,

plus nice big portions. Difficult to believe that the same kitchen would not send out one large green salad, and remiss of the waiter who reported this to bustle us into ordering two without pointing out that one dish was going to come with a generous salad of its own – he had seen it before, we had not. There was rather too much hard-selling going on.

OPEN: Mon-Sat. **HOURS:** 12.00pm-12.00am. **CLOSED:** Bank Holidays. **CREDIT CARDS ACCEPTED:** All major cards. **NUMBER OF SEATS:** 120. **SERVICE:** 12.5%. **SET PRICE DINNER:** £10.75. No smoking area. Private room seats 40. **NEAREST TUBE STATION:** Covent Garden. MAP REF: 12/D2

Smokey Joe's Diner

131 Wandsworth High Street, SW18

081-871 1785 **£8 (Bring your own wine)**

'No frills, plenty of trills!'

The eponymous Joe, who seems actually to be called Charlie Phillips, came with his parents from Jamaica to London in the early fifties. A decade later they opened the first Caribbean eating place in London in Portobello Road. At his own Wandsworth Diner, in operation now for about five years, customers, says Joe/Charlie, are treated 'like they were in my living room'. One of the aspects of this is much inter-action between chef and punters. It is not a place for the reticent. Having secured a seat in the small premises that also serve as a busy take-away, you order by writing your choice on a pad, the system once used in the dining cars of American railways. You are urged to consider the blackboard daily specials – calalloo and saltfish, red beans, stew rice and salad, ackee and saltfish, jerk chicken, various curries with roti, braised oxtail – and order at least two courses. You might start with peppered prawns, barbecue ribs or charcoal-broiled corn (sometimes over-cooked). Desserts are of the ice cream and cake variety. What Joe produces is slightly hit and miss, but he is a natural cook and the result feels more genuinely Caribbean and full of soul than you find elsewhere. Take your own wine (no corkage) or content yourself with punch or pop, but be prepared to party.

OPEN: Mon-Sun. **HOURS:** 12.00-3.00pm and 6.00-11.00pm (12.00-11.00pm Sat; 3.30-10.00pm Sun). **CLOSED:** Bank Holidays and Christmas. **CREDIT CARDS ACCEPTED:** None. **NUMBER OF SEATS:** 15. **SERVICE:** Optional; cover charge to eat in. **NEAREST BR STATION:** Wandsworth Town. MAP REF: 8/B3

Snows on the Green

166 Shepherd's Bush Road, W6

071-603 2142 £24

'Worth drifting into'

A wintery – but explicable – name for a restaurant that has walls painted terracotta and hung with photographs of Provence. The owners, (chef) Sebastian and (manager) Melissa Snow, succeed in bringing sunlight to dingy Shepherd's Bush Road. With the exception of the super richness of foie gras and fried egg (the pan juices mixed with balsamic vinegar), an eccentric combination often on the menu, most of the inspiration is southerly. Pistou, pasta, aubergines, mozzarella, anchovies, gremolada and garlic are all key ingredients and garnishes on a constantly permutating menu. Making reference to Snow's stint at Bistrot 190 (q.v.) working alongside Antony Worrall Thompson, some dishes, particularly the stuffed pastas, layered vegetable terrines and feuilletés, suffer from an embarrassment of riches clamouring for attention from your palate. The composed salads – say chicken wings with rocket – and the robust casseroles, such as knuckle of lamb served with cabbage and mash or bacon on the bone with haricot beans cooked with herbs and tomatoes, is the more orthodox avenue down which to go, and the most orthodox of all is the well-executed steak frites. Dessert tends to centre on tarts. Lemon is excellent, as is bitter chocolate. The wine list has been skilfully compiled to give variety and value at prices that make sense given the aims and ambitions of this gentle establishment. Set lunches are a bargain. Snows on the Green won the 1993 Wine Magazine/Muscadet Most Sympathique Restaurant Award, which was judged by people who know what they are talking about.

OPEN: LUNCH: Sun-Fri. DINNER: Mon-Sat. **HOURS:** 12.00-3.00pm and 7.00-11.00pm. **CLOSED:** Bank Holidays, 2 weeks in August and 2 weeks after Christmas. **CREDIT CARDS ACCEPTED:** Visa, Access, Switch. **NUMBER OF SEATS:** 65. **SERVICE:** Optional. **SET PRICE LUNCH:** £10.50-£12.50 (£12.50-£15.50 Sundays). Wheelchair access (but not lavatory). Private room seats 22. **NEAREST TUBE STATION:** Hammersmith. MAP REF: 8/B2

Sofra Restaurant

18 Shepherd Street, W1

071-493 3320 £19

'Healthy Turkish food in Shepherd Market'

I have met the owner of this Turkish restaurant. He is a keen proponent of healthy eating. This becomes immediately apparent in the set price menus which are entitled Healthy Lunch and Healthy Dinner. Middle Eastern is, of course, fundamentally a healthy cuisine with many of the dishes, particularly in the first course, based on pulses, grains, nuts, vegetables, herbs, garlic, lemon juice and olive oil; the very ingredients and the fibre we are counselled to ingest. The standard of preparation at Sofra is high. I can recommend a particularly fine humuz (their spelling), tabbouleh heavy on parsley and sparse with crushed wheat and kisir, dolma lacking the school mackintosh quality they so often reveal, zeytin yagli bakla, broad beans cooked in olive oil and dill served with yogurt, garlic and coriander, falafel, minced meat mixed with cracked wheat and spices. Sofra also offers my favourite Turkish snack, lahmacun, pitta spread with minced lamb mixed with onions, tomatoes, peppers and pine kernels and grilled.

After such an array, best is steamed fish or simply grilled meat, such as chicken tenderized in milk or fillet of lamb or, if your appetite can handle it, a slow-cooked dish such as incik, a knuckle of lamb braised on the bone. There are some junkety confections that are said to be a more authentic dessert than syrup-soaked pastries but I nevertheless prefer the latter. Service is usually polite but has been known to exhibit grumpiness. Note that there is a cover charge (£1.50) but note also the accommodating hours; daily midday to midnight.

OPEN: Mon-Sun. **HOURS:** 12.00pm-12.00am. **CREDIT CARDS ACCEPTED:** All major cards. **NUMBER OF SEATS:** 66. **SERVICE:** 12.5%, £1.50 cover charge. **SET PRICE LUNCH:** £8.45. **SET PRICE DINNER:** £9.95. Wheelchair access (but not lavatory). 6 tables outside. **NEAREST TUBE STATION:** Green Park/Hyde Park Corner.   MAP REF: 12/A4

Soho Soho Restaurant & Rotisserie

11-13 Frith Street, W1

071-494 3491   **RESTAURANT £30; ROTISSERIE £17**

'So good they named it twice? Not necessarily'

Soho Soho is a split level operation by Groupe Chez Gerard Ltd that occupies a modern revamp of a Soho corner site. Downstairs is a big, brash no-booking rotisserie and cafe-bar much utilized from breakfast time onwards with tables spilling onto the pavement in summer months. In the rotisserie, pastas, omelettes (nicely baveuse), composed salads and various grills are competently done plus there are a couple of casseroles, one vegetarian, one based on shin of lamb. In the more expensive, more spacious upstairs restaurant with its mannered decor and child of Cocteau murals, a menu is offered that you could, if you wanted to, classify as modern Niçoise. It is Mediterranean with specific references to Italy and the South of France. If you believe in the healthy properties of olive oil and, indeed, balsamic vinegar, you will thrive here. Typical dishes are tagliolini mixed with herbs, shredded Treviso, spinach and roasted pine nuts; a roll of radicchio and Bayonne ham grilled and dressed with vinaigrette; reverie du Sud, a frittata of artichokes, sun-dried tomatoes and shiitaki mushrooms; estocaficada, a fish stew that includes cod stock; magret de canard aux fruits du soleil (mango and lime).

Standards of cooking have been extraordinarily variable (although at the time of writing there is news of a change of chef). A possible explanation for this is perhaps a certain amount of central buying and preparation foisted on the kitchen by the ownership. However, some of the scope for mistakes – in the long-cooked dishes – seems to have been removed. Vichyssoise, rarely really well-made or cold enough in the cold version, is both those things. A fillet of daurade is nicely charred in the grilling and served with a smoked tomato purée. Both these benefited from simplicity. Some dishes suffer from too many elements vying with each other. The most interesting of the desserts – a fairly standard list – is compote de fruits d'hiver tiède served warm with caramelized biscuits. French cheeses are well-chosen. The wine list features French country wines and is divided by the Rhône into areas east and west of that river. A cover charge of £1.50 in the restaurant delivers salted almonds, marinated olives and home-made bread.

RESTAURANT: OPEN: LUNCH: Mon-Fri. DINNER: Mon-Sat. **HOURS:** 12.30-3.00pm and 6.00pm-1.00am. **CLOSED:** Bank Holidays. **NUMBER OF SEATS:** 65. Private room seats 60. **ROTISSERIE: OPEN:** Mon-Sun. **HOURS:** 8.00am-2.00am (11.00am-11.00pm Sun). **CLOSED:** Boxing Day, 27th December and New Year's Day. **NUMBER OF SEATS:** 60. Wheelchair access (but not lavatory). 5 tables outside. **CREDIT CARDS ACCEPTED:** Access, AmEx, Diner's Card, Mastercard, Visa. **SERVICE:** 12.5%, £1.50 cover charge in restaurant. No smoking area. **NEAREST TUBE STATION:** Tottenham Court Road/Leicester Square.   MAP REF: 12/C2

Le Soufflé

Inter-Continental Hotel,
1 Hamilton Place, W1

071-409 3131   **£40**

'Haute hotel dining'

As far as I am concerned the food has to be phenomenally good to persuade me that eating in a luxury modern hotel with the attendant high prices and inflated wine cost, the usually rather dull business-oriented clientele and the risk of a cocktail pianist playing Lloyd Webber's greatest hits, is a better idea than going to an independent restaurant. Peter Kromberg, at the Inter-Continental, a skilled and intelligent head chef, also has to contend with a windowless dining room, pleasantly but vapidly decorated. However, his menu is impressive and has much besides the eponymous soufflés, a theme, a name and a reliance on a cooking method which now could well be allowed to fade and a better name dreamt up.

Kromberg's touch is light and the combinations assured. Typical dishes from the main menu might include bouillabaisse du Nord en salade; home made pâté of foie gras with a Sauternes jelly set around diced vegetables; minestrone de homard et caviar, accompagné de ses minis pizzas; petite grillade de loup de mer et rouget à l'encre de calamar; tian de veau aux pâtes fraîches et aux capres; soufflé aux noisettes croquant et praline. There is an additional menu entitled Cuisine de Vie prepared with an eye to wholesome ingredients and healthy cooking methods and with less reliance on the trappings of culinary luxury such as foie gras and lobster. A set price lunch at £25.50 or the seven course Choix de Chef at £43 would be the canny way to try Kromberg's cooking but with wine, you would still need a flexible friend as company. Staff at Le Soufflé are notably agreeable and anxious that you should have a good time. This applies even to women eating together.

A SOUND, WELL-BALANCED wine list, better for Bordeaux (including fine old bottles back to 1916) than for Burgundy. There's little truly inventive buying, though, and large producers like Mondavi, Torres and Brown Brothers supply much outside the classic areas. Is there really a demand for Piesporter Michelsberg and Mateus Rosé in restaurants of this calibre?

OPEN: LUNCH: Tues-Fri, Sun. DINNER: Tues-Sun. **HOURS:** 12.30-2.45pm (12.00-4.00pm Sun) and 7.00-10.30pm (7.00-11.15pm Sat). **CLOSED:** August. **CREDIT CARDS ACCEPTED:** All major cards. **NUMBER OF SEATS:** 75. **SERVICE:** Optional. **SET PRICE LUNCH:** £25.50. **SET PRICE DINNER:** £43. No smoking area. Wheelchair access. **NEAREST TUBE STATION:** Hyde Park Corner.   MAP REF: 12/A4

The Square

32 King Street, SW1

071-839 8787   **£35**

'Neither dull, nor masonic; an elegant modern restaurant'

The design of The Square by David Collins Associates (q.v. The Canteen and La Tante Claire) with its use of gilt and strong jewel-like colours manages to be both brash and luxurious. The food of chef Philip Howard (who has worked with the Roux brothers, Marco Pierre White and Simon Hopkinson) is a matching exercise in clarity and dash. He has a modern, focused style centred on his main ingredient which comes surrounded by well-judged but subsidiary elements. Terse menu descriptions turn out to be beautifully presented dishes that, more to the point, are vibrantly flavoured. Fish and shellfish, impeccably fresh, might be presented as a 'soup' (Howard has fun in various ways with the basic concept of soup) of several species heaped up and surrounded by a creamy anise sauce or with Thai spices. Red mullet with its skin made crisp is a favourite starting point. Roasted meat comes with suitably simple support which might include artichoke purée or wonderful, properly prepared mash. Howard seems to have less success than some of his peers with the challenge of domesticating offal. A sausage of oxtail and pigs' trotter was a lacklustre affair but I suspect the clientele does not encourage his experimentation. Sometimes the likeability of fried ingredients is too heavily relied upon, particularly in the composed salads. Desserts are ace. His caramel crackling seems to be about as good as a dessert can get. And for those whose sweet tooth quivers for chocolate rather than caramel, there is a plate that will satisfy. The Square has made a success of a site that seemed doomed. Its location in St. James's attracts a chic crowd, especially at lunchtime, who value artistry – they seem to have rejected the idea of The Square Meal based on grilled fish or meat. Wear a drop dead jacket and drop some names but regardless of turnout, the warmth of welcome seems unpredictable and there have been complaints of less than delightful service. There is a good wine list.

OPEN: LUNCH: Sun-Fri. DINNER: Mon-Sun. **HOURS:** 12.00-3.00pm and 6.00-11.45pm (10.00pm Sun). **CREDIT CARDS ACCEPTED:** All major cards. **NUMBER OF SEATS:** 65. **SERVICE:** Optional. Wheelchair access. Private room seats 25. **NEAREST TUBE STATION:** Piccadilly Circus/Green Park.   MAP REF: 12/B4

Standard Indian Restaurant

21-23 Westbourne Grove, W2

071-229 0600 £15

'What "going out for an Indian" ought to be like'

The menu in this long-established, perennially popular Indian restaurant holds out no promises in the way of regional specialities or the chef's inspirations. It is, as the name conveys, a standard list. However, the dishes are notably well-prepared and attractively priced and despite considerable competition building up in the area since its inception, you often have to queue for a table at the Standard. Dishes I have enjoyed include dal gosht, mutton mughlai, butter chicken, Jaipuri chicken, mutter paneer (a notable example of cheese and peas), and the kulcha (bread) stuffed with spiced egg and onions. The dish you should not omit to order is chana masladar, the chick-peas almost gritty with spices. Service has counted them in and counted them out for many a long year.

OPEN: Mon-Sun. **HOURS:** 12.00-3.00pm and 6.00pm-12.00am. **CLOSED:** Christmas Day. **CREDIT CARDS ACCEPTED:** All major cards except Diner's Club. **NUMBER OF SEATS:** 130. **SERVICE:** Optional. **SET PRICE LUNCH:** £7.55. No smoking area. Wheelchair access (but not lavatory). Private room seats 50. **NEAREST TUBE STATION:** Bayswater/Queensway. MAP REF: 11/E

Star of India

154 Old Brompton Road, SW5

071-373 2901 £20

'A visitor from some mysterious constellation'

Whether or not the Star of India ever really did have flocked wallpaper and play taped sitar music, its transformation over the years into a baroque fantasy is the stuff of local legend. At one stage it went designer grey, and now there are wonderful trompe l'oeil classical scenes on the walls and very proper service and table settings, though still with the flamboyant, entertaining Reza who is part of the proprietorial family doing the greeting and managing. Though not quite such a challenge to received ideas as the decor, the cooking here has always been good and capable of highlighting certain spices rather than producing a stereotypical curry. Cumin chicken and lamb with fenugreek are examples that appeal, plus a lamb tikka with an unusual marinade including coconut, ginger and poppy seeds, a small vegetable dish of sweet courgettes with coriander leaf and ginger; superior fancified rice pungent with cardamom; and, to end on, spiced Indian tea. Prosperity has brought delicate, home-made chutneys to begin the meal with, a long list of snack food starters (pakoras and samosas), breads and vegetable dishes, the use of very lean meat and a minimum of cooking fat. Eating at the Star of India is not cheap, but it is certainly not bad value either, and this restaurant has a character and verve that more self-consciously innovative or luxurious Indian specialists lack. And a huge selection of tapes of music from sixties thriller movies.

OPEN: Mon-Sun. **HOURS:** 12.00-3.00pm and 6.00pm-12.00am (7.00-11.30pm Sun). **CREDIT CARDS ACCEPTED:** All major cards. **NUMBER OF SEATS:** 95. **SERVICE:** Optional. Wheelchair access (but not lavatory). Private room seats 12. **NEAREST TUBE STATION:** Gloucester Road.   MAP REF: 14/A3

Stephen Bull

5-7 Blandford Street, W1

071-486 9696   £32

'The upmarket face of good value'

Stephen Bull, former advertising executive who many years ago saw the pilot light, believes that eating out should not be surrounded by fuss and fashion and fiddle-de-dee. That conviction comes through loud and clear in the minimalist decor of his Marylebone restaurant. The walls are a hesitant shade of white, apparently achieved by mixing wax with plaster, although coats of paint seem to have gone on since the early days. Decoration is mainly through a clever use of lighting and the reflections from mirrors. Nowadays Bull is most often to be found cooking at his Bistro and Bar (q.v.) but his style is well-interpreted by chef Jon Bentham. Dishes are thought right through and consequently come fully garnished, a detail along with a general fair-minded approach to pricing, that qualifies Stephen Bull for the description good value. The cooking shows no traces of the legacy of nouvelle cuisine nor any involvement with the notion of art on a plate. It is forthright in conception and emphatic in its flavours.

There is insouciant borrowing from other cuisines, as for example in a first course of crab and black bean wontons in a sauce fortified with sherry and coriander and there is a healthy preoccupation with pulses, root vegetables and grains. Certain favoured dishes – e.g. twice-cooked goat's cheese soufflé – have become fixtures on the daily changing menus. There is an agreeable lack of snobbishness as regards the staple ingredient of a dish. A lunch menu might feature neck of lamb with fresh pasta, white beans and pesto or grilled breast of veal with a porcini risotto. A more pretentious restaurant might have chosen a more expensive (but duller) cut of veal. A dinner menu might upgrade a cliché of a dish, usually elsewhere sloppily made, such as huevas rancheros, poached eggs with tomato and chilli sauce, served here with an avocado and sweetcorn salsa. Not every idea or garnish comes off wholly successfully, but that is the penalty of pace and invention as opposed to honing and perfecting fixed specialities. Desserts seem always to please; there is plenty of chocolate involved for those people who find the words synonymous. A more sugar-conscious soul might choose, say, de-moulded gooseberry soufflé with poached gooseberries and gooseberry ice cream. The wine list is well-chosen with likeable house wines and priced in accordance with the idea of affordable eating out.

A STRAIGHTFORWARD LISTING of almost one hundred wines by region, with plenty of variety in the selection and – excellent idea – different wines open each week for sale by the glass. House wines include Cetto's brawny Petite Syrah from Mexico (£11) and the dependably herby Domaine de Belvezet from Côtes du Vivarais (£10.50); for £29 you could treat yourself to one of Australia's best Chardonnays, the 1986 of Leeuwin, while £26 would enable you to compare Bonny Doon's 1989 Cigare Volant with one of its role models: 1985 Vieux Télégraphe.

OPEN: LUNCH: Mon-Fri. DINNER: Mon-Sat. **HOURS:** 12.15-2.15pm and 6.30pm-12.00am. **CLOSED:** Bank Holidays and 1 week at Christmas. **CREDIT CARDS ACCEPTED:** Access, Visa. **NUMBER OF SEATS:** 60. **SERVICE:** Optional. **SET PRICE LUNCH:** £14. Wheelchair access (but not lavatory). **NEAREST TUBE STATION:** Bond Street.

MAP REF: 11/D

Stephen Bull's Bistro

71 St John Street, EC1

071-490 1750   **£20**

'High-tech feeding in a needy area'

Saturnine Stephen Bull, proprietor of the eponymous, more expensive Marylebone restaurant, has been one of the most successful exponents of finding more diversion in giving the people what they want where they want it. The location of his bistro and bar, north of Smithfield, is not exactly a desert in restaurant terms but nor is it a herbaceous border. The stylish architectural interior and the vivacious ever-changing menu give customers the agreeable sensation of being flattered for their taste in choosing to come here. The menu features light, modern dishes, some at two portions, two prices. There is a knowledgeable, creative use of vegetables as in leek, fennel and tarragon broth, the chargrilled veg. served on foccacia, grilled asparagus with dandelion and Parmesan shavings and spinach and ricotta parfait with raw tomato sauce. Main courses are substantially garnished, viz. chick-peas and grilled polenta with a casserole of venison. Bull and his chef Steve Carter like exploring Oriental spicing but sometimes get in a muddle and there can be unfortunate striving for original effect, as in cured salmon with melon and pineapple. Better is evidence of just canny shopping as in delicacies from Spain (Serrano ham, chorizo, Manchego cheese, olives and quince jelly). Desserts understand their function to the extent of some like brown sugar meringue with bananas, ice cream and hot fudge sauce appealing to the inner child. Wines are well-chosen with a good range offered by the glass. Service can sometimes get grumpy under pressure.

OPEN: LUNCH: Mon-Fri. DINNER: Mon-Sat. **HOURS:** 12.00-2.15pm and 6.00pm-12.00am (6.00-11.00pm Sat). **CLOSED:** Bank Holidays and 1 week at Christmas. **CREDIT CARDS ACCEPTED:** Visa, Access. **NUMBER OF SEATS:** 90. **SERVICE:** Optional. Wheelchair access (but not lavatory). **NEAREST TUBE STATION:** Farringdon.

MAP REF: 8/C2

Suntory

72-73 St James's Street, SW1

071-409 0201 £60

'For when you have a yen – plenty of them'

With Japanese food now available in London almost on a fast food basis, some of the reverence we westerners have for the cuisine can be re-examined. It is true that a visit to Suntory will give you some of the best and most expensive Japanese food in town but consider the cheapest teppanyaki set meal on offer here; small appetiser (and believe me it is small), dobin-mushi soup (steamed soup with dried mushroom), seafood and steak griddled on the hotplate (a partnership or sequence that induces profound understanding of Jewish dietary laws), salad (usually token), rice, dessert (probably fresh fruit) and green tea; £48 per person. You could spend £56 or £64 on other slightly embellished teppanyaki 'courses'. Suntory is a place to go if you are into ceremony and subtlety and spending money and/or if you truly understand and love Japanese food.

In the discreetly decorated restaurant on the ground floor where you eat à la carte, you are poised to discover more arcane and interesting dishes, most of them among the chef's suggestions. These change according to season and are well worth trying. For those whose appreciation of a Japanese meal is enhanced by the presence of a demure handmaiden to help with the cooking, there are the stock-pot and grill-pan dishes of shabu-shabu, sukiyaki and yose-nabe (mixed seafood and fresh vegetables cooked in a ceramic pan and seasoned with special sauce for £38 per sucker, sorry, person). Suntory has a following among British chefs and I can understand why. There is profound sagacity to be appreciated in some of the food and its preparation but I nevertheless feel that as these chaps dangle a piece of expensive but quite straightforwardly grilled eel from their chopstick, they think, why can't it be this easy and lucrative for us? Given the Suntory ownership of the eponymous brewing and distilling empire, you would be foolish to drink wine. Stick to beer or whisky. Lunch is a much cheaper meal if you stay with the set-price deals. Suntory is not the place to go for sushi.

OPEN: Mon-Sat. **HOURS:** 12.00-3.00pm and 7.00-11.00pm. **CLOSED:** Bank Holidays. **CREDIT CARDS ACCEPTED:** Access, AmEx, Diner's Club, JCB, Visa. **NUMBER OF SEATS:** 120. **SERVICE:** Optional. **SET PRICE LUNCH:** From £15. **SET PRICE DINNER:** From £48. Private room seats 7. **NEAREST TUBE STATION:** Green Park.
MAP REF: 12/B4

Le Suquet

104 Draycott Avenue, SW3

071-581 1785 **£30**

'An incorrigibly French fish restaurant'

I have heard complaints about Le Suquet, nearly always concerning off-hand service. All I can say is that, as a customer, it is worth perservering because once they get to know you, the staff might be pleasant. Or they might not. What I like about the place is that, like its owner Pierre Martin, it is without pretension or bullshit. The restaurant is there to serve fresh shellfish and fish in an atmosphere that does as good a job at conveying a small restaurant in Cannes as anyone could probably achieve in South Kensington. It attracts a glamorous clientele of a certain age – with usually a couple of introspective men eating alone at the bar – and my spirits always lift when I go there. The most dramatic first course is the plateau de fruits de mer (£15), a cork board heaped with raw shellfish with which you can happily play with your bucket and spade for most of the meal. Alternatives would be a composed salad, a feuilleté, a soupe de poisson, a crêpe de fruits de mer, frogs legs or harengs pommes à l'huile. Main course fish is according to the market. There is usually an expensive variety, say, fillet of turbot in a champagne sauce, and a more humble offering, say, cod Provençale. Lobsters are plucked from the vivier and are priced at £4.80 per 100g. If bass or bream are on offer, they are best simply and precisely grilled. Each day there are two or three meat dishes; perhaps rognons de veau, magret de canard or civet de lièvre. Salad tends to be a better choice than the vegetables, but the latter are included in the price. The desserts are little more than functional and sorbets are probably the best bet. Le Suquet has been trading in much the same fashion for over fifteen years; a good, glamorous formula well-executed – but I can't speak for eating on the first floor.

OPEN: Mon-Sun. **HOURS:** 12.00-11.30pm. **CREDIT CARDS ACCEPTED:** AmEx, Diner's Club, Visa. **NUMBER OF SEATS:** 50. **SERVICE:** 15%. **SET PRICE DINNER:** £26. 4 tables outside. Private room seats 10-16. **NEAREST TUBE STATION:** South Kensington.

MAP REF: 14/C2

Sweetings

39 Queen Victoria Street, EC4

071-248 3062 **£24**

'A City institution that thrives'

Were I to formulate for a visitor to London an itinerary for a culinary tour, I would include an early or late weekday lunch at Sweetings, the Victorian fish 'ordinary' that has been at these Queen Victoria Street premises since 1906. Avoiding peak mealtimes (no bookings are taken) is to avoid the worst of the crowd of pinstriped City gents who patronize the agreeably functionally decorated place for its slightly nursery interpretations of British fish cooking. As first courses there is much with which not much can go wrong – potted shrimps, soused herring and smoked versions of salmon, trout, cod's roe and eel. For a main course it is advisable to choose simply cooked fish and not rely on sauces or salads for diversion. A tranche of opalescently fresh grilled turbot with new potatoes and a dab of mustard sauce is a spiffing lunch when followed with steamed syrup pudding or a savoury such as Welsh rarebit. It was a fresh-faced, red-braced young Gekko type who demonstrated to me rarebit technique. You cross-hatch the melted cheese with your knife, shake on Worcester sauce which dribbles away into the runnels, cut up and eat with a glass of house port. No coffee is served although 'favourites' – such as restaurant critics who are rumbled – are ceremoniously presented with a cup of Nescafé. The wine list is short but champagne is served by the glass as is Black Velvet to accompany the West Mersea oysters.

OPEN: Mon-Fri. **HOURS:** 11.00am-3.00pm. **CLOSED:** 25th December to 2nd January. **CREDIT CARDS ACCEPTED:** None. **NUMBER OF SEATS:** 70. **SERVICE:** Optional. Wheelchair access (but not lavatory). **NEAREST TUBE STATION:** Mansion House/Bank.

MAP REF: 8/C2

The Tageen

12 Upper Saint Martin's Lane, WC2

071-836 7272   £24

'A rare London sighting of Moroccan food'

Moroccan food is a passion of mine and one not wholly satisfied by the cooking at this relatively new restaurant. Most of what you would think would be offered is; vegetable salads, briouats and briks (stuffed envelopes of pastry), minced lamb kebabs, couscous, bastela (bisteeya approximates the pronunciation) and, of course the eponymous casseroles cooked in earthernware conical pots, the tageens. However, Moroccan cooking properly done – as it is more likely to be in a domestic setting – is labour intensive, many-layered in flavour, as intricate as the lanes of a souk. Here it is as if gestures are only made. The flavours of the ingredients in the tageens – meat or poultry is often partnered with fruit – have not melded. In the bastela chicken is used in place of pigeon and the curdy stock-flavoured lemony omelette layer barely discernible. The dish is worth ordering though, as you will be hard pressed to find it elsewhere in London and some of the impact of the thrilling icing sugar sweetness and cinnamon smokiness on crisp pastry enclosing a savoury filling is there. With the couscous be sure to ask for harissa, an enlivening pureé. For dessert, there are more pastries, many of them honey-drenched. In conveying Moroccan, the decor and the staff outfits make more visible effort than the kitchen. Decorative tiles, brass lamps, leather cushions and fezes do their bazaar bit. The waitresses try hard but sometimes are linguistically challenged. Rabbi Jacob wine is a curiosity – one you might take to the next barmitzvah to which you are invited.

OPEN: LUNCH: Mon-Fri. DINNER: Mon-Sat. **HOURS:** 12.30-3.00pm and 6.00-11.30pm. **CLOSED:** Bank Holidays, 1st and 2nd January. **CREDIT CARDS ACCEPTED:** AmEx, Visa, Access, Diner's Club. **NUMBER OF SEATS:** 90. **SET PRICE LUNCH:** £12. **SET PRICE DINNER:** £12 (to 7.00pm only). Wheelchair access (but not lavatory). Private room seats 50. **NEAREST TUBE STATION:** Covent Garden/Leicester Square.

MAP REF: 12/C3

Tandoori Lane

131a Munster Road, SW6

071-371 0440 **£18**

'Worth wandering down'

I have this fantasy about The Great Indian Restaurant Meal shimmering somewhere in the distance forever eluding my grasp. Turned on by a review of another restaurant critic, I went to Tandoori Lane with high hopes. Whilst not having found culinary nirvana, I do think the food here notably superior to the average Indian restaurant experience. The ingredients seem better bought and the spicing possessed of greater thrust and immediacy. Recommended dishes from the long menu, complete with sections of house and chef's specialities, are the gracelessly named kebab cocktail, a patty of tandoori-grilled spiced minced meat topped with a salad of chopped fresh vegetables closely resembling a Mexican salsa, onion bhaji; prawn puri; king prawn delight with its uncanonical ingredient of red wine in the sauce but squeaky-fresh prawns; chicken dhansak; lamb jalfarezi. The chutneys are good but the breads could be better. So could some of the customers. On a visit to Tandoori Lane I overheard one actually saying to one of the waiters, 'My good man, bring me a port'. As he left, this same chap handed the barman a card, invited him to a cricket match and said something along the lines of: 'My name is Nerdo Somerset-Wiltshire and I'm most frightfully rich'. I imagined him repairing to one of the two-up, two-down terraced houses in this under-Volvoed part of Fulham. For dessert try the pistachio kulfi, but do not be seduced by the individually presented bunsen burner coffee pots – which eventually bring the liquid to a rolling boil – into thinking that it is worth ordering coffee.

OPEN: Mon-Sun. **HOURS:** 12.00-2.30pm and 6.00-11.30pm. **CLOSED:** Christmas Day and Boxing Day. **CREDIT CARDS ACCEPTED:** All major cards. **NUMBER OF SEATS:** 48. **SERVICE:** Optional. **SET PRICE LUNCH:** £7.95. **SET PRICE DINNER:** £8.95. **NEAREST TUBE STATION:** Parsons Green/Fulham Broadway. MAP REF: 8/B2

La Tante Claire

68 Royal Hospital Road, SW3

071-352 6045 **£35-£70**

'Now endorsed by The Michelin Men as "exceptional cuisine, worth a special journey"'

After too long a wait – in the opinion of many in the biz – this year (1993) Pierre Koffmann, chef/proprietor of La Tante Claire was awarded three stars by *The Michelin Guide*. With the demotion of Le Gavroche to two, this makes La Tante Claire the only restaurant so honoured in London. Typically Koffman is publicly only gruffly pleased by the recognition but he does admit that the customers he is now getting are ordering better – more expensive – wines. To do such a thing, and there is considerable scope on the wine list, demonstrates a belief that a fine meal merits a price beyond rubies;

a first course here will set you back between £18 and £24 and that just sets the pace. Is it worth it? When Koffmann is on form it is. His Gascon heritage on which is overlaid natural artisan skills, good taste and single-mindedness produce some masterpiece dishes although occasionally a desire either to show off or alleviate boredom or simply be seen to be doing enough to justify the price, make some creations over-elaborate and over-rich. The assiette canardière aux deux sauces, with duck conjured up four different ways, laid on bases of three quite different types of ingredient and sauced twice is a case in point. To appreciate what are always prime ingredients, it is better to approach them more straightforwardly, as in pigonneau rôti aux truffes, chapon et choux; tranches de filet de boeuf aux echalotes, fumet de ceps. It is also sometimes apparent that his self-confessed difficulty with delegation in the kitchen can lead to rough edges due to oft-changing staff.

Koffman enjoys play with initially unprepossessing ingredients as in his now famed pied de cochon aux morilles, purée de pois cassés, or conversely using a luxurious ingredient in a conventionally homely setting, as in garbure de turbotin au confit de canard. In the first course it is tempting to choose the pride of Gascony, foie gras, which Koffmann prepares knowledgeably, but ragoût of langoustines with a healthy amount of vegetables and herbs or the sensational griddled, caramelized scallops with a sauce based on squid ink are fierce competitors for your attention. There seems few if any slips or lapses of attention in the dessert course. They are invariably ravishing to look at as well as delicious. Try croustade de pommes caramelisées or soufflé aux pistaches et sa glâce.

Most people know this, but the set-price lunch menus at £24.50 – more or less the price of a main course à la carte – for three courses and coffee are one of London's gastronomic bargains. The light dining room with its blonde wood, sunny yellow chairs and pastel pictures induces a feeling of wellbeing and there seems no overload of corporate entertaining among the clientele. The service is led by a great general in Jean-Pierre Durantet, but sometimes with slightly straggling troops.

THE STRENGTHS OF this wine list are its good selection of half bottles (four pages towards the end) and its willingness to look beyond Bordeaux and Burgundy out into 'deep' France (as in ancient Cahors, modern Corbières or the timeless Jura). But there is nothing, port aside, from outside France; prices are funereally serious (Krug Grande Cuvée £181.50 here; £146 at Le Gavroche); the fine wines don't have quite the historical depth they might; and the list looks rather unappealing, as if hammered out on a second-hand typewriter.

OPEN: Mon-Fri. **HOURS:** 12.30-2.00pm and 7.00-11.00pm. **CLOSED:** Christmas and New Year. **CREDIT CARDS ACCEPTED:** Access, AmEx, Diner's Club, Visa. **NUMBER OF SEATS:** 45. **SERVICE:** Optional. **SET PRICE LUNCH:** £24.50. Wheelchair access. **NEAREST TUBE STATION:** Sloane Square. MAP REF: 14/C4

Tate Gallery Restaurant

Millbank, SW1

071-834 6754   **£25**

*'A look at the paintings followed by a great bottle
in the restaurant is a London treat'*

The Whistler mural, The Expedition in Pursuit of Rare Meats, remains a
delight in the restaurant of the Tate but there is something very staff canteen
about the service, a problem that could almost be solved at a stroke by
moving elsewhere the desk by the doorway where bills are totted up and
waitresses congregate to chat. The food, which at one point in the past got
bogged down in the unproductive alley of researching and reproducing
historical English dishes – which presumably fell from favour because they
were horrid – has improved considerably. It is now modern European but
with enough for the tourists; poached salmon in jellied Muscadet, roast
sirloin of beef with Yorkshire pudding, summer pudding, gooseberry and
elderflower tart. All puddings are served with a complimentary glass of
champagne which tends to encourage ordering. The institutional aspect to
the catering tends to show up in details such as vegetables and salad
dressings. The wine list is famous and still offers classic French bottles at
prices that require a note on the list to the effect that wine can only be
purchased for consumption in the restaurant. It is usual to see members of
the government – and the opposition – making good use of this facility.

STILL A PLACE to come to drink the great and the pretty damn good at
razor-edge prices (Vincent Leflaive's 1987 Chevalier-Montrachet, now
approaching maturity, is £75.60 here compared with £120 at Harveys, or
£85 for a half-bottle at Le Gavroche). Not much from outside France's
classic areas, but with classed growths aplenty under £20, who cares? Some
strange old spirits, too – wartime whisky, Rhône marc, that kind of thing.

OPEN: Mon-Sat. **HOURS:** 12.00-3.00pm. **CLOSED:** Christmas, New Year's Day, Good
Friday and May Day Holiday. **CREDIT CARDS ACCEPTED:** All major cards. **NUMBER OF
SEATS:** 100. **SERVICE:** Optional. No smoking area. Wheelchair access. **NEAREST TUBE
STATION:** Pimlico.   MAP REF: 8/C2

TGI Friday's

6 Bedford Street, WC2

071-379 0585   **£20**

'A slick slice of middle Americana transported to Britain'

Apparently the most profitable or one of the most profitable catering
ventures in the land, TGIF cleverly manages to sustain simultaneously a
strong family image and a lively singles bar scene – the latter presumably one
day feeding into the former. The menu is vast – Oriental, Mexican, salads,
sandwiches, steaks, burgers, build your own omelette, potato skins and so
on. It is probably the biggest non-Chinese menu in the city. Cocktails are

lavish and entertainingly made. Service at TGIF is a major plus factor. Lapses into the pre-programmed 'Have a nice day' mode may occur as the bright-eyed, bushy-tailed waitperson kneels down to take your order, but the delivery is always friendly, quick and efficient. The food lives up to modulated expectations. My own children, when teenagers, marvelled at a restaurant that seemed to be so unsparing in its efforts to have on offer the sort of things they liked. Prices are on the high side. Many more grown up places could learn from the style of service, the staff training and the sheer enthusiasm.

OPEN: Mon-Sun. **HOURS:** 12.00-11.30pm (12.00-11.00pm Sun.) **CLOSED:** Christmas Day and New Year's Eve. **CREDIT CARDS ACCEPTED:** All major cards except Diner's Club. **NUMBER OF SEATS:** 250. **SERVICE:** Optional. No smoking area. Wheelchair access. **NEAREST TUBE STATION:** Charing Cross. MAP REF: 12/D3

The Thai Garden

249 Globe Road, E2

081-981 5748 £20

'A very green restaurant at Bethnal'

It is a properly restoring experience to arrive on a rainy night at a restaurant offering something unusual (Thai vegetarian and fish dishes) on the fringes of Bethnal Green and find it full of happy customers. The Thai Garden is a little box of a place on two storeys, decorated in grey and black and made pretty by stylish food photographs and tasteful oddments. 'Most of our vegetarian recipes come from *Thai Vegetarian Cooking* by Vatcharin Bhumichitr' a sign announces. This author owns the Chiang Mai restaurant in Frith Street. What fun would be had were all Michelin star contenders to become as candid. 'You will find the original at Troisgros' . . . somehow it seems unlikely. Not so small dishes offered as starters include fiery som tum (a salad of papaya and raw vegetable); prawns, squid and vegetables in tempura batter; hot and sour seafood salad and little vegetable samosas with a rich, raisin flavour. A cauliflower and coconut soup was like an inspired, galangal-flavoured version of cauliflower cheese. The vegetarian version of the massaman (named after the Southern Thai Muslims) curry is very addictive, made with dissolving yellow bean curds, potatoes and a peanut and coconut sauce. Other main courses include goong kratiem (prawns stir-fried with white pepper and garlic) and aubergine with black beans and so much Thai basil that it really was perfumed. Pahd Thai noodles are good and the portions are large. Observations which are not really criticisms are that mushrooms are used as frequently on the vegetarian menu as prawns are on the seafood list, and that the wine list is not particularly exciting. Drink beer and don't take anyone who isn't a fungi to be with.

OPEN: LUNCH: Mon-Fri. DINNER: Mon-Sat. **HOURS:** 12.00-3.00pm and 6.00-11.00pm. **CLOSED:** Bank Holidays. **CREDIT CARDS ACCEPTED:** Access, Barclaycard. **NUMBER OF SEATS:** 32. **SERVICE:** 10%. **SET PRICE LUNCH:** £6.50. **SET PRICE DINNER:** £14.50-£19. No smoking area. Wheelchair access (but not lavatory). Private room seats 14. **NEAREST TUBE STATION:** Bethnal Green. MAP REF: 8/C2

Thai Kitchen Restaurant

108 Chepstow Road, W2

071-221 9984   **£18**

*'Just about the only place in Notting Hill not serving
Thai crab cakes'*

The names are not really the right way around here. The Thai Garden in E2
has a plain, eat at the kitchen table sort of appeal whereas the Thai Kitchen
in W2 goes in for the botanical look, though not on a big budget. The
Kitchen is a consistently polite, welcoming place but it seems that some
customers lingered too long and too stingily because there is now a
requirement to spend £10 each (excluding drinks) at dinner. When everyone
in the neighbourhood has tired of their bizarre diet of trendy bread, sub-
standard Caribbean cooking plus sun-dried tomatoes, this is where they
repair. A consolation is that such customers do support a wine list which
includes a few bold reds. Recently the food, too, seems to have grown bolder
in seasoning and choice: a salad of crisply fried fish stomach (crunchy but
flavourless) with cashew nuts and shrimps in a chilli-hot dressing; fish
casseroled with lemon grass and salted plum; rice combined with the
unforgettable flavour of shrimp paste, dried shrimp and sweet pork. Fried
noodle dishes are full of the advertised ingredients and very sustaining. Duck
in red curry is good, as are the beef salad, green curry and piercing soups. A
short vegetarian menu is also offered.

OPEN: Mon-Sat. **HOURS:** 12.00-2.30pm and 6.30-11.00pm. **CLOSED:** Christmas
Day, Boxing Day and New Year's Day. **CREDIT CARDS ACCEPTED:** Visa, Access, AmEx,
Mastercard. **NUMBER OF SEATS:** 46. **SERVICE:** Optional. **SET PRICE LUNCH:** £5.95 (on
request). **SET PRICE DINNER:** £13.95. **NEAREST TUBE STATION:** Westbourne Park

MAP REF: 11/E

Thailand Restaurant

15 Lewisham Way, SE14

081-691 4040   **£20**

'Laotian specialities and bagpipes'

This diminutive restaurant is like – and indeed is – somebody's front room,
in this case that of Glaswegian Victor Herman and his wife Khamkhong
Kambungoet whose birthplace is the part of Thailand that was once Laos. It
is decorated with some of Herman's paintings and what looks like many
happy hours spent with a stained glass kit. The long menu features some Lao
dishes and if the repetitiousness of Thai food as served in so many of
London's restaurants is getting to you, then make a booking here and order
some of them. There is a salad of hot and sour green papaya with lime, garlic,
chilli, fish sauce and mudfish that is quite extraordinary, and an assembly of
rice balls with minced pork cooked with lime juice, chillies and Thai herbs
with lettuce to wrap that would please anyone. Other dishes I can
recommend are the hot and sour seafood, the crabshell stuffed with minced

pork, crab and black pepper and the pungent accompaniment of chilli sauce based on shrimp paste. It is essential to order sticky rice and eat as much as possible with your fingers, having kneaded the rice into a sort of scoop. From the eighty-one savoury dishes, I have tried relatively few. My advice to maximize experimentation is to skip the fairly conventional first courses. Wines are well chosen to match the food which is not for the chilli-shy. Mr Herman is an amiable host, apt to pipe in someone's birthday cake on his bagpipes or offer you one of his many malt whiskies to try. Worth a journey if, to you, New Cross means a journey.

OPEN: Tues-Sat. **HOURS:** 6.00-11.00pm. **CREDIT CARDS ACCEPTED:** AmEx, Mastercard, Visa. **NUMBER OF SEATS:** 25. **SERVICE:** Optional. **SET PRICE DINNER:** £20. **NEAREST TUBE STATION:** New Cross Gate. MAP REF: 8/C3

Tokyo Diner
2 Newport Place, WC2

071-287 8777 £8

'Cheap Japanese meals in the heart of Chinatown'

Here is a commendable idea, a plain little Japanese cafe which declares its intention to serve food that is 'affordable, satisfying and fun'. There are three red lanterns by the door and a notice saying 'Cash only' which avoids any confusion. The welcome is warm and the atmosphere cheerful. On offer are Bento lunch boxes in which compartments hold rice, salmon sashimi with a potato salad, soya sauce marinaded vegetables and a prawn, plus the protein of your choice; breaded, crisply fried pork, chicken or salmon; salmon or chicken teriyaki; beef with a ginger sauce. A simple box of rice with egg, spring onion and dashi stock is another alternative, or there are soup noodles, or a course of mixed (nigiri) sushi pieces. The soup noodles are nothing like as full of flavour as Wagamama's, and indeed other dishes lack clarity, but the prices are decent and the place very likeable.

OPEN: Mon-Sun. **HOURS:** 12.00pm-12.00am. **CREDIT CARDS ACCEPTED:** None. **NUMBER OF SEATS:** 70. No smoking area. Wheelchair access (but not lavatory). **NEAREST TUBE STATION:** Leicester Square. MAP REF: 12/C2

Topkapi
25 Marylebone High Street, W1

071-486 1872 £15

'Easy-going hours for Turkish food in a fairly uptight area'

You may have forgotten, but Topkapi have not; in 1984 they were voted Restaurant of the Year in a search conducted by Capital Radio in conjunction with what used to be called The Ad-Lib column in the *Evening Standard*. Topkapi was the overall winner as well as the winner in the

mid-price category. Value is still paramount, especially in the first courses –
which could be summarized as Ottoman's greatest hits – all at one price.
After grazing among cacik, hummus, taramasalata, tabbouleh, stuffed
pastries and so forth, move on to lamb, minced lamb or chicken charcoal-
grilled. These are a better bet than items such as moussaka. The long room
with the inevitable cold cabinet at its head has a sort of gloomy glamour,
accentuated in the winter when a coal-effect gas fire flickers into action.
Topkapi is a long-standing decent place but I doubt that Azil Nadir will risk
an encounter with the SFO to try it.

OPEN: Mon-Sun. **HOURS:** 12.00pm-12.00am. **CLOSED:** Christmas Day and Boxing
Day. **CREDIT CARDS ACCEPTED:** Visa, Access, AmEx, Diner's Club. **NUMBER OF SEATS:**
50. **SERVICE:** 10%. **SET PRICE LUNCH AND DINNER:** £12.50. Wheelchair access (but not
lavatory). **NEAREST TUBE STATION:** Baker Street/Bond Street.   MAP REF: 12/A1

Turner's

87-89 Walton Street, SW3

071-584 6711   **£50**

*'A gastronomic good deed in an increasingly
capricious world'*

Brian Turner is a chef who knows how to work a room. Unlike those of his
compatriots who, apparently on the verge of tears or temper, ask you
grudgingly everything has been to your liking. He is a warm, buoyant host
much liked, I get the feeling, both by the canny ladies who lunch off the set
price menu and by the chaps who are willing to pay out more, much more, in
the evenings. Turner is the first to admit that the day-to-day responsibility
in the kitchen is that of his chef Alan Thompson, but when not cooking on a
North Sea oil rig for the TV programme *Food and Drink,* or some other such
ploy, he is very much a presence.

The food at Turner's, which retains vestiges of a style – particularly in
terms of presentation – that might once have been called nouvelle cuisine,
could strike some as old hat but there is nothing antiquated about the
execution of dishes such as petite salade de langoustines au saumon fumé;
terrine de lapereau à la compote d'aubergines; rôti de lotte aux olives et
nouilles vertes; coeur de filet de boeuf au raifort et gingembre or croûte aux
pommes caramelisées. It is cooking, despite the stubborn use of French,
representative of modern British elegance and excellence. It also suits the
recently redecorated small, pretty, feminine room. With new competition on
the block in the shape of Daphne's, Turner's might come across as staid and
terribly expensive but it is worth bearing in mind that the prices are fully
inclusive of tax and service and that at lunchtime two courses, say, petite
salade de faisan rôti aux girolles followed by délice de saumon marine grillé,
sauce aux asperges, will set you back only £9.95. And the petits fours that
accompany coffee (£2.50) will stand in for dessert. The prices on the
somewhat unadventurous wine list are not, however, by any means a
bargain.

NOTABLE CHIEFLY FOR thirteen different 1989, 1990 and 1991 Chablis from
a single grower, William Fèvre, who has vineyards in all the right places and

belongs to the oakist tendency – giving a richer style (others prefer the severity of steel). It's not often you get a chance to compare five different Premiers Crus (£26-£35) and five Grands Crus (£47-£49); there's eleven halves, too. Burgundy stays good, Bordeaux and Champagne are passable, there's a few other French bits and pieces, then it's thank you and goodnight.

OPEN: LUNCH: Sun-Fri. DINNER: Mon-Sun. **HOURS:** 12.30-2.30pm (12.30-2.00pm Sun) and 7.30-11.15pm (7.30-10.00pm Sun). **CLOSED:** 25th-30th December and Bank Holidays. **CREDIT CARDS ACCEPTED:** Access, AmEx, Diner's Club, Visa. **NUMBER OF SEATS:** 52. **SERVICE:** Optional. **SET PRICE LUNCH:** £15.75-£18.50. **SET PRICE DINNER:** £23.50-£29.50. Wheelchair access (but not lavatory). **NEAREST TUBE STATION:** South Kensington/Knightsbridge.   MAP REF: 14/C2

Two Brothers Fish Restaurant

297-303 Regents Park Road, N3

081-346 0469   **£14-£16**

'Popular to the point of bursting and dazzlingly efficient'

The motors parked outside this fish and chip restaurant in furthest Finchley are dazzling – Bentleys, old Jags and various expensive Italian and German imports. Two Brothers is that most unusual of things, a dressy chippy, its attractive blue interior done out just like a brasserie and a fair proportion of the customers done up to match. The polite and speedily proficient service would not be out of place in some of central London's most fashionable restaurants, indeed the proprietors of two or three would be well-advised to pay a visit and attempt to poach the staff. At the heart of the operation there is respect for tradition: bread rolls are automatically served with the fish and chips just in case more calories are called for, and there is the option of drinking tea and ordering mushy peas, and a glass of fruit juice as a starter. The choice of fish includes skate, lemon sole, halibut, Dover sole and rock eel (which turns out to be another alias of the dog fish) as well as the traditional trio of cod, haddock or plaice. An enormous piece coated in faultless batter or a fine matzo meal crust and served with large, very crisp chips and their own tartare sauce is the standard serving, but then other options are offered such as having little fried goujons or ordering any fish steamed or grilled, perhaps with an abstemious salad or some Hollandaise sauce. Or, indeed, not having fish at all – the menu offers chicken or steak, an unusually big choice of starters and an even bigger selection of ice cream sundaes and creamy puddings. There is a fairly priced wine list and a policy of not taking bookings.

OPEN: Tue-Sat. **HOURS:** 12.00-2.30pm and 5.30-10.15pm. **CLOSED:** Bank Holidays, day following a Bank Holiday, 2 weeks in August and any time the fish market is closed. **CREDIT CARDS ACCEPTED:** Visa, Mastercard, AmEx. **NUMBER OF SEATS:** 90. **SERVICE:** Optional. No smoking area. **NEAREST TUBE STATION:** Finchley Central.
                                                            MAP REF: 8/B2

The Upper Street
Fish Shop

324 Upper Street, N1

071-359 1401 £10 (Bring your own wine)

'Eat too much in cheerful surroundings'

An almost invariably crowded fish and chip restaurant which is something of a local landmark. Islington is justifiably proud of supporting two fine fish shops, Steve Hatt's fishmongery in the Essex Road and this restaurant and take-away which is certainly one of the best in London. The fish is just right but the chips are not quite up there, in this Guide's opinion. Upper Street Fish Shop is often nicknamed Olga's after the vivacious proprietress who organises the queues for take-aways and tables. Her place looks more like a bistro than a chippy, an unorthodox but agreeable scheme. The chummy mood and massive portions of plaice, cod, haddock or huss attract an interesting mix of customers, some of whom have picked up a bottle of champagne en route (there is no licence); thesps lament the ten o'clock closure, longing to call in after work at The Almeida or King's Head. Starters of Pacific oysters, fish soup, fried mussels or salmon pâté are recommended to the hugely hungry or hard-working, as are good old fashioned puds. As alternatives to battered fish there are poached salmon or haddock with salad, and grilled Dover sole or steak.

OPEN: LUNCH: Tues-Sat. DINNER: Mon-Sat. **HOURS:** 12.00-2.00pm (12.00-3.00pm Sat) and 5.30-10.00pm. **CLOSED:** Bank Holidays. **CREDIT CARDS ACCEPTED:** None. **NUMBER OF SEATS:** 48. **SERVICE:** Optional. Wheelchair access (but not lavatory). **NEAREST TUBE STATION:** Angel. MAP REF: 8/C2

Vasco & Piero's Pavilion

15 Poland Street, W1

071-437 8774 £25

'A hidden treasure'

If, like me, you still regret the closure of The Academy Cinema in Oxford Street, a visit to Vasco & Piero's Pavilion will have a certain poignancy. The Poland Street restaurant is the re-creation, under the same ownership, of the Angus McBean designed original that was housed in the same building as The Academy. There is reference to the theme of a striped tent but now less dramatically so. The Italian food which has moved with the times is sound and steady, cooked for the most part with skill and a light touch. Daily changing set price meals at lunch and dinner are eminently reasonable and the dishes more inventive than the average trattoria supplies, viz. salad of baby spinach, chorizo and pecorino shavings; home made salt cod ravioli with butter and fresh herbs, farfalle with calamari and peas; polpette of veal (meatballs) with anchovies and mozzarella; poached skate wings with fennel sauce; roast rabbit with oyster mushrooms; grilled slices of salmon with pesto and vinaigrette. It doesn't really pay, in any sense, to stray onto the à la carte. The partners are dignified hosts. V & P's Pavilion seems a sort of backwater restaurant, but agreeably so. Located quite near theatreland and West End cinemas, it is a place to keep in mind to keep the price of an evening in check.

Open: Mon-Fri. **Hours:** 12.00-3.00pm and 6.00-11.00pm. **Closed:** Bank Holidays. **Credit cards accepted:** All major cards. **Number of seats:** 55. **Service:** Optional. **Set price dinner:** £12.95. No smoking area. Wheelchair access (but not lavatory). Private room seats 30. **Nearest tube station:** Oxford Circus.
MAP REF: 12/B2

Vegetarian Cottage

9 Haverstock Hill, NW3

071-586 1257   **£15**

'A place to try "zhai" Buddhist cuisine and more'

The introduction to the menu at this Chinese vegan, vegetarian and fish restaurant invokes the ideal of a healthy mind in a healthy body. It mentions the cancer-preventing properties of the Chinese vegetarian diet and, one way and another, does not prepare you at all for the delight to be found in the cooking here. When choosing first courses it is important to concentrate so as not to find that everything you order comes deep-fried, a favoured mode. But do try deep-fried buns with vegetable stuffing, little money-bags of thin pastry with a savoury filling. Other ways of wrapping diced and shredded vegetables are with leaves of iceberg lettuce, a dish listed as crispy lettuce wrap, or in a soya bean sheet doused with soy-based sauce known as fu pai roll. The Buddhist vegetarian 'zhai' cuisine uses wheat gluten, soya bean sheets or yam to imitate fish or duckling. I thought 'duckling' a qualified success as a piece of gastronomic forgery. Much better is the more up-front, confrontational fried bean curd with mushrooms, stir-fried mangetouts and enough garlic to lower the cholesterol level of NW3. Singapore rice noodles have the most ingenious faux-viande constituent part; strips of what seem like barbecued pork. For those who will admit fish into their bodies, steamed scallops and sea bass, in line with all the other dishes, are notably reasonably priced. There is a relatively enterprising wine list and sweet service in the small, modern dining room.

Open: Lunch: Sun. Dinner: Mon-Sun. **Hours:** 6.00-11.30pm (12.00-11.30pm Sun). **Closed:** Christmas. **Credit cards accepted:** Mastercard, Visa. **Number of seats:** 70. **Service:** Optional. Wheelchair access (2 steps). Private room seats 20. **Nearest tube station:** Belsize Park/Chalk Farm.   MAP REF: 10/A

Villandry Dining Room

89 Marylebone High Street, W1

071-224 3799 £25

'Appetizing lunches at the back of a glorious grocery'

Villandry is a dream of a shop with cheeses sitting out in the open on wooden counters and bread which can be touched. It is a wonder some officious Environmental Health Officer has not stepped in and spoilt it. At the back is a plain, school room of a place to have lunch, an even more tactile experience because tables are packed in and plates have to be passed overhead. A different sort of lady who lunches likes it here – gals of any age who know about food, eat plenty of it, and have interesting lives to discuss. Breakfast and tea are also served, though sometimes all the cakes have been eaten by 4.00pm. The lunch menu is edited highlights from the shop, items such as a plate of dried sausages and ham, or complicated salads with unusual leaves. Hunks of the wonderful loaves sold here arrive first. Soups and savoury tarts are good, and the puddings are bliss. There are also hot main courses such as lamb couscous or roast poultry, but after three courses the bill begins to resemble what might be run up in a spacious and less frenetic restaurant. With wines from a small list of good quality, the damage is about the same. Smoking is banned and dinner is a movable feast held once a month.

OPEN: Mon-Sat. **HOURS:** 9.30-11.30am and 12.00-5.30pm (dinner on the 3rd Thursday of each month only). **CLOSED:** Bank Holidays. **CREDIT CARDS ACCEPTED:** Visa, Access, Switch. **NUMBER OF SEATS:** 60. **SERVICE:** Optional. **SET PRICE LUNCH:** £6.50. No smoking throughout. Wheelchair access (but not lavatory). Private room seats 44, evenings only. **NEAREST TUBE STATION:** Baker Street/Great Portland Street/Regent's Park. MAP REF: 12/A1

Vrisaki

73 Myddleton Road, N22

081-881 2920 £15

'Order the meze and let wave after wave
of dishes wash up on your table'

The Greek/Cypriot manager of a BMW garage in the West End told me that the best Greek/Cypriot food in town is at Vrisaki in Wood Green. It is good and if not necessarily the best, Vrisaki must take first prize for spirit of largesse in the meze. Ordered for two, the dishes keep coming – after twenty-five I stopped counting – and among them are some items not frequently offered elsewhere, for example the green leafy vegetable known as horta, pickled vegetables, two kinds of dried beans, some excellent grilled field mushrooms and, presumably as a gesture of extra munificence, two little rolls of smoked salmon. Charcoal grills are well-handled. There is the chance of grilled fish as well as meat and also bastourma (smoked sausage), haloumi (cheese) and large prawns. The big dining room with its long tables, hidden behind what looks simply a fairly ordinary take-away, is ideal for parties or large family gatherings and that is how it is frequently used by the local community. The waiters have seen it all and then some.

OPEN: Mon-Sat. **HOURS:** 12.00-3.00pm and 5.30pm-12.00am. **CLOSED:** 2 weeks at end of August. **CREDIT CARDS ACCEPTED:** None. **NUMBER OF SEATS:** 130. **SERVICE:** 10%. **SET PRICE DINNER:** £12. Wheelchair access. Private room seats 20. **NEAREST TUBE STATION:** Bounds Green.   MAP REF: 8/C1

Wagamama

4 Streatham Street, WC1

071-323 9223   **£11**

'Join the queue for the way of the noodle'

Queues up the stone staircase and out into the street are a feature of this ramen (noodle) bar. Health-conscious food, lively spicing, fair prices, minimalist but striking design, cheerful energetic staff are the factors that persuade customers that a wait is worthwhile. The turnover is brisk, galvanized by the staring faces of the yet-to-be-seated. When your time comes you sit at long wooden tables. The dishes you ask for, mostly based on noodles in soup or beds of rice, are brought in no particular order but just when they have been prepared at the kitchen counter running down one side of the restaurant. My favourite, chilli beef ramen, is a bowlful of noodles topped with chargrilled sirloin, green chillies, onions, coriander, mint, shallots and spring onions, garnished with bean sprouts and lime. Noodles also come fried garnished with either vegetables alone or a mixture of meat, seafood and vegetables. Donburi is rice tricked out in much the same way. Avoid the dumplings which taste as if filled with minced-up leftovers. Raw juices are the PC accompaniment but fortunately wine, Japanese beers and sake are also served. Free Japanese tea completes the palpably beneficial experience.

OPEN: Mon-Sat. **HOURS:** 12.00-2.30pm (1.00-3.30pm Sat) and 6.00-11.30pm. **CREDIT CARDS ACCEPTED:** None. **NUMBER OF SEATS:** 104. **SERVICE:** Optional. No smoking. **NEAREST TUBE STATION:** Tottenham Court Road.   MAP REF: 12/C2

Wakaba

122A Finchley Road, NW3

071-586 7960 or 071-722 3854   **£30**

'Wear your Yamamoto to be comme les garçons'

Few people are indifferent to John Pawson's typically, dramatically minimalist design for the Japanese restaurant Wakaba. I love the elegant discretion of the curved glass frontage and the clean-cut lines and absence of colour of the interior, but it seems many don't. A palpable drawback is that a totality of hard surfaces leads to noise and reverberating clatter; best to go to Wakaba with someone to whom you have a minimal amount to say. The menu is long and requires careful study but should this lead you to order a set meal, you will not be gastronomically short-changed. The menus provide a thorough sampler of ingredients and cooking styles. Wakaba is a place to order sushi. It is concisely constructed by an imposing sushi chef. Sashimi is also good. The ragoût/fondue style dishes cooked at the table seem popular with customers but more illuminating food, suzukuri, thinly-sliced raw turbot with ponzu sauce, can be found by trawling through the menu. Green tea, sake or beer, rather than wine, make for a well-rounded meal.

OPEN: Mon-Sat. **HOURS:** 6.30-11.00pm. **CLOSED:** 3rd week of August, 4 days at Christmas and Easter. **CREDIT CARDS ACCEPTED:** Access, AmEx, Diner's Club, Visa. **NUMBER OF SEATS:** 55. **SERVICE:** Optional. **SET PRICE DINNER:** £23. Wheelchair access. **NEAREST TUBE STATION:** Finchley Road.   MAP REF: 10/B

Walsh's Seafood & Shellfish Restaurant

5 Charlotte Street, W1

071-637 0222   £25

*'A fish restaurant created by the granddaughter
of the founder of Wheeler's'*

Bernard Walsh founded Wheeler's restaurants when he opened the first of the group in 1929 in Old Compton Street. The vicissitudes of the chain in recent years are probably known to anyone who believes that the ideal meal is oysters, grilled Dover sole and a bottle of Chablis. Walsh's in Charlotte Street, the venture of Bernard's granddaughter, Elaine Emmanuel, is designed to be an establishment in keeping with the spirit of former times. Christopher German, formerly chef at Odin's, masterminds a fundamentally traditional fish menu. As of old, it is divided by species of fish and starts with oysters. Hors d'oeuvres include smoked fish, various shellfish cocktails and salads, asparagus, caviar and the more contemporary lobster ravioli. Prices which are inclusive of tax and service are relatively reasonable, particularly for the Dover soles which are offered a dozen ways, the best of which, on short acquaintance with the restaurant, seeming to be Bonne Femme – the fillets served with mushrooms and their reduction incorporated into a white wine sauce, the plate bordered with piped mashed potato. German's Scampi Provencale would cause apoplexy among long-standing Wheeler's customers but that is to the benefit of the dish from which flour (to dust the fish) is excluded and a deep-fried tangle of vegetable threads imposed to provide contrasting texture. Basil leaves and fresh tomato concassée are additional uncanonical accoutrements. Savouries are probably a better and certainly a more traditional ending than dessert. Wines are fairly priced and in the style of the original Wheeler's there is not only a house Chablis but a house Meursault. The front room of Walsh's is designed as an oyster bar.

OPEN: LUNCH: Mon-Fri. DINNER: Mon-Sat. **HOURS:** 12.00-2.30pm and 6.00-11.00pm. **CLOSED:** Bank Holidays. **CREDIT CARDS ACCEPTED:** All major cards. **NUMBER**

OF SEATS: 70 and 8 at oyster bar. **SERVICE:** Optional. No smoking area on request. Wheelchair access (but not lavatory). Private room seats 12. **NEAREST TUBE STATION:** Goodge Street, Tottenham Court Road. MAP REF: 12/B1

The White Tower

1 Percy Street, W1

071-636 8141 £30

'A charmer in an almost unbroken line from 1938 –
and the birthplace of taramasalata in London'

It was a happy day in April 1993 for Friends of The White Tower when Miss Mary and George returned to reclaim their rightful places as manageress and sommelier and, in addition, the owners of a new twenty year lease at The White Tower. Miss Mary Dunne is the niece of Eileen and the late John Stais, owners of the restaurant since 1938. She joined them as receptionist in 1959, seven years after George Metaxas had arrived to take up the position as sommelier. At the dinner I enjoyed post The Restoration, every one of the customers who had been seated in the ground floor rooms was on cheek-grazing terms with Miss Mary. The White Tower is a restaurant that inspires loyalty and devotion and I am one of its devotees. I go and read the verbose menu originally written by Daniel George when he was working as an editor at the publishing house of Jonathan Cape, then in nearby Bedford Square, and then I choose more or less the same things: to start, the taramasalata and the chicken (or duck) liver pâté served with crudités, or sometimes the fish salad made with turbot trimmings, to follow either the duck stuffed with cracked wheat, nuts, dried fruit and seasonings – order when booking – or the baby chicken treated in much the same way. Neither of these dishes would be complete without green peas. Many years ago The White Tower was dropped from *The Good Food Guide* for serving frozen peas. That vegetable is, to my mind, almost reason enough to make the trip to Percy Street.

Years before it was common currency the menu of The White Tower was referring to diet consciousness and something they call the anabolic and catabolic nature of foodstuffs. Charcoal-grilled spring chicken is a suggestion for a light meal as is the poached poularde, its broth thickened with egg yolks. Both those dishes are also good choices. I am less keen on the moussaka and stuffed vegetables with the exception of stuffed aubergine, called imam bayeldi. Finish a meal with fruit salad or pancakes filled with rose petal jam, then coffee and Turkish delight. Relying on George for wine advice is the most pleasurable way to approach a not particularly inspiring list. The cluttered surroundings were mercifully left unchanged during the recent hiccup and the collection of heroic Greek pictures, firearms, and plates remains firmly in place.

OPEN: LUNCH: Mon-Fri. DINNER: Mon-Sat. **HOURS:** 12.30-2.30pm and 6.30-10.30pm. **CLOSED:** Bank Holidays, last 2 weeks in August and 1 week at Christmas. **CREDIT CARDS ACCEPTED:** All major cards. **NUMBER OF SEATS:** 75. **SERVICE:** Optional. Private room seats 16. **NEAREST TUBE STATION:** Tottenham Court Road/Goodge Street. MAP REF: 12/C1

Wilson's

236 Blythe Road, W14

071-603 7267   **£20-£30**

*'For that moment when you feel like
some Scottish food'*

This is an oddity; a rather lugubrious Scottish-themed restaurant run by a chap who seems to be acting out the part of an unkind prep school headmaster. Much of the allure, I suspect, lies more in the all-inclusive modest pricing and the set menus with a note to the effect that 'no other payments or gratuities are required or necessary', than in tartan tablecloths – disturbingly cut from a woolly fabric – the antlers projecting from some panelling or indeed the cooking. To eat an ethnic meal you could try finnan haddock pudding, best end of lamb with a haggis stuffing with the pan juices finished with whisky and atholl brose, more whisky this time whipped with cream, oats and heather honey, but most of the menu is not MacDishes but a slightly effortful attempt at British bistro food. Wines are also modestly priced and you get a large slug of a single malt whisky for £4. This can easily lead to silliness at the back of the class.

OPEN: Mon-Sun. **HOURS:** 12.30-2.30pm and 7.30-10.30pm. **CLOSED:** Christmas, Easter and Bank Holidays. **CREDIT CARDS ACCEPTED:** All major cards except Diner's Club. **NUMBER OF SEATS:** 58. **SERVICE:** Included. **SET PRICE LUNCH:** £10 (3 courses). Wheelchair access (but not lavatory). **NEAREST TUBE STATION:** Hammersmith/ Shepherd's Bush/Goldhawk Road.   MAP REF: 11/F

Wiltons Restaurant

55 Jermyn Street, SW1

071-629 9955   **£40**

*'Max Hastings, a regular, observed that if you
have to read the bill at Wilton's, you can't afford
the lunch'*

Wiltons, nowadays, managed by The Savoy Group, likes to date its inception to 1742 when George William Wilton opened as a shellfishmonger in Cockspur Street. As a restaurant originally described as Oyster Rooms, which it became in 1840, it made several moves, always in the St James's area. Wiltons has been at the Jermyn Street address only since 1984 but the traditional Edwardian interior, with some parts of it having survived the upheavals, is designed to muffle that fact. Wiltons is a haunt for the rich and influential in politics, business and journalism. They like the discretion, the formal staff, some of whom dress as nannies, and doubtless the straightforwardness of much of the cooking, mainly based on fish and game. The daily specialities tend to involve slightly more imaginative treatments of raw materials. I've seen ginger used as a flavouring for grilled sea bass and a pimento and coriander dressing for chargrilled tuna. Refugees from the gentlemen's clubs nearby probably scoff at these departures and stick to oysters or smoked salmon followed by grilled Dover sole or mixed grill followed by sherry trifle and a savoury. A meal at Wiltons is extremely expensive and its clubby atmosphere may work against enjoyment for a casual visitor, but I have to admit it is somewhere I am always delighted to be taken.

OPEN: LUNCH: Mon-Fri. DINNER: Mon-Sat. **HOURS:** 12.30-2.30pm and 6.30-10.30pm. **CLOSED:** Bank Holidays. **CREDIT CARDS ACCEPTED:** All major cards. **NUMBER OF SEATS:** 80. **SERVICE:** Optional. Wheelchair access (but not lavatory). Private room seats 18. **NEAREST TUBE STATION:** Green Park. MAP REF: 12/B3

Wódka

12 St Albans Grove, W8

071-937 6513 £20-£25

'New wave Polish place with plenty of spirit'

The restaurant trade has very few sayings, ones that are repeatable anyhow, but one truism is that the three main ingredients for success are location, location and location. Of this the current restaurant boom in W8 and W11 is abundant proof. A great swathe beginning below the park and pushing towards the boundary of the West Way (Ultima Thule!) has seen openings, spin-offs and extensions at a frantic pace. Wódka expanded into the neighbouring building last June, making it look more like a proper restaurant than the cosy little drinking den colleagues from the *Evening Standard* were so fond of. There is still a magnificent range of vodka: bison grass, rowan, pepper, plum and honey, the last a sovereign remedy if taken at the onset of colds. Also provided is an attractive list of wines in the £9-£20 bracket, and no doubt many more will now be sold to accompany the Polish cooking which is much improved in execution and variety. There is barszcz (Polish borsch) and herrings with dill and black pudding with cabbage or stuffed cabbage as a main course (golabki) and rich beef olives (zrazy). A few unashamedly Mediterranean dishes are offered as alternatives but die-hards will stick to their blinis with keta (salmon caviare) and several shots of vodka.

OPEN: LUNCH: Sun-Fri. DINNER: Mon-Sat. **HOURS:** 12.30-2.30pm (1.00-3.30pm Sun) and 7.00-11.15pm. **CLOSED:** Bank Holidays. **CREDIT CARDS ACCEPTED:** Access, AmEx, Visa. **NUMBER OF SEATS:** 50. **SERVICE:** Optional. Wheelchair access (but not lavatory). Private room seats 30. **NEAREST TUBE STATION:** Kensington High Street.

MAP REF: 11/F

Woodlands

77 Marylebone Lane, W1

071-486 3862 £12

'Virtuous food near loutish Leicester Square'

Southern Indian vegetarian food is now making incursions into new territories (q.v. Mamta in Fulham) and thus taking on a kind of fashionability. The Woodlands chain with branches in India and the USA remains a worthy, sober, purveyor of iddli, rasa vada, dosa, paper masala dosa, utappam – try it mixed when it is served with a topping of tomato, onions and coconut – and the pickle, chutneys and raitas that further enliven these crafty ways with breads, fermented batters and pulses. For the uninitiated or idle, there are thalis, trays containing a range of dishes (cheaper at lunchtime). The virtuous quality of the food – and its deliciousness – is particularly welcome in the Panton Street branch near tawdry Leicester Square.

ALSO AT: 402a High Road, Wembley, Middx (081-902 9869).
37 Panton Street, W1 (071-839 7258).

OPEN: Mon-Sun. HOURS: 12.00-3.00pm and 6.00-11.00pm. CLOSED: Christmas Day and Boxing Day. CREDIT CARDS ACCEPTED: All major cards. NUMBER OF SEATS: 70. SERVICE: 12.5%. SET PRICE LUNCH AND DINNER: £9.95. NEAREST TUBE STATION: Bond Street.
MAP REF: 12/A2

Zen

Chelsea Cloisters,
85 Sloane Avenue, SW3

071-589 1781 or 584 9219 £35

'The original Zen experience'

This Zen on the ground floor of Chelsea Cloisters is PRM (pre-Rick Mather) and in appearance has a certain vulgar, nightclubby charm. The menu is long and inventive with a list of thirty-two appetizers hot and cold to decide among before getting down to business of a meal. There are various ways round this; going alone, taking a dreary companion whom you can ignore while studying the list at length, opting for one of the set meals, leaving it all up to the waiter, having the restaurant fax you a menu to study beforehand at home or visiting often enough to work your way through and decide what you really like. The last is ideal but impractical, save for the improvident. The set meals (from £18-£38 per person) are in fact less tame assemblies than usual and would provide a good first tasting of Zen. Recommended à la carte are the assorted dim sum, lobster cold tossed with jelly fish (order in advance), Szechuan duck's tongues, properly made Peking duck, sea-spice Dover sole, baked quail with spicy hot sauce, chopped pork with dried scallops and water chestnut, Tao Peng prawn balls and French beans foo yung. Incidentally, there is quite a lot on the menu suited to vegetarians.

The caveat about almost all Chinese restaurants concerning fluctuating standards also applies here although the volume of custom would seem to indicate that the variation is never drastic. Service is quick on its feet but never quick enough to justify the credit card slip being left open after 15% service charge has automatically been added, as has been known to happen.

OPEN: Mon-Sun. **HOURS:** 12.00-3.00pm and 6.00-11.30pm (12.00-11.00pm Sat-Sun). **CLOSED:** Christmas Day. **CREDIT CARDS ACCEPTED:** All major cards. **NUMBER OF SEATS:** 110. **SERVICE:** 15%. **SET PRICE LUNCH:** £9.50 (3 courses, Mon-Fri only). **SET PRICE DINNER:** £18, £28, £33 and £38. Private room seats 22. **NEAREST TUBE STATION:** South Kensington.   MAP REF: 14/C3

Zen Central Restaurant

20-22 Queen Street, W1

071-629 8103/8089   **£40**

'Capable of the best, chic Chinese food in town'

This Mayfair restaurant was the second 'new-style' Zen designed by Rick Mather, following after ZENW3. An unpromising site, formerly a post office, has been made bright and sinuous through Mather's trademark use of glass and steel. When the group's top chef is in place and not on secondment to a Zen that needs to buckle down or brace up, the food can be ace; seductive and inventive. The crisp menu layout is an invitation to interesting ordering and if there are enough of you – or you have enough money – at least one choice should be made from each section. Hot Appetisers might deliver deep-fried crispy tofu with sesame fragrance; Dumplings to try are fried mustard spiced chicken in batter and deep-fried minced prawn balls; Wrapped should be lettuce around diced chicken and herbs; Cold Appetisers that live up to the name are either Imperial hors d'oeuvres (to share) or sliced rice wine-marinated chicken and pig's trotter; a fine Soup is shark's fin and seafood; Zen's Specials are many but I particularly like lobster baked with tangerine peel and crushed garlic or steamed sea bass with ginger and spring onion; among the Poultry and Meat dishes veal cutlets in black pepper sauce and hand-cut pork with dried shredded scallops stand out; quick fried seasonal Vegetables are, in my view, the best vegetables and steamed Rice all you need with such an intricate order.

Zen Central attracts an international clientele. The Japanese contingent order Shao Hsing rice wine and add sugar to it. If that does not appeal you must content yourself with a wine list that could be better thought through in terms of flattering Chinese food. On form, Zen Central cracks the problem of combining the buzz of a glamorous restaurant with reckonable Chinese food.

OPEN: Mon-Sun. **HOURS:** 12.15-2.30pm and 6.30-11.30pm (6.30-11.00pm Sun). **CLOSED:** Christmas Eve, Christmas Day and Boxing Day. **CREDIT CARDS ACCEPTED:** All major cards. **NUMBER OF SEATS:** 90. **SERVICE:** Optional. **SET PRICE LUNCH:** £25. **SET PRICE DINNER:** £30-£45. Wheelchair access (but not lavatory). 70 tables outside. Private room seats 18. **NEAREST TUBE STATION:** Green Park.
MAP REF: 12/A4

ZENW3

83-84 Hampstead High Street, NW3

071-794 7863/4   **£25**

*'A monosodium glutamate and Chinese lantern
free zone'*

The Hampstead Zen – still striking in appearance – was the first fruit of the collaboration between Zen's owner Lawrence Leung, architect Rick Mather and designer Howard Waller. It established a corporate image of clean, uncluttered lines, health-conscious Chinese food and stylish graphics. The short, concise menu was a departure from the usual long laundry list of dishes and quickly ZENW3 became a North London place to see and be seen. Food here is notably fresh-tasting. Favourite dishes include: pot stickers (Peking ravioli in a hot sauce); bean curd in peppercorn salt; soft shell crabs; prawns steamed with fennel seeds; steamed sea bass and something they call salt and pepper pork chops (offered on a separate card). Among the more interesting than usual vegetable dishes, sea-spice aubergine stands out. Fresh exotic fruit makes the best dessert. ZENW3 is not immune to the peripatetic nature of Chinese chefs, in this case sometimes a result of re-shuffles within the group, so standards can vary. Mather has managed the tricky feat of making neither floor preferable as a place to be, but at lunchtime, when the business is quieter, it is pleasant to sit on the ground floor by the floor-to-ceiling window and watch the Hampstead world go by.

OPEN: Mon-Sun. **HOURS:** 12.00-11.30pm. **CLOSED:** Christmas Day. **CREDIT CARDS ACCEPTED:** All major cards. **NUMBER OF SEATS:** 135. **SERVICE:** 12.5%. **SET PRICE LUNCH:** £9.50. Wheelchair access (but not lavatory). 32 tables outside. Private room seats 24. **NEAREST TUBE STATION:** Hampstead.   MAP REF: 10/A

Ziani

45 Radnor Walk, SW3

071-351 5297   **£25**

*'Named after an aristocratic Venetian family –
they would stand out in this crowd'*

Originally conceived and financed by a cabal of young Chelsea bucks, the clientele has always reflected the clout of their collective address books. However, above-average Italian food justifies the popularity and the noisy, crowded atmosphere. As I said in my original review of Ziani, every table in the L-shaped space is the worst table in the room – unless coveting your neighbour's wife is your particular weakness. Pastas and risottos are carefully prepared. The figure-conscious eater is well-catered for with various carpacci, bresaola, spinach salad, artichoke with bagna caôda and grilled fish. The derivation of Ziani is Venetian – referring to a twelfth century family who helped shape the city – and an influence is just about discernible in the menu, most notably in the central panel of daily specialities. Ziani is situated in a pretty little Chelsea street. In summer the residents must wish that it wasn't.

OPEN: Mon-Sun. **HOURS:** 12.30-2.45pm (12.30-3.15pm Sun) and 7.00-11.30pm (7.00-10.30pm Sun). **CLOSED:** Bank Holidays. **CREDIT CARDS ACCEPTED:** All major cards. **NUMBER OF SEATS:** 60. **SERVICE:** Optional. **SET PRICE LUNCH:** £10 when available. **SET PRICE DINNER:** £15 when available. Wheelchair access. **NEAREST TUBE STATION:** Sloane Square. MAP REF: 14/C3

Zoë

St Christopher's Place,
3-5 Barrett Street, W1

071-224 1122 £23

'All the ingredients for excess'

A-n-other restaurant opened by the irrepressible Antony Worrall Thompson, the man who has a finger in every polenta pot. Zoë is what once was Coconut Grove, the flamenco pink cocktail bar off St Christopher's Place, and very briefly Zen Cargo. It has changed its colours. The decor is hectic (likeably so) but however many different, bold colours have been used the pigments cannot compete with the multiplicity of ingredients produced by the kitchen. One of Wozza's skills is to write a very fashionable menu. Here dishes are divided between 'City' and 'Country', a separation which does not make a great deal of sense but probably appeals to the sort of people who like to classify themselves – as you must, for example, when composing an ad for a lonely hearts' column. Also a concentration of casseroles in 'Country' and grills in 'City' helps to stop the garrulous list of modish ingredients – blue corn quesadilla chilli jelly hand-rolled mozzarella smoked butter Hollandaise black-eyed peas wild greens asparagus peelings sweetbread ravioli grilled rabbit saddle roast pumpkin rolling into one uncontrollable conglomeration. That said there are clever conceits such as cold-smoked and burned butters that with a small gesture can transform a dish. Chef Konrad Melling seems to enjoy and be a master of the style but on sunny days when tables can be set up outside, simpler less attention-grabbing food would be an asset. The ground floor room and bar beside serve a snack version of the downstairs menu. Service can get muddled and bookings (and companions) have been known to be mislaid. Zoë, by the way, is the Greek word for life.

OPEN: Mon-Sat. **HOURS:** 11.00am-11.30pm. **CLOSED:** Some Bank Holidays. **CREDIT CARDS ACCEPTED:** All major cards. **NUMBER OF SEATS:** 180. **SERVICE:** Optional. **SET PRICE LUNCH AND DINNER:** £7.50-£10. No smoking area. Wheelchair access (but not lavatory). 6 tables outside. **NEAREST TUBE STATION:** Bond Street. MAP REF: 12/A2

Eros Awards*

Beth's (nepotism)
Bibendum
Bistrot Bruno
The Brackenbury
Le Caprice
Chez Moi
Chutney Mary

The French House
   Dining Room
Fung Shing
Le Gavroche
The Ivy
Le Petit Max
Quaglino's

Riva
The River Cafe
Les Saveurs
Le Suquet
La Tante Claire
The White Tower
Zen Central

Newcomers

L'Accento
Albero & Grana
Alexandra
The Argyll
Beauchamp Place
Belgo
Beth's *
Bice
Bistrot Bruno *
Bodali
Bonjour Vietnam
Brixtonian Backyard
Café des Arts
Cafe Lazeez
Caffe Graffiti
The Canteen
Cheneston's
China Court
Chopstix Xchange

Christopher's
   American Grill
Daphne's
del Buongustaio
dell'Ugo
The Dog House
Downstairs at One-
   Ninety
L'Escargot
Fifth Floor
The French House
   Dining Room *
Granita
Imperial City
Indian Connoisseurs
The Lansdowne
   Public House
The Lexington
The Lobster Pot

Mamta
Marché Mövenpick
Mezzaluna
Nosh Brothers
O'Keefe's
Le Palais du Jardin
Pavilion Restaurant
Le Petit Max *
Pied-à-Terre
Prost
Quaglino's *
Winter Garden at the
   Regent Hotel
La Semillante
The Square
Tokyo Diner
Vegetarian Cottage
Wagamama
Walsh's
Zoë

Restaurants by Cuisine

AFGHAN:

Buzkash
Caravan Serai

AFRICAN:

Calabash

AFRO-CARIBBEAN:

Brixtonian Backyard
Smokey Joe's Diner

THE AMERICAS:

Cafe Pacifico
Cheneston's
Christopher's
   American Grill
Deals

Down Mexico Way
Foxtrot Oscar
Hard Rock Cafe
Joe Allen
Kenny's Cajun Creole
   Bar & Restaurant
Kettners
PJ's Bar & Grill
Rock Island Diner
TGI Friday's

BELGIAN:

Belgo

BRITISH:

The Grill Room,
   Dorchester Hotel

The French House
   Dining Room *
Gilbert's
The Greenhouse
Green's
The Quality Chop
   House
Ransome's Dock
The Rib Room
The Ritz
Rules
The Savoy Grill
Simpson's-in-the-
   Strand
Wiltons

CHINESE:

China Court
Chopstix Xchange
Feng Shang
Fung Shing *
Green Cottage
Harbour City
Ho Ho
Imperial City
Ley-On's
Mandarin Kitchen
Ming
Mr Kong
Now & Zen
The Oriental,
    Dorchester Hotel
Poons
Royal China
Zen Central *
Zen
ZENW3

CHINESE VEGETARIAN:

Vegetarian Cottage

EAST EUROPEAN:

Caviar Kaspia
The Gay Hussar
Ognisko Polskie
Prost
Wódka

FISH:

L'Altro
Bibendum Oyster Bar
Cafe Fish
Chez Liline
Downstairs at One-
    Ninety
La Gaulette
Geales
Green's Oyster Bar
The Lobster Pot
Lou Pescadou
Manzi's
Le Suquet *
Sweetings
Two Brothers
Walsh's

FISH AND CHIPS:

Brady's
Nautilus

Seafresh
Seashell
Upper Street Fish Shop

FRENCH:

Alexandra
Les Associés
Au Jardin des
    Gourmets
Brasserie Faubourg
Le Cadre
Le Café du Marché
Café Flo
Café Rouge
Cafe Royal Grill Room
Chez Gerard
Chez Moi *
Connaught Hotel
L'Escargot
L'Estaminet
Four Seasons
Le Gavroche *
Gavvers
Grill St Quentin
Le Midi
Mijanou
Mirabelle
Mon Petit Plaisir
Mon Plaisir
Monkeys
Le Muscadet
Oak Room
Le Palais du Jardin
Le Petit Max *
Le P'tit Normand
Pied-à-Terre
River Restaurant
Les Saveurs *
La Semillante
Le Soufflé
St Quentin
La Tante Claire *
Turner's

GREEK:

Greek Valley
Kalamaras
Lemonia
Vrisaki
The White Tower

INDIAN:

Ali's Indian Cuisine

Bodali
Bombay Brasserie
Cafe Lazeez
Chutney Mary *
Gate of India
Gopal's of Soho
Indian Connoisseurs
Jashan
Khan's
Lahore Kebab House
Ma Goa
Old Delhi
Ragam
The Red Fort
Salloos
Standard Indian
Star of India
Tandoori Lane

INDIAN VEGETARIAN:

Chutneys
Geeta
Mamta
Mandeer
Rani
Sabras
Woodlands

ITALIAN:

Academia Italiana
L'Accento
Alba
Al San Vincenzo
Arts Theatre Cafe
Bertorelli's
Bice
Billboard Cafe
La Capannina
Caruso
Casale Franco
Cibo
Daphne's
del Buongustaio
The Eagle
Emporio Armani
    Express
Florians
La Fontana
Granita
The Halkin
L'Incontro
Mezzaluna
Neal Street Restaurant

Olivo
Orso
Osteria Antica
  Bologna
Il Passetto
Riva *
The River Cafe *
Santini
Scalini
Vasco & Piero's Pavilion
Ziani

JAPANESE:
Gonbei
Inaho
Neshiko
Suntory
Tokyo Diner
Wagamama
Wakaba

KOREAN:
Bu-San
Jin

LEBANESE:
Al Basha
Al Bustan
Al Hamra
Meshwar
Phoenicia

**MALAYSIAN
& INDONESIAN:**
Melati
Nusa Dua
Singapore Garden

MODERN BRITISH:
Alastair Little
The Argyll
Beauchamp Place
The Belvedere in
  Holand Park
Beth's *
Bibendum *
Bistrot Bruno *
Bistrot 190
Blakes
Blue Print Cafe
Boyd's
The Brackenbury *
Brasserie du Marché
  aux Puces

Café des Arts
Cafe Royal Brasserie
Caffe Graffiti
Camden Brasserie
Canal Brasserie
The Canteen
Capital Hotel
Le Caprice *
Chinon
Clarke's
The Criterion
The Dog House
dell'Ugo
The Enterprise
Fifth Floor
First Floor
The Footstool
Halcyon Hotel
Harvey's Cafe
Hilaire
The Ivy *
Joe's Cafe
Kensington Place
The Lansdowne
  Public House
Launceston Place
The Lexington
Mélange
Le Metro
Motcombs
Museum Street Cafe
N.B.
Newton's
Nosh Brothers
Odette's
O'Keefe's
192
Pavilion Restaurant
Le Pont de la Tour
Quaglino's *
Winter Garden at the
  Regent Hotel
RSJ
Smith's
Snows on the Green
Soho Soho
The Square
Stephen Bull
Stephen Bull's Bistro
Tate Gallery
  Restaurant
Villandry Dining Room
Zoë

MOROCCAN:
Laurent
The Tageen

NEPALESE:
Great Nepalese

PIZZAS:
La Delizia
Kettners
Pizza Express
Pizza on the Park
Pizzeria Castello

PORTUGUESE:
O Fado

SCANDINAVIAN:
Anna's Place
The Causerie

SCOTTISH:
Wilson's

SPANISH:
Albero & Grana
La Copita
Galicia
Rebato's

SWISS:
Marché Mövenpick

THAI
Bahn Thai
Blue Elephant
Esarn Kheaw
Sabai Sabai
Thai Garden
Thai Kitchen
Thailand

TUNISIAN
Adam's Cafe

TURKISH
Efes Kebab House
Istanbul Iskembecisi
Sofra
Topkapi

VIETNAMESE
Bonjour Vietnam
Saigon

Restaurants under £25 per person

Academia Italiana
L'Accento
Adam's Cafe
Al Bustan
Ali's Indian Cuisine
Anna's Place
Arts Theatre Cafe
Bahn Thai
Belgo
Bertorelli's
Billboard Cafe
Bistrot 190
Bodali
Bonjour Vietnam
The Brackenbury *
Brady's
Brasserie du Marché
    aux Puces
Bu-San
Le Cadre
Café des Arts
Cafe Fish
Café Flo
Cafe Lazeez
Cafe Pacifico
Café Rouge
Cafe Royal Brasserie
Caffe Graffiti
Calabash
Camden Brasserie
Canal Brasserie
Caravan Serai
Casale Franco
China Court
Chopstix Xchange
Chutneys
La Copita
The Criterion
Deals
del Buongustaio
La Delizia
dell'Ugo
Down Mexico Way
Dragon Inn
The Eagle
Efes Kebab House
Emporio Armani
    Express
The Enterprise
Florians

The Footstool
Foxtrot Oscar
The French House
    Dining Room *
Galicia
Gate of India
Gavvers
Geales
Geeta
Gilbert's
Gonbei
Gopal's of Soho
Granita
Great Nepalese
Greek Valley
Green Cottage
Harbour City
Hard Rock Cafe
Harvey's Cafe
Ho Ho
Inaho
Indian Connoisseurs
Istanbul Iskembecisi
Jashan
Joe Allen
Kalamaras
Kenny's
Kettners
Khan's
Lahore Kebab
    House (BYO)
The Lansdowne
    Public House
Laurent
Lemonia
Ley-On's
Lou Pescadou
Ma Goa
Mamta
Mandeer
Marché Mövenpick
Mélange
Melati
Meshwar
Le Metro
Mezzaluna
Le Midi
Ming
Mr Kong
Museum Street Cafe

Nautilus
N.B.
Newton's
Nosh Brothers
Now & Zen
Nusa Dua
O Fado
O'Keefe's
Old Delhi
Osteria Antica
    Bologna
Le Palais du Jardin
Pavilion Restaurant
Le Petit Max * (BYO)
Le P'tit Normand
Phoenicia
Pizza Express
Pizza on the Park
Pizza Castello
PJ's Bar & Grill
Le Pont de la Tour
    (Grill)
Poons
Prost
The Quality Chop
    House
Ragam
Rani
Rebato's
The Winter Garden
    at the Regent Hotel
Rock Island
Diner
Sabai Sabai
Sabras
Saigon
Seafresh
Seashell
Smokey Joe's Diner
    (BYO)
Snows on the Green
Sofra
Soho Soho
    (Rotisserie)
Standard Indian
Star of India
Stephen Bull's Bistro
Sweetings
The Tageen
Tandoori Lane

TGI Friday's
Thai Garden
Thai Kitchen
Thailand
Tokyo Diner

Topkapi
Two Brothers
The Upper Street Fish
   Shop
Vegetarian Cottage

Vrisaki
Wagamama
Wódka
Zoë

Restaurants between £25 and £50

Alastair Little
Alba
Al Basha
Albero & Grana
Alexandra
Al Hamra
L'Altro
Al San Vincenzo
The Argyll
Les Associés
Au Jardin des
   Gourmets
Beauchamp Place
The Belvedere in Holland
   Park
Beth's *
Bibendum Oyster Bar
Bice
Bistrot Bruno *
Blue Elephant
Blue Print Cafe
Bombay Brasserie
Boyd's
Brasserie Faubourg
Brixtonian Backayard
Le Café du Marché
Cafe Royal, Grill
   Room
The Canteen
La Capannina
Capital Hotel
Le Caprice *
Caruso
The Causerie
Caviar Kaspia
Cheneston's
Chez Gerard
Chez Moi *
Chinon
Christopher's American
   Grill
Chutney Mary *
Cibo
Clarke's
Connaught Hotel

Daphne's
The Dog House
The Grill Room,
   Dorchester Hotel
Downstairs at One-
   Ninety
Esarn Kheaw
L'Escargot
L'Estaminet
Feng Shang
Fifth Floor
First Floor
La Fontana
Four Seasons
Fung Shing *
La Gaulette
The Gay Hussar
The Greenhouse
Green's
Grill St Quentin
Halcyon Hotel
The Halkin
Hilaire
Imperial City
The Ivy *
Jin
Joe's Cafe
Kensington Place
Launceston Place
The Lexington
The Lobster Pot
Mandarin Kitchen
Manzi's
Mijanou
Mirabelle
Monkeys
Mon Petit Plaisir
Mon Plaisir
Motcombs
Le Muscadet
Neal Street Restaurant
Neshiko
Odette's
Ognisko Polskie
Olivo

192
The Oriental,
   Dorchester Hotel
Orso
Il Passetto
Pied-à-Terre
Le Pont de la Tour
Quaglino's *
Ransome's Dock
The Red Fort
The Ritz
Riva *
The River Cafe *
River Restaurant
Royal China
RSJ
Rules
St Quentin
Salloos
Les Saveurs *
Scalini
La Semillante
Simpson's-in-the-
   Strand
Singapore Garden
Smith's
Soho Soho
   (Restaurant)
Le Soufflé
The Square
Stephen Bull
Le Suquet *
Tate Gallery
   Restaurant
Vasco & Piero's Pavilion
Villandry Dining Room
Wakaba
Walsh's
The White Tower *
Wilson's
Wiltons
Zen
Zen Central *
ZENW3
Ziani

Restaurants over £50

Bibendum
    Restaurant *
Blakes
Le Gavroche *

L'Incontro
Oak Room
The Rib Room
Santini

The Savoy Grill
Suntory
La Tante Claire *
Turner's

Restaurants by Area

ALDGATE:
Imperial City

BARNES:
Gate of India
Riva *

BATTERSEA:
Osteria Antica
    Bologna
Ransome's Dock

BAYSWATER:
Al San Vincenzo
Indian Connoisseurs
Kalamaras
Khan's
Mandarin Kitchen
Old Delhi
Royal China
Standard Indian

BELGRAVIA/ ST JAMES:
Al Bustan
Cafe Fish
Le Caprice *
Fifth Floor
La Fontana
The Footstool
Gavvers
Green's
The Halkin
L'Incontro
Mijanou
Motcombs
Olivo
Pizza on the Park
Quaglino's *
Santini
Seafresh
The Square
Suntory
Tate Gallery Restaurant
Wiltons

BETHNAL GREEN:
Thai Garden

BLACKFRIARS:
Sweetings

BLOOMSBURY:
Gonbei
Museum Street Cafe
Wagamama

CAMDEN TOWN & CHALK FARM /EUSTON:
Ali's Indian Cuisine
Belgo
Camden Brasserie
Chutneys
Feng Shang
Great Nepalese
The Lansdowne
    Public House
Lemonia
N.B.
Odette's

CHELSEA & KNIGHTSBRIDGE:
Albero & Grana
The Argyll
Beauchamp Place
Bibendum *
Capital Hotel
Daphne's
La Delizia
Emporio Armani
    Express
The Enterprise
Foxtrot Oscar
Grill St Quentin
Joe's Cafe
Le Metro
Monkeys
O Fado
PJ's Bar & Grill

The Rib Room
St Quentin
Salloos
Scalini
Le Suquet *
La Tante Claire *
Turner's
Zen
Ziani

CHILD'S HILL:
Laurent

CLAPHAM:
Newton's

COVENT GARDEN/ LEICESTER SQUARE/ HOLBORN:
Arts Theatre Cafe
Bertorelli's
Brixtonian Backayard
Café Flo
Cafe Pacifico
Calabash
Chez Gerard
Christopher's
    American Grill
L'Estaminet
Fung Shing *
The Ivy *
Joe Allen
Manzi's
Mélange
Mezzaluna
Mr Kong
Mon Plaisir
Neal Street
    Restaurant
Now & Zen
Orso
Le Palais du Jardin
Il Passetto
Poons

River Restaurant
Rules
The Savoy Grill
Simpson's-in-the-
　Strand
Smith's
The Tageen
TGI Friday's
Tokyo Diner

EARL'S COURT:
La Delizia
Lou Pescadou
Star of India

**FARRINGDON/
SMITHFIELD:**
Alba
Café du Marché
The Eagle
The Quality Chop
　House
Stephen Bull's
　Bistro

FINCHLEY:
Rani
Two Brothers

FINSBURY PARK:
Chez Liline

FULHAM:
Blue Elephant
Bonjour Vietnam
Café Flo
Caruso
Mamta
Le Midi
Nosh Brothers
Tandoori Lane

HAMMERSMITH:
The Brackenbury *
The River Cafe *
Sabai Sabai
Snows on the Green

**HAMPSTEAD/
BELSIZE PARK:**
Beth's *
Café des Arts

Café Flo
Caffe Graffiti
Green Cottage
Kenny's
Vegetarian Cottage
Wakaba
ZENW3

HAMPTON WICK:
Le Petit Max *

HIGHBURY:
Bodali

HOLLOWAY:
Bu-San

**HORNSEY/
CROUCH END:**
Les Associés
Le Cadre
Florians
Jashan

**ISLINGTON/
KING'S CROSS:**
Anna's Place
Café Flo
Casale Franco
Granita
Neshiko
The Upper Street Fish
　Shop

KENNINGTON:
The Lobster Pot

**KENSINGTON
HIGH STREET:**
Al Basha
The Belvedere in
　Holland Park
Boyd's
Café Flo
Cheneston's
Clarke's
Geales
Kensington Place
Launceston Place
Mon Petit Plaisir
Phoenicia
Wódka

**KENSINGTON (NORTH)/
LADBROKE GROVE:**
L'Altro
Brasserie du Marché
　aux Puces
The Canal Brasserie
Galicia

KENSINGTON (SOUTH):
Academia Italiana
Bistrot 190
Blakes
Bombay Brasserie
Cafe Lazeez
Downstairs at One-
　Ninety
Gilbert's
Hilaire
Ognisko Polskie

KENSINGTON (WEST):
Chinon
Cibo
Wilson's

**KILBURN/
WEST HAMPSTEAD:**
Billboard Cafe
Geeta
Nautilus
Singapore Garden

MARBLE ARCH:
Meshwar

MARYLEBONE:
Le Muscadet
The Winter Garden at
　the Regent Hotel
Stephen Bull
Villandry Dining
　Room

MERTON:
Alexandra

NEW CROSS:
Thailand

NOTTING HILL:
L'Accento
Chez Moi *

First Floor
Halcyon Hotel
Inaho
192
Prost
Thai Kitchen

PUTNEY:
Buzkash
del Buongustaio
Ma Goa

RICHMOND:
Café Flo

SHEPHERD'S BUSH:
Adam's Cafe
La Copita
Esarn Kheaw

**SOHO/OXFORD
STREET/MAYFAIR:**
Alastair Little
Al Hamra
Au Jardin des
   Gourmets
Bahn Thai
Bice
Bistrot Bruno *
Cafe Royal
La Capannina
Caravan Serai
The Causerie
Caviar Kaspia
Chez Gerard
China Court
Connaught Hotel
The Criterion
dell'Ugo
The Dog House
Dorchester Hotel
Down Mexico Way
Dragon Inn
Efes Kebab House
Efes II
L'Escargot
Four Seasons
The French House
   Dining Room *
La Gaulette
Le Gavroche *
The Gay Hussar

Gopal's of Soho
The Greenhouse
Harbour City
Hard Rock Cafe
Ho Ho
Jin
Kettners
The Lexington
Ley-On's
Mandeer
Marché Mövenpick
Melati
Ming
Mirabelle
Nusa Dua
Oak Room
O'Keefe's
Pavilion Restaurant
Pied-à-Terre
Ragam
The Red Fort
The Ritz
Rock Island Diner
Saigon
Les Saveurs *
La Semillante
Sofra
Soho Soho
Le Soufflé
Topkapi
Vasco & Piero's
   Pavilion
Walsh's
The White Tower *
Woodlands
Zen Central *
Zoë

ST JOHN'S WOOD:
Greek Valley
Seashell

SOUTH BANK:
Blue Print Cafe
Pizzeria Castello
Le Pont de la Tour
RSJ

SPITALFIELDS:
Lahore Kebab House

STOKE NEWINGTON:
Istanbul Iskembecisi

**TOTTERIDGE &
WHETSTONE:**
Chopstix Xchange

**VAUXHALL/
QUEENSTOWN ROAD:**
Brasserie Faubourg
Rebato's

WANDSWORTH:
Brady's
Le P'tit Normand
Smokey Joe's Diner

WEST BROMPTON:
The Canteen
Chutney Mary *
Deals
Harvey's Cafe

**WILLESDEN/
HARLESDEN:**
Sabras

WOOD GREEN:
Vrisaki

Restaurants with No Smoking Areas

CHECK RESTAURANT
ENTRIES FOR DETAILS

Academia Italiana
Au Jardin des
   Gourmets
Beauchamp Place
Bertorelli's
Bice
Brixtonian Backayard
Le Cadre
Cafe Fish
Cafe Lazeez
Cafe Pacifico
Calabash
La Capannina
Caravan Serai
Caruso
Chez Gerard
Chutney Mary *
Clarke's
L'Escargot
L'Estaminet
The Footstool

Geeta
Gilbert's
Gopal's of Soho
Hard Rock Cafe
Indian Connoisseurs
Joe Allen
Launceston Place
The Lexington
Mamta
Marché Mövenpick
Mezzaluna
Mijanou
Ming
Mirabelle
Motcombs
Museum Street Cafe
Newton's
O Fado
Orso
Pavilion Restaurant
Pizza Express, Coptic
   Street
Pizza on the Park

PJ's Bar & Grill
Prost
Rani
Winter Garden at the
   Regent Hotel
Sabras
Seashell
Smith's
Soho Soho
Le Soufflé
Standard Indian
Tate Gallery
   Restaurant
TGI Friday's
Thai Garden
Tokyo Diner
Two Brothers
Villandry Dining
   Room
Wagamama
Walsh's
Zoë

Restaurants with Last Orders After 11.30pm

CHECK RESTAURANT
ENTRIES FOR DETAILS

Al Basha (12.00am)
Albero & Grana
   (bar: 12.00am)
Ali's Indian Cuisine
   (12.00am Mon-Fri;
   12.15am Sat-Sun)
Beauchamp Place
   (12.00am Mon-Sat)
Billboard Cafe
   (12.45am)
Bistrot 190
   (12.30am Mon-Sat)
Blue Elephant
   (12.00am)
Bombay Brasserie
   (12.00am)
Cafe Lazeez
(12.30am Mon-Sat)
The Canteen
   (11.45pm Mon-Sat)
Le Caprice (12.00am)
Daphne's (11.50pm)

La Delizia (11.45pm)
dell'Ugo (12.30am
   restaurant)
The Dog House
   (12.00am restaurant)
Down Mexico
   Way (11.50pm)
Downstairs at One-
   Ninety (12.00am)
Dragon Inn (11.45pm)
Gate of India (12.00am)
Greek Valley (12.00am)
Harbour City
   (11.50pm Sat)
Hard Rock Cafe
   (12.30am Sun-Thu;
   1.00am Fri-Sat)
Indian Connoisseurs
   (12.00am)
Istanbul Iskembecisi
   (4.30am)
The Ivy (12.00am) *
Joe Allen
   (12.45am Mon-Sat;

11.45pm Sun)
Kalamaras (12.00am)
Kenny's (11.45pm)
Kettners (11.55pm)
Khan's (1.45am)
Lahore Kebab
   House (12.00am)
Lou Pescadou
   (12.00am)
Marché Mövenpick
   (12.00am)
Meshwar (12.00am)
Ming (11.45pm)
Mr Kong (1.45am)
O Fado (12.30am)
Orso (11.50pm)
Le Palais du
   Jardin (11.45pm)
Phoenicia (11.45pm)
Pizza Express (12.00am)
Pizza on the
   Park (12.00am)
PJ's Bar &
   Grill (12.00am)

Le Pont de la Tour
  (12.00am Mon-Sat)
Quaglino's (12.00am
  Mon-Sat) *
The Quality Chop
  House

(12.00am Mon-Sat)
Ransome's Dock
  (12.00am Sat)
Rules (11.45pm)
Scalini (11.45pm)
Sofra (12.00am)

Soho Soho (12.00am)
The Square (11.45pm)
Standard Indian
  (11.45pm)
Star of India (12.00am)

Restaurants with Wheelchair Access

CHECK RESTAURANT ENTRIES
FOR DETAILS OF ACCESS TO
FACILITIES

Academia Italiana
L'Accento
Adam's Cafe
Alba
Al Basha
Al Hamra
Ali's Indian Cuisine
L'Altro
Anna's Place
Les Associés
Au Jardin des
  Gourmets
Bahn Thai
Belgo
The Belvedere in
  Holland Park
Bertorelli's
Beth's *
Bibendum *
Bice
Billboard Cafe
Blakes
Blue Elephant
Blue Print Cafe
Bodali
Bombay Brasserie
Bonjour Vietnam
The Brackenbury
Brady's
Brasserie du Marché
  aux Puces
Brasserie Faubourg
Brixtonian Backayard
Bu-San
Le Cadre
Café des Arts
Le Café du Marché
Cafe Fish
Café Flo
Cafe Lazeez

Cafe Pacifico
Café Rouge
Cafe Royal
Camden Brasserie
The Canal Brasserie
The Canteen
Capital Hotel
Le Caprice *
Caruso
Casale Franco
The Causerie
Caviar Kaspia
Chez Moi *
Chinon
Chopstix Xchange
Chutneys
Cibo
Clarke's
Connaught Hotel
La Copita
The Criterion
Daphne's
Deals
The Grill Room,
  Dorchester Hotel
Down Mexico Way
  (Bar)
Dragon Inn
The Eagle
Efes Kebab House
Emporio Armani
  Express
The Enterprise
L'Escargot Brasserie
Feng Shang
Fifth Floor
Florians
La Fontana
Four Seasons
Foxtrot Oscar
Fung Shing *
Galicia
La Gaulette

Gavvers
The Gay Hussar
Geales
Geeta
Gilbert's
Granita
Great Nepalese
Greek Valley
Green Cottage
Halcyon Hotel
The Halkin
Harbour City
Hard Rock Cafe
Hilaire
Ho Ho
Imperial City
L'Incontro
Istanbul Iskembecisi
The Ivy *
Jashan
Jin
Joe's Cafe
Kalamaras
Kenny's
Kensington Place
Kettners
Khan's
The Lansdowne
  Public House
Launceston Place
Laurent
Lemonia
The Lexington
The Lobster Pot
Lou Pescadou
Ma Goa
Mamta
Mandarin Kitchen
Manzi's
Melati
Mezzaluna
Mijanou
Monkeys

Mon Plaisir
Le Muscadet
Museum Street Cafe
N.B.
Neal Street Restaurant
Newton's
Nosh Brothers
Oak Room
Odette's
Ognisko Polskie
O'Keefe's
Old Delhi
Olivo
The Oriental,
 Dorchester Hotel
Orso
Osteria Antica
 Bologna
Le Palais du Jardin
Il Passetto
Pavilion Restaurant
Le Petit Max *
Le P'tit Normand
Phoenicia
Pied-à-Terre
Pizza on the Park
Pizzeria Castello
PJ's Bar & Grill
Le Pont de la Tour
Poons
Quaglino's *

The Quality Chop
 House
Ragam
Rani
Ransome's Dock
Rebato's
The Red Fort
Winter Garden at the
 Regent Hotel
The Rib Room
The Ritz
Riva *
The River Cafe *
River Restaurant
Rock Island Diner
Royal China
RSJ
Rules
Sabai Sabai
Sabras
St Quentin
Santini
The Savoy Grill
Seafresh
La Semillante
Simpson's-in-the-
 Strand
Snows on the Green
Sofra
Soho Soho (Rotisserie)
Le Soufflé

The Square
Standard Indian
Stephen Bull
Stephen Bull's Bistro
Sweetings
The Tageen
La Tante Claire *
Tate Gallery
 Restaurant
TGI Friday's
Thai Garden
Tokyo Diner
Topkapi
Turner's
The Upper Street Fish
 Shop
Vasco & Piero's
 Pavilion
Vegetarian Cottage
Villandry Dining
 Room
Vrisaki
Wakaba
Walsh's
Wilson's
Wiltons
Wódka
Zen Central *
ZENW3
Ziani
Zoë

Restaurants with Live Music

THIS IS OFTEN OCCASIONAL.
PLEASE TELEPHONE
RESTAURANTS FOR DETAILS

Al Basha
Billboard Cafe
Bombay Brasserie
Brixtonian Backayard
Le Café du Marché
Cafe Fish
Cafe Lazeez
Cafe Pacifico
Calabash
Le Caprice *
La Copita
Down Mexico Way
 (Bar)
Downstairs at One-
 Ninety

First Floor
Harvey's Cafe (Bar)
Imperial City
L'Incontro
Joe Allen
Kalamaras
Kenny's
Kettners
The Lexington
Mezzaluna
Oak Room
O Fado
Le Palais du Jardin
Pavilion Restaurant
Pizza on the Park
Pizzeria Castello
Le Pont de la Tour
Quaglino's *

Rebato's
The Rib Room
The Ritz
River Restaurant
Rock Island Diner
Simpson's-in-the-
 Strand (Bar)
Smith's
Soho Soho (Rotisserie)
Le Soufflé
Star of India
Villandry Dining
 Room

Restaurants with Tables Outside

CHECK RESTAURANT
ENTRIES FOR DETAILS

L'Accento
Al Basha
Al Bustan
Alexandra
Al Hamra
L'Altro
Anna's Place
The Belvedere in
  Holland Park
Beth's *
Blue Print Cafe
The Brackenbury *
Brasserie du Marché
  aux Puces
Brixtonian Backayard
Le Cadre
Café des Arts
Cafe Fish
Café Flo
Cafe Lazeez
Caffe Graffiti
The Canal Brasserie

Casalę Franco
Chez Gerard
Chinon
Daphne's
Deals
dell'Ugo
The Eagle
Efes Kebab House
The Enterprise
Florians
Halcyon Hotel
Hard Rock Cafe
Kalamaras
Lahore Kebab House
The Lansdowne
  Public House
Lou Pescadou
Marché Mövenpick
Mezzaluna
Mijanou
Mon Petit Plaisir
Motcombs
N.B.
Newton's

Odette's
Ognisko Polskie
O'Keefe's
Old Delhi
Osteria Antica
  Bologna
Le Palais du Jardin
Pizza Express, Coptic
  Street
Pizza on the Park
PJ's Bar & Grill
Le Pont de la Tour
Poons
Ransome's Dock
The Ritz
Riva *
The River Cafe *
Singapore Garden
Sofra
Soho Soho (Rotisserie)
Le Suquet *
Zen Central *
Zoë

Restaurants with Private Areas

SEE INDIVIDUAL ENTRIES
FOR DETAILS

Academia Italiana
L'Accento
Adam's Cafe
Alastair Little
Al Basha
Albero & Grana
Alexandra
Ali's Indian Cuisine
Au Jardin des
  Gourmets
Bahn Thai
Beauchamp Place
Billboard Cafe
Bistrot 190
Blakes
Blue Elephant
Bonjour Vietnam
Brasserie du Marché
  aux Puces
Brixtonian Backayard
Le Café du Marché

Cafe Lazeez
Cafe Royal
La Capannina
Capital Hotel
Caravan Serai
Caruso
Caviar Kaspia
Cheneston's
Chez Gerard
China Court
Chopstix Xchange
Christopher's
  American Grill
Chutneys
Cibo
Connaught Hotel
La Copita
The Criterion
Deals
dell'Ugo
The Dog House
Downstairs at One-
  Ninety

Dragon Inn
L'Escargot
L'Estaminet
First Floor
Florians
Foxtrot Oscar
Fung Shing *
La Gaulette
Le Gavroche *
The Gay Hussar
Geeta
Great Nepalese
Greek Valley
Green Cottage
Green's
Halcyon Hotel
The Halkin
Harbour City
Hard Rock Cafe
Harvey's Cafe
Hilaire
Ho Ho
Imperial City

L'Incontro
Indian Connoisseurs
The Ivy *
Jin
Kalamaras
Kettners
Lahore Kebab House
The Lansdowne
  Public House
Launceston Place
Lemonia
The Lexington
Lou Pescadou
Mandeer
Marché Mövenpick
Mélange
Melati
Meshwar
Le Midi
Mijanou
Ming
Mirabelle
Monkeys
Mon Plaisir
Motcombs
N.B.
Neal Street Restaurant
Newton's
The Nosh Brothers
Now & Zen
Nusa Dua
Odette's
O Fado
Ognisko Polskie
Old Delhi
192
The Oriental
Le Palais du Jardin
Pied-à-Terre
Pizza on the Park
PJ's Bar & Grill
Le Pont de la Tour
Poons
Prost
Quaglino's *
Rani
The Red Fort
The Rib Room
The Ritz
River Restaurant
Royal China
RSJ

Rules
Sabai Sabai
Saigon
St Quentin
Les Saveurs *
Seafresh
La Semillante
Simpson's-in-the-
  Strand
Singapore Garden
Smith's
Snows on the Green
Soho Soho
The Square
Standard Indian
Star of India
Suntory
Le Suquet *
The Tageen
Thai Garden
Vasco & Piero's
  Pavilion
Vegetarian Cottage
Villandry Dining
  Room
Vrisaki
Walsh's
The White Tower *
Wiltons
Wódka
Zen
ZENW3